T0321960

Principles, Policies, and Applications of Kotlin Programming

Duy Thanh Tran
*University of Economics and Law, Ho Chi Minh City, Vietnam
& Vietnam National University, Ho Chi Minh City, Vietnam*

Jun-Ho Huh
Korea Maritime and Ocean University, South Korea

A volume in the Advances in
Systems Analysis, Software
Engineering, and High Performance
Computing (ASASEHPC) Book Series

Published in the United States of America by
 IGI Global
 Engineering Science Reference (an imprint of IGI Global)
 701 E. Chocolate Avenue
 Hershey PA, USA 17033
 Tel: 717-533-8845
 Fax: 717-533-8661
 E-mail: cust@igi-global.com
 Web site: http://www.igi-global.com

Library of Congress Cataloging-in-Publication Data

Names: Tran, Duy Thanh, 1984- author. | Huh, Jun-Ho, 1984- author.
Title: Principles, policies, and applications of Kotlin programming / by
 Duy Thanh Tran and Jun-Ho Huh.
Description: Hershey, PA : Engineering Science Reference, an imprint of IGI
 Global, [2023] | Includes bibliographical references and index. |
 Summary: "This book is a guide to learning and understanding the Kotlin
 programming language"-- Provided by publisher.
Identifiers: LCCN 2022023479 (print) | LCCN 2022023480 (ebook) | ISBN
 9781668466872 (h/c) | ISBN 9781668466889 (s/c) | ISBN 9781668466896
 (ebook)
Subjects: LCSH: Kotlin (Computer program language) | Android (Electronic
 resource) | Smartphones--Programming.
Classification: LCC QA76.73.K68 T73 2023 (print) | LCC QA76.73.K68
 (ebook) | DDC 005.13/3--dc23/eng/20220804
LC record available at https://lccn.loc.gov/2022023479
LC ebook record available at https://lccn.loc.gov/2022023480
This book is published in the IGI Global book series Advances in Systems Analysis, Software Engineering, and High Performance Computing (ASASEHPC) (ISSN: 2327-3453; eISSN: 2327-3461)

British Cataloguing in Publication Data
A Cataloguing in Publication record for this book is available from the British Library.
All work contributed to this book is new, previously-unpublished material.
The views expressed in this book are those of the authors, but not necessarily of the publisher.
For electronic access to this publication, please contact: eresources@igi-global.com.

Advances in Systems Analysis, Software Engineering, and High Performance Computing (ASASEHPC) Book Series

ISSN:2327-3453
EISSN:2327-3461

Editor-in-Chief: Vijayan Sugumaran, Oakland University, USA

MISSION

The theory and practice of computing applications and distributed systems has emerged as one of the key areas of research driving innovations in business, engineering, and science. The fields of software engineering, systems analysis, and high performance computing offer a wide range of applications and solutions in solving computational problems for any modern organization.

The **Advances in Systems Analysis, Software Engineering, and High Performance Computing (ASASEHPC) Book Series** brings together research in the areas of distributed computing, systems and software engineering, high performance computing, and service science. This collection of publications is useful for academics, researchers, and practitioners seeking the latest practices and knowledge in this field.

COVERAGE

- Performance Modelling
- Human-Computer Interaction
- Enterprise Information Systems
- Computer System Analysis
- Metadata and Semantic Web
- Virtual Data Systems
- Network Management
- Distributed Cloud Computing
- Software Engineering
- Parallel Architectures

IGI Global is currently accepting manuscripts for publication within this series. To submit a proposal for a volume in this series, please contact our Acquisition Editors at Acquisitions@igi-global.com or visit: http://www.igi-global.com/publish/.

Titles in this Series

For a list of additional titles in this series, please visit:
http://www.igi-global.com/book-series/advances-systems-analysis-software-engineering/73689

Advanced Applications of Python Data Structures and Algorithms
Mohammad Gouse Galety (Catholic University in Erbil, Iraq) Arul Kumar Natarajan (CHRIST (Deemed to be University), Bangalore, India) and A. V. Sriharsha (MB University, India)
Engineering Science Reference • © 2023 • 320pp • H/C (ISBN: 9781668471005) • US $270.00

Adaptive Security and Cyber Assurance for Risk-Based Decision Making
Tyson T. Brooks (Syracuse University, USA)
Engineering Science Reference • © 2023 • 243pp • H/C (ISBN: 9781668477663) • US $225.00

Novel Research and Development Approaches in Heterogeneous Systems and Algorithms
Santanu Koley (Haldia Institute of Technology, India) Subhabrata Barman (Haldia Institute of Technology, India) and Subhankar Joardar (Haldia Institute of Technology, India)
Engineering Science Reference • © 2023 • 323pp • H/C (ISBN: 9781668475249) • US $270.00

Handbook of Research on Quantum Computing for Smart Environments
Amit Kumar Tyagi (National Institute of Fashion Technology, New Delhi, India)
Engineering Science Reference • © 2023 • 564pp • H/C (ISBN: 9781668466971) • US $325.00

Concepts and Techniques of Graph Neural Networks
Vinod Kumar (Koneru Lakshmaiah Education Foundation (KL Deemed to be University), India) and Dharmendra Singh Rajput (VIT University, India)
Engineering Science Reference • © 2023 • 320pp • H/C (ISBN: 9781668469033) • US $270.00

For an entire list of titles in this series, please visit:
http://www.igi-global.com/book-series/advances-systems-analysis-software-engineering/73689

701 East Chocolate Avenue, Hershey, PA 17033, USA
Tel: 717-533-8845 x100 • Fax: 717-533-8661
E-Mail: cust@igi-global.com • www.igi-global.com

Table of Contents

Detailed Table of Contents

This chapter introduces Kotlin programming language and its strengths, such as brevity, saftey, versatility, and interoperability features. Readers will discover how to install Kotlin programming tools, how to create projects, program sample projects and check the output results. At the same time, this chapter also presents the types of notes when programming such as single-line comment, multi-line comments, and KDoc comments; comments are one of the important requirements of the software industry. Readers will be familiar with simple and easy-to-understand examples so that readers can practice after reading and using the functions in the IntelliJ IDEA programming tool. Finally, there are exercises listed at the end of the chapter to help readers practice more programming skills with Kotlin.

In the process of programming, understanding data types and variable declaration plays an important role in software development. When choosing the right data type and managing variables well, this will help the software to be optimized and memory, making the customer experience for the software better. The chapter will present the data types of the Kotlin language, data types will be grouped some category to make it easy for learners to remember and compare, data explicit conversion and implicit conversion are mentioned. Also, important operators for data types covered in this chapter include unary operators, basic arithmetic, assignment, comparison, Logic, increment and decrement operators, etc. This chapter also guides how to input data into the software from the keyboard to help readers easily test the cases during the programming process. For each content, this chapter provides simple and easy-to-understand sample code for easy access, and at the end of the chapter there are practice exercises to improve programming skills.

Chapter 3

Almost every programming language has to use conditional constructs to handle the business of the software. Basically, the operating mechanism of these conditional structures is the same, but with the Kotlin programming language, it has added a lot of extended and very convenient features, it helps programmers more optimal options in the process of processing business. This chapter will present conditional constructs about simple if statement, if/else statement, nested conditionals, expression and block form { }, and when structure. The when structure has been greatly improved in Kotlin, it provides a lot of use cases so that programmers can easily handle business tasks more optimally, such as when with if/else statement, group multiple conditions. For each conditional structure, this chapter provides simple examples and detailed explanations to help readers understand the working mechanism of the conditional structure and apply them to specific business handling. At the end of the chapter, there is a list of exercises to help readers improve programming skills on conditional structures.

Chapter 4

Similar to the conditional structure, in all software, programmers have to use loop structures to handle repetitive tasks according to certain rules. When dealing with list data such as character strings, numeric arrays, list of objects, etc. then loops will be used. Kotlin provides loop controls such as for, while, do while and abnormal loop termination. The loop executions are greatly improved, such as for loops that are divided many types such as closed range, half-open range, step and downTo navigation. And these kinds cover most of the loop handling cases, making it easy for programmers to use them optimally. This chapter also demonstrates how to handle break statement and continue statement in abnormal loop termination, these are very important statements in loop handling. This chapter also provides complete code and detailed explanations for each loop, making it easy for learners to understand and practice loops. At the end of the chapter, there are exercises to help readers practice programming skills for loops and consolidate the knowledge in previous chapters.

Chapter 5

In the process of programming, most of mistakes can be raised. And making errors while programming is inevitable. Therefore, programmers need to have ways to distinguish the types of errors and how to handle errors. This chapter will present error levels such as compiler error, runtime exception error, and exception logic error. This chapter also provides techniques for catching errors such as try catch structure and throw exception technique. Illustrative codes are presented for how to handle this error for readers to easily grasp. However, most programming tools support debugging functions, and this tool makes it easy for programmers to find errors and from there it helps programmers easily find the solutions to fix errors quickly and accurately, so this chapter presents IntelliJ IDEA's debugging tool. At the end of the chapter there are exercises to help readers improve the skills in exception handling.

Chapter 6

Every programming language has a set of libraries that will help programmers quickly solve certain tasks, and programmers must certainly use it because programmers either cannot write some libraries or it takes a long time; so programmers must know how to use them. These libraries may be in the JVM or KotlinJavaRuntime or in any other external library. In this chapter, the book will present some commonly used libraries, such as numeric data processing library, date processing library, math processing library, random number processing library, and string processing library. And there are many other processing libraries—readers can do more research about those libraries. At the end of the chapter there are exercises to help readers improve the skills in important libraries commonly.

Chapter 7

In all programming languages, string processing is extremely important. This chapter will present how to declare strings and summarize the commonly used functions of strings, such as indexOf, lastIndexOf, contains, substring, replace, trim, compare, plus, split, upper case and lowercase functions, etc. Each function has sample code along with detailed explanations that make it easy for readers to understand how to use basic string functions. In this chapter, the book will present some of the most commonly used functions in the string. At the end of the chapter there are exercises to help readers improve the skills in string processing.

Chapter 8

Array is one of the very important data in software processing, it will be used to store data in the form of a list. Almost all programming languages support array processing, and so does the Kotlin language. However, with Kotlin, arrays are a very powerful data type, which overcome many disadvantages compared to other programming languages such as C++, C#, Java, etc. The book has briefly mentioned some of the array types that are built-in in Kotlin, such as: CharArray, BooleanArray, ByteArray, ShortArray, IntArray, LongArray, FloatArray, and DoubleArray. Depending on the purpose of use, programmers can choose different types of arrays; to help readers easily understand how to declare and use one-dimensional arrays in Kotlin, the book will use IntArray to illustrate in the examples below. Other types of arrays Readers can infer. At the end of the chapter, there are exercises to help readers improve programming skills to handle arrays.

Chapter 9

Similar to other programming languages, arrays and collections are indispensable data types in the process of processing list data. In the previous chapter presented about arrays, there are some benefits of arrays, but in some cases, arrays do not meet requirements and are difficult to implement. Usually, the data has no change in quantity, no deleting or changing the position of data, then it is appropriate to use an array, but when it comes to cases where the data changes continuously, or the number of elements is not known in advance, or the position in the list can be shuffled, using arrays is no longer optimal, so collections are more optimal. This chapter will present hierarchical collections so that readers have an overview of collections, and then Mutable and Immutable collection are presented. The chapter also provides code and detailed explanation to help readers easily grasp the working mechanism, as well as be able to implement the collection in practice. At the end of the chapter, there are exercises to help readers improve collection processing programming skills.

Chapter 10

Object-oriented programming (OOP) is a programming technique that allows programmers to abstract objects in reality and create those objects in code, this programming technique is based on the concept of classes and objects. Objects include properties and methods, properties are information, specific characteristics of each object; Methods are operations that an object is capable of performing. A class is a data type that includes many predefined properties and methods. Each class acts as a unit of combined methods and properties. Kotlin is like other programming languages that support object-oriented programming. OOP is a general concept; programming language is just one of the tools to implement that concept. This means that if readers already understand OOP, then C #, Java, Kotlin, etc. will share this concept for implementation. The chapter provides illustrative and detailed explanations to help readers easily understand OOP. And at the end of the chapter, there are exercises to help readers practice and improve OOP skills as well as review the knowledge in previous chapters.

Chapter 11

During software deployment, different kinds of file will be used depending on the specific case. The book will show the series of four file types: Text File, Serialize File, XML File, JSon File so that readers have more options in file processing. Why does program have to store data? As computer architecture is mentioned, a program wants to work, every resource must be loaded into memory, namely the RAM (Random Access Memory). The principle of RAM is the clipboard, when the software is turned off the data in the memory will no longer there. Assuming customers are entering 100 products, and the power is suddenly cut, if there is no mechanism to save data from RAM memory to the hard drive, customers will be losing all the data. Kotlin uses JVM libraries to interact with the file, so programmers can invoke these libraries. This chapter provides examples of handling saving and reading files with different cases, which help readers to cover most of the processing cases in practice. At the end of the chapter, there are exercises to improve readers skills with file processing.

Chapter 12

For customers, providing interactive user interfaces is very important because customers can only manipulate on the intuitive screen. There are many types of interfaces provided by different programming languages and dependent on the case that programmer used. In addition, with the development of programming languages, it is possible to use interfaces between different programming languages. This chapter presents graphic user interface, guides learners on how to write classes that inherit interfaces as well as how to drag and drop controls on the interface to get the desired interface. In this chapter, readers will discover layout, basic controls label, button, etc. and list, table, tree, etc. For each type of control, detailed instructions are provided, which makes it easy for readers to grasp the theory and implement the practical parts. The chapter also presents how to create executables for Kotlin. At the end of the chapter, there are exercises to help readers practice user interface handling skills.

Chapter 13

Kotlin as well as other programming languages can be applied to writing service APIs. This chapter presents a new framework called Vert.X. It is considered as one of the powerful frameworks. It can support the implementation of many services including Restful API. Kotlin is used as the main programming language of Android mobile. When deploying Mobile, Restful API is used to interact with data on the server, so how to create Restful APIs is very important. Using Vert.X will help programmers save a lot of time, and Vert.X is considered to be very optimal when deploying services. This chapter will demonstrate the knowledge of how to build and deploy Restful APIs using Vert.X and demonstrate how to write code in Kotlin to call these APIs and how Postman platform interacts the API. This chapter includes brief of Restful API, overview Vert.X, creating Restful API by Kotlin in Vert.X, calling API in Postman, and authentication for Restful API. At the end of the chapter, there are exercises to help readers improve their programming skills using Vert.X to create Restful API.

Preface

Kotlin is a form of programming language designed and standardized according to its own rule system, it can be programmed stand-alone or integrated with the Java programming language. Kotlin has now become a popular language for Android programming, increasingly interested in the programming community. There are many advantages that the Kotlin programming language offers such as the ability to overcome the weaknesses of Java. Currently, Java is one of the preferred programming languages when developers implement Android projects, but it still has certain limitations. One of the biggest lingering problems in Java is the lack of extensibility and inability to support functional programming. Kotlin is developed with features all inherited from Java, so programmers can use Kotlin as well as exploit all platforms from the existing Java class Library.

The Kotlin programming language is built with a low-code system that makes it easy for programmers to read, write, and work with. Beginners can easily absorb the specific knowledge of this language. The reduction of the amount of code has helped Kotlin bring a more enjoyable user experience compared to other languages like Java. Kotlin is designed to be able to reduce and eliminate most of the Null reference sources based on the null-safety mechanism. Therefore, according to experts, using Kotlin programming language will become safe. Much more complete than Java. Kotlin has high interoperability, now, Android developers have the ability to use Java class library right after using Kotlin to be able to write code and vice versa. In addition, Kotlin applications will work on different operating systems, such as iOS, Android, macOS, Windows, Linux, watchOS, and others.

Kotlin and Java are the best pairing, in our opinion; readers should learn Java well in the first place in order to master Kotlin programming language. These two languages will mutually support each other in coding. Google has recognized Kotlin as the main language for deploying Android projects, so this language has tremendous potential. We deliberately compiled to the level of difficulty in order from low to high, so you should study each lesson and we hope you will try your best to study Kotlin. Mastering Kotlin will give readers invaluable chances in the future, because in the future there will be a sin wave of recruiting Android programmers who are good at Kotlin.

With the desire to share knowledge about Kotlin programming language, we published the book *Principles, Policies, and Applications of Kotlin Programming* to provide comprehensive knowledge of Kotlin programming, the book that introduces the benefits of Kotlin programming, core of Kotlin, how to use programming tools, data types and variables, conditional and loop executions. Addition, the exception handling, important libraries commonly, string processing, array and collection processing are explained in the book. Especially knowledge of Object Oriented Programming in Kotlin, file processing, graphic user interface and Vert.X for Kotlin Restful API also implemented. Readers will gain a sufficient amount of knowledge about Kotlin to be able to continue implementing real projects, which can be applied to Restful API programming as well as Android programming.

Here are the main summaries of Kotlin programming knowledge presented in the 13 chapters that we cover in this book.

Chapter 1. Kotlin Introduction

This chapter introduces Kotlin programming language, readers will discover how to install Kotlin programming tools, how to create projects. This chapter also presents the types of notes when programming such as single-line comment, multi-line comments and KDoc comments, comments are one of the important requirements of the software industry. Readers will be familiar with simple and easy-to-understand examples so that readers can practice after reading and using the functions in the IntelliJ IDEA programming tool.

Chapter 2. Data Types and Variables

In the process of programming, understanding data types and variable declaration plays an important role in software development. The chapter presents the data types of the Kotlin language, data conversion. Also, important operators for data types covered in this chapter include unary operators, basic arithmetic, assignment, comparison, Logic, increment and decrement operators, etc. This chapter also guides how to input data into the software from the keyboard to help readers easily test the cases during the programming process.

Chapter 3. Conditional Execution

This chapter presents conditional constructs about simple if statement, if/ else statement, nested conditionals, expression and block form { }, and when structure. The when structure has been greatly improved in Kotlin, it provides a lot of use cases so that programmers can easily handle business tasks more optimally, such as when with if/ else statement, group multiple conditions. For each conditional structure, this chapter provides simple examples and detailed explanations to help readers understand the working mechanism of the conditional structure and apply them to specific business handling.

Chapter 4. Loop Executions

When dealing with list data such as character strings, numeric arrays, list of objects, etc. then loops will be used. Kotlin provides loop controls such as for, while, do while and abnormal loop termination. The loop executions are greatly improved, such as for loops that are divided many types such as closed range, half-open range, step and downTo navigation. And these kinds cover most of the loop handling cases, making it easy for programmers to use them optimally. This chapter also demonstrates how to handle break statement and continue statement in abnormal loop termination, these are very important statements in loop handling. This chapter also provides complete code and detailed explanations for each loop, making it easy for learners to understand and practice loops.

Chapter 5. Exception Handling

In the process of programming, most mistakes can be raised. And making errors while programming is obvious. Therefore, programmers need to have ways to distinguish the types of errors and how to handle errors. This chapter presents error levels such as Compiler error, Runtime exception error, Exception logic error. The techniques for catching errors such as try catch structure, throw exception technique, and illustrative codes are presented for how to handle this error for readers to easily grasp in this chapter. The IntelliJ IDEA's debugging tool is used in this book.

Chapter 6. Important Libraries Commonly

Every programming language has a set of libraries that will help programmers quickly solve certain tasks, and programmers must certainly use it because programmers cannot write some libraries or it spends long time, so programmers must know how to use it. These libraries may be in the JVM or KotlinJavaRuntime or in any other external library: Numeric Data Processing Library, Date processing library, Math processing library, Random number processing library, String processing library.

Chapter 7. String Processing

In all programming languages, string processing is extremely important, almost all of which are related to string processing. This chapter presents how to declare strings and summarize the commonly used functions of strings, such as indexOf, lastIndexOf, contains, substring, replace, trim, compare, plus, split, upper case and lowercase functions, etc. Each function has sample code along with detailed explanations that make it easy for readers to understand how to use basic string functions.

Chapter 8. Array Processing

Array is one of the very important data in software processing, it will be used to store data in the form of a list. Almost programming languages support array processing, and so does the Kotlin language. However, with Kotlin, arrays are a very powerful data type, which overcomes many disadvantages compared to other programming languages such as C++, C#, Java, etc. In chapter data type, the book has briefly mentioned some of the array types that are built-in in Kotlin, such as: CharArray, BooleanArray, IntArray, FloatArray, DoubleArray, etc. The book also presents multiple-array with IntArray type.

Chapter 9. Collections

Arrays do not meet and difficult to implement, because the data usually has no change in quantity, no deleting or changing the position of data, then it is appropriate to use an array, but when it comes to cases where the data changes continuously, or the number of elements is not known in advance, or the position in the list can be shuffled, using arrays is no longer optimal, so collections are more optimal. This chapter presents hierarchical collections so that readers have an overview of collections, and then Mutable and Immutable collection are presented. The chapter also provides code and detailed explanation to help readers easily grasp the working mechanism, as well as be able to implement the collection in practice.

Chapter 10. Object-Oriented Programming in Kotlin

Object-oriented programming (OOP) is an important programming technique that allows programmers to abstract objects in reality and create those objects in code, this programming technique is based on the concept of classes and objects. Objects include properties and methods, properties are information, specific characteristics of each object; Methods are operations that an object is capable of performing. A class is a data type that includes many predefined properties and methods, each class acts as a unit of combined methods and properties. Kotlin is like other programming languages that support object-oriented programming, the chapter provides illustrative and detailed explanations to help readers easily understand OOP concept.

Chapter 11. File Processing

During software deployment, different kinds of file will be used depending on the specific case. The book presents the series of four file types: Text File, Serialize File, XML File, JSon File so that readers have more options in file processing. The Kotlin uses JVM libraries to interact with the file, so programmers can invoke these libraries. This chapter provides examples of handling saving and reading files with different cases, which help readers to cover most of the processing cases in practice.

Chapter 12. Graphic User Interface

For customers, providing interactive user interfaces is very important, because customers almost manipulate on the intuitive screen. There are many types of interfaces provided by different programming languages, and depending on the case that programmer can use. In addition, with the development of programming languages, it is possible to use interfaces between different programming languages. This chapter presents graphic user interface, guide learners how to write classes that inherit interfaces as well as how to drag and drop controls on the interface to get the desired interface. This chapter, readers will discover about Layout, basic controls Label, Button, etc. and advanced like List, Table, Tree, etc. For each type of control, detailed instructions and instructions are provided, which makes it easy for readers to grasp the theory and implement the practical parts.

Chapter 13. Vert.X for Kotlin Restful API

Kotlin as well as other programming languages can be applied to writing Restful APIs. This chapter presents a new framework called Vert.X. It is considered as one of the powerful frameworks, it can support the implementation of many services including Restful API. Kotlin is used as the main programming language of Android mobile. When deploying Mobile, Restful API is used to interact with data on the Server, so how to create Restful APIs is very important. Using Vert.X will help programmers save a lot of time, and Vert.X is considered to be very optimal when deploying services. This chapter presents the knowledge of how to build and deploy Restful APIs using Vert.X, and demonstrate how to write code in Kotlin to call these APIs and how Postman platform interacts the API, and the Authentication for Restful API also mentioned.

Duy Thanh Tran
University of Economics and Law, Ho Chi Minh City, Vietnam & Vietnam National University, Ho Chi Minh City, Vietnam

Jun-Ho Huh
Korea Maritime and Ocean University, South Korea

Acknowledgment

We would like to thank the University of Economics and Law, Vietnam National University, Ho Chi Minh City, and the National Korea Maritime and Ocean University for supporting us during this book.

Chapter 1
Introducing Kotlin Programming Language

ABSTRACT

This chapter introduces Kotlin programming language and its strengths, such as brevity, saftey, versatility, and interoperability features. Readers will discover how to install Kotlin programming tools, how to create projects, program sample projects and check the output results. At the same time, this chapter also presents the types of notes when programming such as single-line comment, multi-line comments, and KDoc comments; comments are one of the important requirements of the software industry. Readers will be familiar with simple and easy-to-understand examples so that readers can practice after reading and using the functions in the IntelliJ IDEA programming tool. Finally, there are exercises listed at the end of the chapter to help readers practice more programming skills with Kotlin.

KOTLIN INTRODUCTION

This chapter introduces Kotlin programming language, its strengths such as Brief, Safe, Versatile, Interoperability features. Readers will discover how to install Kotlin programming tools, how to create projects, program sample projects and check the output results. At the same time, this chapter also presents the types of notes when programming such as single-line comment, multi-line comments and KDoc comments, comments are one of the important requirements of the software industry. Readers will be familiar with simple

DOI: 10.4018/978-1-6684-6687-2.ch001

and easy-to-understand examples so that readers can practice after reading and using the functions in the IntelliJ IDEA programming tool. Finally, there are exercises listed at the end of the chapter to help readers practice more programming skills with Kotlin.

Should We Study Kotlin?

Recently, the name Kotlin has created on May 17, 2012, and Google has announced that Kotlin will become the official Android programming language in 2017. From Android version 3.0, developers can use this language (Jemerov et al., 2017).

Figure 1. Kotlin language

The table below shows a summary of the official Kotlin versions published over the years.

Table 1. Kotlin version history

Kotlin version	Release Date	Main Features
Kotlin 1.0.0	February 15, 2016	The first officially stable release, and JetBrains compatibility starting with this version.
Kotlin 1.2.0	November 28, 2017	Sharing code between JVM and JavaScript platforms.
Kotlin 1.3.0	October 29, 2018	Bringing the coroutines for Asynchronous programming technique.
Kotlin 1.4.0	August 17, 2020	Support for Apple's platforms,such as Objective-C/Swift interop
Kotlin 1.5.0	May 5, 2021	New language features, performance improvements, stabilizing experimental APIs.
Kotlin 1.6.0	November 16, 2021	Continue to put new language and performance improments, APIs.
Kotlin 1.7.0	June 9, 2022	New Kotlin K2 compiler in Alpha for JVM
Kotlin 1.8.0	December 28, 2022	improved kotlin - reflect performance, improved Objective-C/Swift interoperability.
Kotlin 1.8.10	February 2, 2023	A bug fix release for Kotlin 1.8.0.
Kotlin 1.8.20	April 3, 2023	Updating Kotlin K2 compiler, AutoCloseable and Base64 encoding. Set by default for New JVM incremental compilation, put new compiler backend with Kotlin/Wasm.

In addition, Technology experts predict that in the future, there will be a sin wave of recruiting Android programmers who master the Kotlin language, companies will be very thirsty of talents, and you need to study Kotlin right now to go one-step ahead in the forthcoming trend. Google declares that these days over 60 percent of professional Android developers use Kotlin.

If you still reserve an opinion of "Being slow but stable". We think it is no longer true. This modern age is different, you have to be fast and stable to get the best opportunities, do not wait until Kotlin becomes too popular, then you are already the latecomers; try your best now to lead the market!

Have you been interested in Kotlin yet? Back to the day, we have tried our best to drop some lines to introduce Kotlin to you.

Kotlin has many advantages; We just list some of them here for your reference (of course you can find more): Brief, Safe, Versatile, Interoperability.

Figure 2. Kotlin advantages

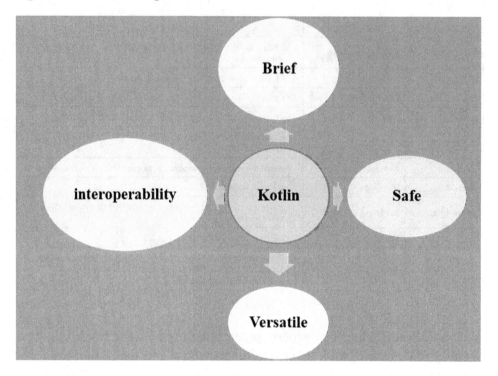

How brief is it?

- We can easily write the POJO (Plain Old Java Object) on one line:

```
data class Product(var id:String, var name: String, var
quantity: Int, var unitPrice: Double)
```

- You can use Lambda to filter data quickly:

```
var list:IntArray= IntArray(3)
list[0]=4
list[1]=5
list[2]=8
val evenNumbers = list.filter { it % 2 == 0 }
for (x in evenNumbers)
    println(x)
```

- We can create objects using SingleTon:

```
object ThisIsASingleton {
    var Name: String = "Viking"
}
```

In addition, there are many more brief programming styles; you take a quick look at https://kotlinlang.org/.

How safe is it?

Kotlin automatically checks for Null pointer exception, the actions on the null data set, and automatically casts the correct type for us, for example.

Table 2. Comparing Kotlin vs Java language

KOTLIN	JAVA

var s1:String?=null
//does not run
//kotlin check s1 is null so method not executed
s1?.trim()
s1="Hello World"
//does runs, because s1 is not null
s1?.trim()
//runs anyway (don't care s1 is null or not null)
s1!!.trim()
var s2:String="I'm Kotlin"
//no need s2? because String instead String?
s2.trim()
	String s1=null;
	//runs and through exception
	//java doesn't check s1 is null or not
	s1.trim();
	s1="Hello World";
	//runs method, because s1 is not null
	s1.trim();
	String s2="I'm Java";
	//runs method, because s2 is not null
	s2.trim();

How versatile is it?

Kotlin can do multiplatform applications. We can build Kotlin for Server-side, for Android, for JavaScript, Native....

How is its interoperability?

Kotlin can use 100% of the libraries from the JVM; we can call Kotlin from Java and call Java from Kotlin. Kotlin helps the programmer reduce their worry about converting coding, increasing the interoperability of the system.

Kotlin can also program easily on a variety of tools: Website, Eclipse, NetBeans, Android Studio, Jet Brains... Document about programming is very rich and easy to find, Kotlin support communities are constantly growing.

Install the Kotlin Programming Tool

In previous lesson, the book showed why you should study Kotlin. In this lesson, we will learn how to install the Kotlin programming tool.

To program Kotlin, you can use the Website to test online https://try.kotlinlang.org/

Alternatively, install IntelliJ IDEA, Eclipse Neon, Command Line Compiler, Build Tools (Ant, Maven, Gradle, Griffon (external support)).

In this lesson, we will show you how to install the IntelliJ IDEA software for Kotlin programming (because throughout the Kotlin programming tutorials, we will use this tool for illustration.)

First, you need to install JDK on your computer (Kotlin running on the JVM, install 1.8 or higher version); Kotlin course is usually for those who are already familiar with Java. Please take this step yourselves.

You download the Community version of IntelliJ IDEA at the following link: https://www.jetbrains.com/idea/download

Figure 3. Download IntelliJ IDEA

At the screen above, select Download Exe in Community, the moment we wrote this tutorial was 2023, so you would have the following results (depending on the time you load that you may have different versions):

Figure 4. IntelliJ IDEA after downloaded

Research (D:) > TranDuyThanh > Software			∨ C Search Software
Name	Date modified	Type	Size
▣ idealC-2023.1.exe	19/04/2023 12:26 AM	Application	647,617 KB

We see that the current version of the file "ideaIC-2021.1.3.exe" has more than 659 MB. To install, double click on the downloaded file:

Figure 5. Welcome to IntelliJ IDEA setup

Click Next to continue, the screen asking where to install will display as below:

Figure 6. Choose install location

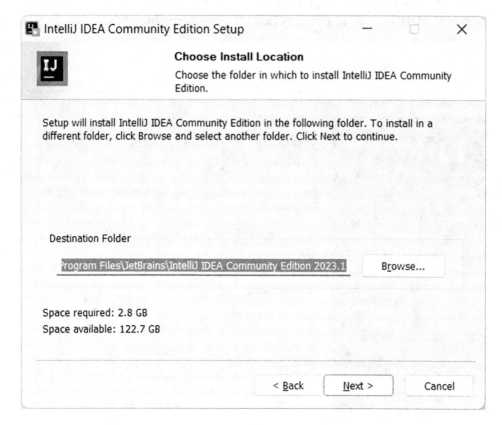

We can choose the default mode and then click Next, the program will display the configuration to be selected during the installation process, select the configuration as above and click next, the installation Options screen appears as below.

Figure 7. Installation options

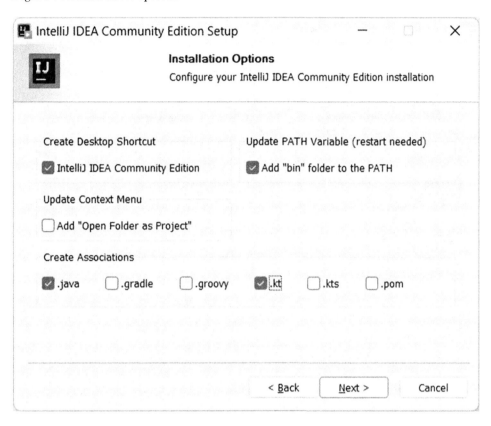

Checked the options as the same screen above and then click Next. Screen required to select Start Menu appears:

Figure 8. Choose start menu folder

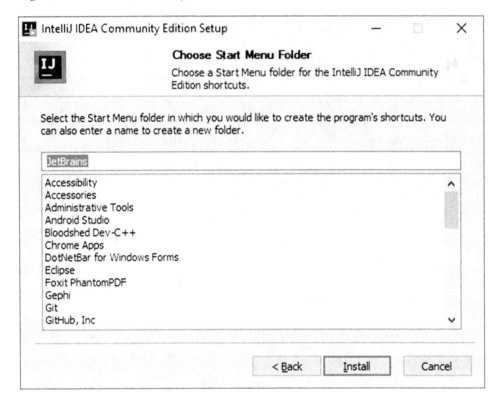

You choose the default mode and then click Install, wait for the program to complete the installation:

Figure 9. Installing

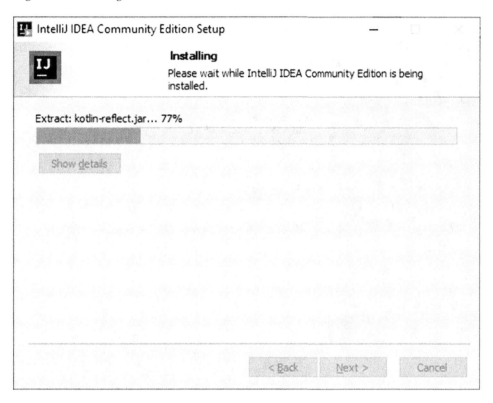

After successful installation, we have the notification screen as below:

Figure 10. Completing IntelliJ IDEA setup

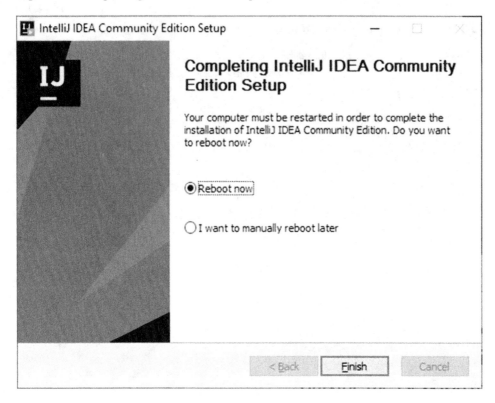

Choose Reboot now and click Finish to complete the installation. In the desktop screen, click on icon "IntelliJ IDEA Community Edition" to run the software. If you are running the software for the first time, you will encounter the following window:

Figure 11. Import IntelliJ IDEA settings

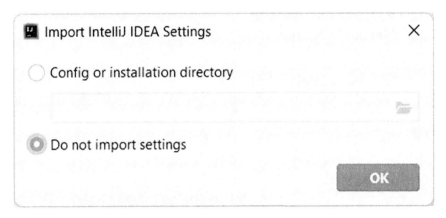

We choose "Do not import settings" and then click OK, the screen asking for the Theme setting the tool appears:

Figure 12. Set UI theme

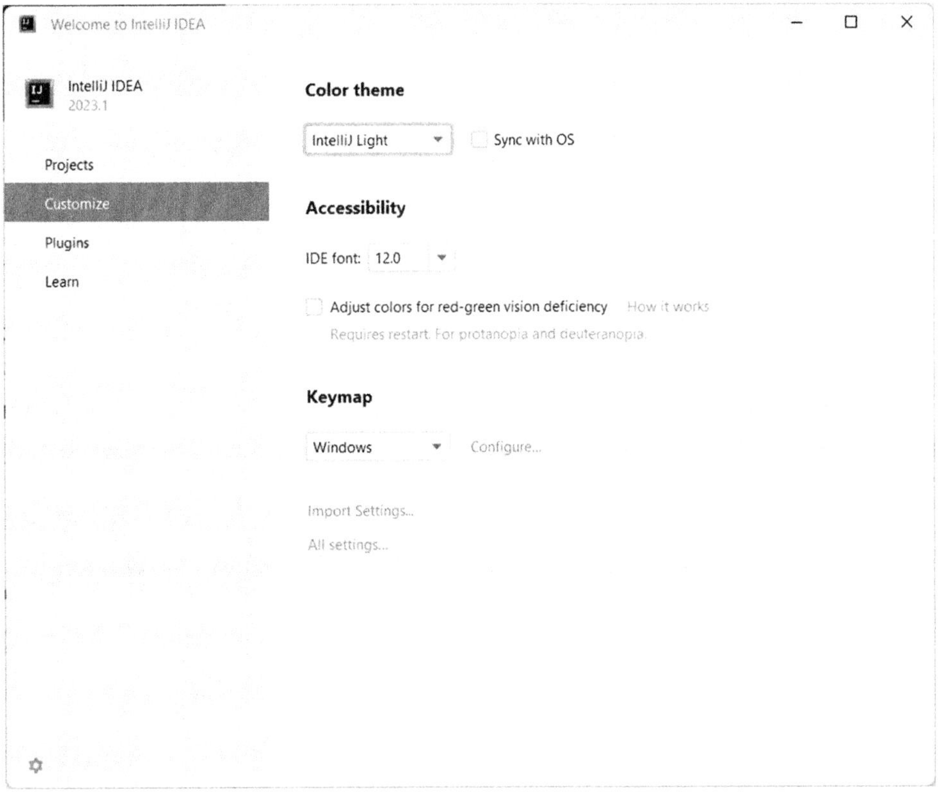

There are three color themes, depending on your choice, then click Skip All and Set Defaults for quick process, below is the screen after you have configured IntelliJ IDEA, the Welcome Screen will be similar:

Figure 13. Welcome to IntelliJ IDEA

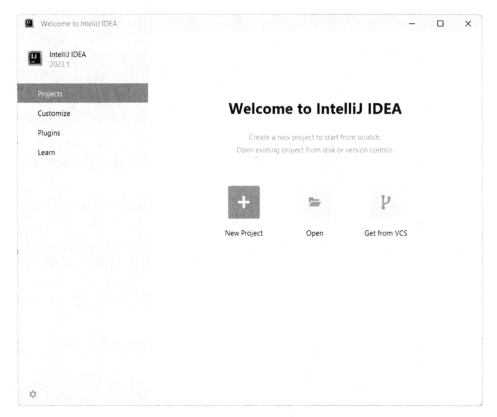

As for now, the book has completed the instructions on how to download and install the Kotlin programming tool, if you have ever done the Android Studio, is the interface very similar?

In the next lesson, the book will show how to create a project HelloWorld Kotlin, to feel programming in this new language. Please pay proper attention to the tutorial.

Create the First Application

Before we go into details about Kotlin, you need to know how to create the first Project Kotlin, we often say in English that it is "Hello World Project". Launch IntelliJ IDEA, from the short cut on the desktop, double click to launch:

Figure 14. Launch IntelliJ IDEA

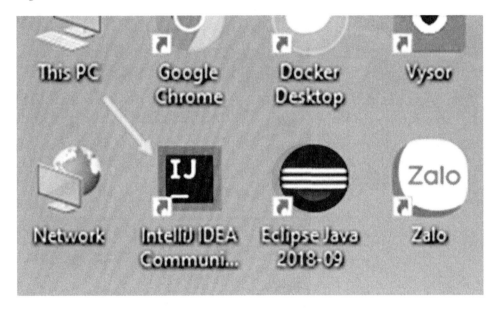

Welcome screen of IntelliJ IDEA, click Create New Project:

Figure 15. Welcome screen of IntelliJ IDEA

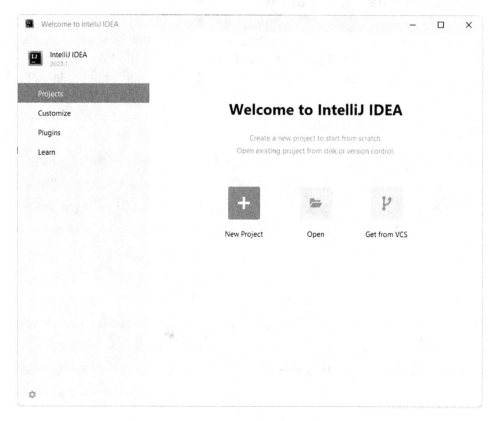

After clicking Create New Project, the New Project screen appears:

Figure 16. New project with Kotlin/JVM

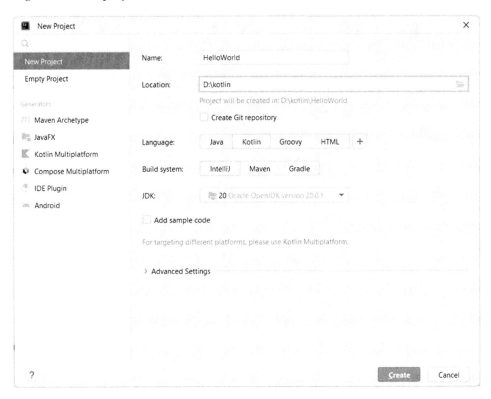

On the New Project screen above, you need to set Project SDK. This is where you select the path where you installed the JDK, click combobox to point to where you have installed (you should install JDK from 1.8 or higher version). Project name is "HelloWorld", language "Kotlin", build system "IntelliJ" and choose location to store, then click Finish.

Here is the screenshot of Project Kotlin created:

Figure 17. Completed creating Kotlin project

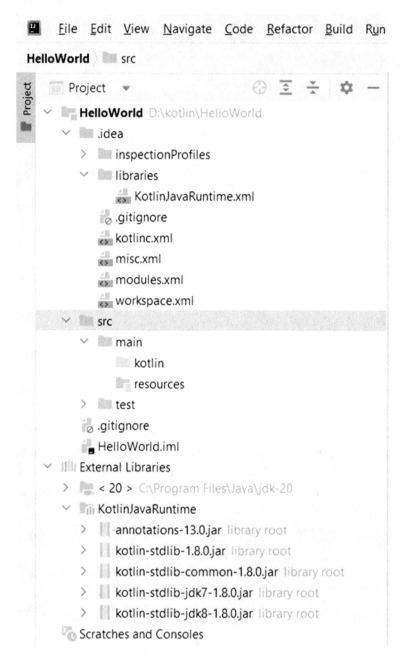

- The ". idea" directory gives us configuration files, library references.

o The "src" directory is where the source code files are stored for the project.

- The File HelloWorld.iml is essentially an XML file, which saves the default configuration parameters for the project.
- **External Libraries:** JDK, KotlinJavaRuntime is required, these libraries will be referenced in the KotlinJavaRuntime.xml file.

To create a Kotlin source code, proceed as follows: Right-click on the "kotlin" directory / select New / select Kotlin Class / File as figure below.

Figure 18. Choose Kotlin class/file

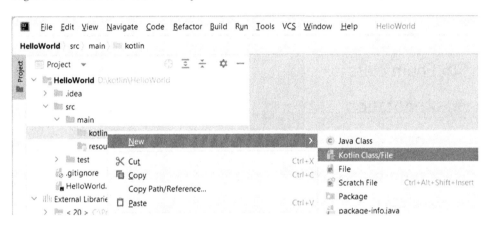

The screen asking to create the Kotlin File appears as below:

Figure 19. Create app Kotlin file

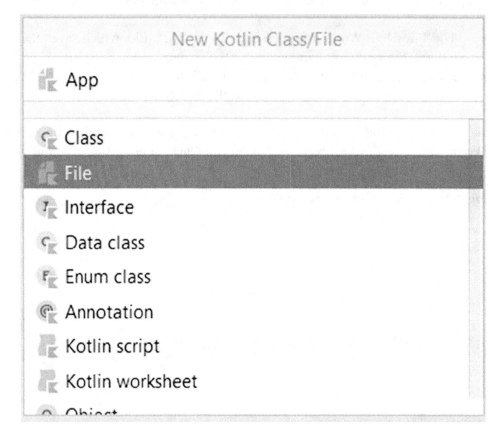

Name: You can set the name as you wish, for example, we choose the name
App.

Kind: Select File (this will select File; the following lesson will be the case
where we select other types in the combo box).

Press Enter to create; we will see the source code structure as follows:

Figure 20. App.kt Kotlin file

So, you see, the extension of Kotlin is kt, we proceed to Coding to export the outstanding message *"Hello World! I am Kotlin"*:

In the coding editor of App. kt, just type main (main method without parameter) or maina (main method with parameter) and press ctrl + space, the full main function will appear:

Figure 21. Create main method

the main () function ==> you just need to press Enter, it will automatically appear full command (this is called Template, you can configure yourself, and there are many IntelliJ IDEA default templates):

Figure 22. Main method

```
App.kt ×
1 ▶    fun main(args: Array<String>) {
2
3      }
```

You have seen the main Function structure, with the fun keyword (i.e., function), and with arguments input inside run when the code is run (often used to pass call parameters between different applications). If you want to export the command prompt to the screen then write inside the main function, for example:

Figure 23. println method

```
App.kt ×
1 ▶    fun main(args: Array<String>) {
2          println("Hello World! I am Kotlin")
3      }
```

In what aspects is this different from Java? Finalizing the statement without a semicolon, isn't it? Now how can we run this command? You can go to Run / Run menu. Alternatively, right-click on App.kt and select Run App. kt as shown below:

Figure 24. Run App.kt

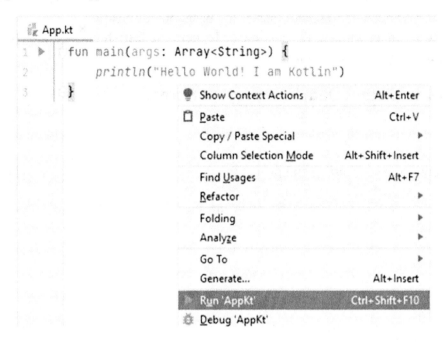

You wait for the program to compile and you will have the output as below:

Figure 25. Process finished for App.kt

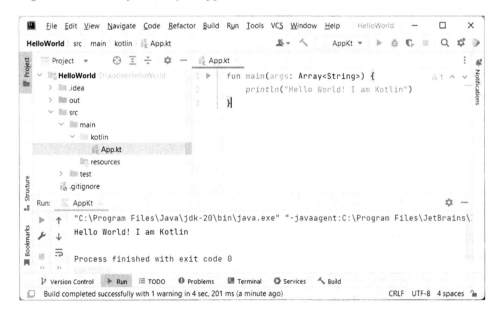

We have shown you how to create a first Project Kotlin, as well as how to run it, you need to do this to master the basic operations first.

You can download the source code here to test: https://github.com/thanhtd32/kotlin/tree/main/HelloWorld

How to Output Data in the Kotlin Screen

In previous lesson, we have learned how to create a Project Kotlin, in this lesson; we will learn how to output data in the Kotlin screen.

You can use println() and print() functions to send output to the standard output (screen) these two functions belong to the kotlin.io library

The println() function is used to display output on different lines, for example:

```
println("Sun")
println("Earth")
println("Moon")
```

Result of the codes:

```
Sun
Earth
Moon
```

The print() function is used to export data on the same line, for example:

```
print("Sun")
print("Earth")
print("Moon")
```

Result of the codes:

```
SunEarthMoon
```

Download source code here:
https://github.com/thanhtd32/kotlin/tree/main/LearnOutput
Kotlin also provides some special characters for navigating the way that data is displayed, such as:

- \n to begin a newline
- \t for indentation

- \" to quote

The coding is shown in the Listing 1.

Listing 1. LearnSpecialCharacter/App.kt

```
1    fun main(args: Array<String>) {
2      println("It sits, poisonous")
3      println("Dripping sorrow over the windowsill")
4      println("\tI drove to the \"Skyway\"")
5      println("\tDropped a heart over the edge.")
6      print("Watched it splash under")
7      print("\nIt took a couple seconds to hit.")
8    }
```

Result of the codes:

```
It sits, poisonous
Dripping sorrow over the windowsill
        I drove to the "Skyway"
        Dropped a heart over the edge.
Watched it splash under
It took a couple seconds to hit.
```

The book has shown how to print strings to the screen, please practice two functions print() and println(). Download source code here:
https://github.com/thanhtd32/kotlin/tree/main/LearnSpecialCh aracter

Comments

Why should we take comments during coding?
From our personal point of view, some of the following reasons need to be taken into account when writing code:

- The purpose of comments is to help explain the semantics of statements, as well as the function of functions and classes. Helps programmers easily re-read, train new employees, create documents from comments
- Projects are usually done by a team, if we do not comment, how can we understand? If you just write, after a long time, it will be forgotten, you must comment to save human resources, time, costs ...

- Practice professionalism in the work process
- Being responsible for the issues that you are assigned to complete, it should be explained so that when you say Goodbye others can understand your codes.

When programming Kotlin, we have three common captioning styles, and these will be ignored during compilation:

- Comment on one line
- Comment on multiple lines
- Comment using KDoc Syntax

Now we go into details.

Comment on One Line

To Comment on a line using the syntax // Comment 1 line

The example for comment 1 line is in the Listing 2.

Listing 2. LearnComments/App_Comment1Line.kt

```
1   fun main(args: Array<String>) {
2     //call plus function for 2 numbers:
3     var t:Int=7.plus(8)
4     println(t)
5   }
```

You see line number 2 has string // call plus function for 2 numbers => this is the comment line. This syntax allows us to comment a line, based on this we can understand what the command below is used for.

Comment on Multiple Lines

This comment will be wrapped by

```
/* Comment line 1
Comment line 2
Comment line n
*/
```

Allow you to make comments on different lines, the Listing 3 shows the example.

Listing 3. LearnComments/App_CommentMultipleLine.kt

```
1    /*
2    This is the main function
3    used to run the program
4    */
5    fun main(args: Array<String>) {
6    //call plus function for 2 numbers:
7     var t:Int=7.plus(8)
8    println(t)
9    }
```

We look at the top of the main function with multiple line comments to explain in detail a command, a block of command or a function (depending on our purpose and style).

Comment KDoc Syntax

This syntax is wrapped by / ** Kdoc Syntax * /

Kotlin has a tool to generate Document; this tool is called <u>Dokka,</u> https://github.com/Kotlin/dokka/blob/master/README.md

KDoc Syntax has some Blog Tag; we need to know:

```
@author: The author
@sample: Sample and example
@param: parameter in function
@return: return result of function
```

KDoc example is shown in the Listing 4.

Listing 4. LearnComments/App_CommentKDoc.kt

```
1    /**
2    * @author Tran Duy Thanh
3    * @param x parameter x
4    * @param y parameter y
5    * @return sum of x and y
6    * @sample x=5, y=6 => 11
7    * This is docs comment
8    */
9    fun Plus(x:Int,y:Int):Int
10   {
11   return x+y
12   }
13   /*
14   This is the main function
15   used to run the program
16   */
17   fun main(args: Array<String>) {
18   //call plus 2 numbers function
19    val t:Int=Plus(7,8)
20   println(t)
21   }
```

The way to write notes in **KDoc** format is very convenient, when using the function, we only need to move the mouse to know the function description, the meaning of the function as well as the arguments in the function. This helps programmers easily understand how to use the function quickly, optimizing time and effort to learn.

The following figure shows at command line 19, we move the mouse to the Plus function, the usage description of this function will be displayed as below:

Figure 26. KDoc example

```
17  ▶     fun main(args: Array<String>) {
18              //call plus 2 numbers function
19              val t:Int=Plus( x: 7, y: 8)
20              println(t)
21         }
22
```

```
App_CommentKDoc.kt
public fun Plus(
        x: Int,
        y: Int
): Int


Params:  x - parameter x
         y - parameter y
Returns: sum of x and y
Author:  Tran Duy Thanh
Samples: x
             x:Int                           ⋮
```

We have completed the comments when programming with Kotlin, please pay attention to the comments. Source code you can download at here:
https://github.com/thanhtd32/kotlin/tree/main/LearnComments

Exercises

1. What is the Kotlin Language?
2. How Kotlin language brief is it?
3. How Kotlin Language safe is it?
4. How Kotlin Language versatile is it?
5. How Kotlin Language is its interoperability?
6. What is the Kotlin Programming Tool?
7. What is the Kotlin file extension?
8. How to create a Kotlin Project in IntelliJ IDEA tool?
9. How to output data in the Kotlin screen?
10. How to print the special characters in Kotlin?
11. How many kinds of comments in Kotlin?
12. Explain the KDoc Syntax.

13. Compare Kotlin and Java programming languages.
14. What types of programming languages are used to program software running on the Android operating system?
15. What is the kotlin.io library used for?

REFERENCES

Jemerov & Isakova. (2017). *Kotlin in Action.* Manning.

Chapter 2
Data Types and Variables

ABSTRACT

In the process of programming, understanding data types and variable declaration plays an important role in software development. When choosing the right data type and managing variables well, this will help the software to be optimized and memory, making the customer experience for the software better. The chapter will present the data types of the Kotlin language, data types will be grouped some category to make it easy for learners to remember and compare, data explicit conversion and implicit conversion are mentioned. Also, important operators for data types covered in this chapter include unary operators, basic arithmetic, assignment, comparison, Logic, increment and decrement operators, etc. This chapter also guides how to input data into the software from the keyboard to help readers easily test the cases during the programming process. For each content, this chapter provides simple and easy-to-understand sample code for easy access, and at the end of the chapter there are practice exercises to improve programming skills.

DATA TYPES AND VARIABLES

In the process of programming, understanding data types and variable declaration plays an important role in software development. When choosing the right data type and managing variables well, this will help the software to be optimized and memory, making the customer experience for the software better. The chapter will present the data types of the Kotlin language, data types will be grouped some category to make it easy for learners to remember

DOI: 10.4018/978-1-6684-6687-2.ch002

and compare, data explicit conversion and implicit conversion are mentioned. Also, important operators for data types covered in this chapter include unary operators, basic arithmetic, assignment, comparison, Logic, increment and decrement operators, etc. This chapter also guides how to input data into the software from the keyboard to help readers easily test the cases during the programming process. For each content, this chapter provides simple and easy-to-understand sample code for easy access, and at the end of the chapter there are practice exercises to improve programming skills.

Data Types

Each programming language provides several types of data that are available for storing. In addition, Kotlin offers a wide range of data types, such as real numbers, integers, characters, strings, logic, and arrays. The fact is that all types of data in Kotlin are object oriented. Understanding the meaning of each type of data helps, we choose how to declare variables of the appropriate type, which helps optimize the system.

Figure 1 shows overview of the built-in data types in Kotlin.

Figure 1. Kotlin data types

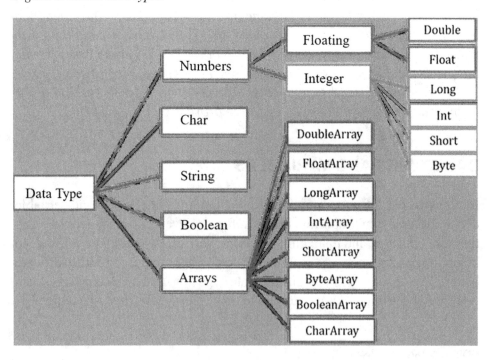

Floating numbers will have two types, Double and Float. If there is a constant to determine that it is a real number, then we can add the letter f or F behind that constant:

For example: 113.5 → Double; 113.5F or 113.5f → Float

There are four types of integers: Long, Int, Short, Byte. Note the case of the Long and Int constants by adding the letter L

For example: 113→ Int number; 113L → Long number

Variables and Assignment

We can declare variables for these types of data as follows:

var Variable_name: Data_Type= Default Value

Listing 1 shows the variables and assignment.

Listing 1. LearnDataType/App.kt

```
1   fun main(args: Array<String>) {
2   var x:Long=100L
3   var y:Double=113.5
4   var f:Float=113.5f
5   var i:Int =113
6   var s:Short=8
7   var b:Byte=1
8   }
```

Please notice that no semicolon is needed at the end of the command.

Character type used to store a character in a single quote.

```
var c:Char='c'
```

The string type used to store character sets is in double quotation strings, using the String object to declare:

```
var name:String="Tran Duy Thanh-thanhtd@uel.edu.vn"
```

In addition, we can declare a string on multiple lines by enclosing three double quotes, see the Listing 2.

Listing 2. LearnDataType/App_String.kt

```
1    fun main(args: Array<String>) {
2    var address:String="""
3    No. 407 Data Science Lab
4    Korea Maritime & Ocean University
5    727 Taejong-ro, Dongsam-dong, Yeongdo-gu, Busan
6    """
7    println(address)
8    }
```

The output of the three double quotes:

```
No. 407 Data Science Lab
Korea Maritime & Ocean University
727 Taejong-ro, Dongsam-dong, Yeongdo-gu, Busan
```

Logical type uses a Boolean object to declare that this type of data will hold true or false value, which is very important to use in conditional checking:

```
var result:Boolean=true
```

With array data types, Kotlin provides us with eight types of arrays for eight data types built into Kotlin (except for String).

To declare and use the data type, please follow these steps:

```
var Array_Name: Data_Type_Array = XXXArrayOf (value 1, value 2,
..., value n)
```

With XXX is the corresponding 8 data types (the first character is usually lowercase), Listing 3 show how to use the array data type.

Listing 3. LearnDataType/App_ArrayData.kt

```
1    fun main(args: Array<String>) {
2    var arrX:IntArray= intArrayOf(1,2,3,5)
3    println(arrX[1])
4    var arrY:DoubleArray= doubleArrayOf(1.5,2.6,9.0,10.3)
5    println(arrY[3])
6    var arrC:CharArray= charArrayOf('a','b','c')
7    println(arrC[0])
8    }
```

The result of the code:

```
2
10.3
a
```

Also, if we want to declare a constant, we use val instead of var. var allowed to change the value of the variable, val is not allowed. We often say mutable when declaring var, read-only when declaring val. Listing 4 shows how to use the val keyword.

Listing 4. LearnDataType/App_constant.kt

```
1   fun main(args: Array<String>) {
2       //PI is a constant
3       val PI:Double =3.14
4       //we get the error:
5       PI=3.15//not allowed because PI is read-only
6   }
```

We have presented the data types and how to declare variables in Kotlin, you remember to do this again to understand more about data types in Kotlin, you should compare the differences in data type as well as how to declare variables to java.

Source code you can download at the link: https://github.com/thanhtd32/ kotlin/tree/main/LearnDataType.

Data Type Conversion

We have a good understanding of the data types as well as how to declare variables, in this lesson, the book will show how to converse data type in Kotlin.

Figure 2. Kotlin type conversion

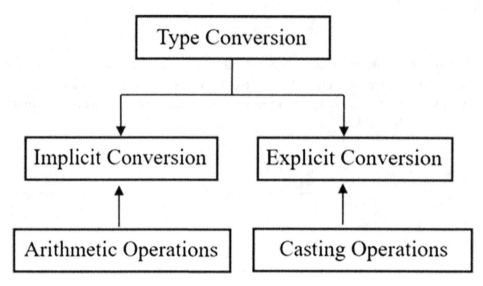

Why should we have to cast?

In the calculation process, the result is no longer the same as the initial data type, so we need to cast. And when conversing, we usually encounter two cases:

Widening conversion

Taken from the conversion of small storage area to the conversion of large storage area. This way avoids data loss.

For example: Byte→Short→Int→Long→Float→Double

Narrowing conversion

Taken from the conversion of large storage area to the conversion of small storage area. This way there maybe loss of data

For example: Double→Float→Long→Int→Short→Byte

How to cast?

In Kotlin, any number data type also has methods available:

- toByte(): Convert data type to Byte
- toShort(): Convert data type to Short
- toInt(): Convert data type to Int
- toLong(): Convert data type to Long
- toFloat(): Convert data type to Float
- toDouble(): Convert data type to Double
- toChar(): Convert data type to Char

Explicit Conversion

These methods are often referred to as explicit conversion (which specifies what type of data is to be conversed).

We try to run the following conversion in Listing 5.

Listing 5. LearnDataConversion/App_Int_to_Double.kt

```
fun main(args: Array<String>) {
var X:Int=10
//Convert value of X from Int data type to Double data type
 var D:Double=X.toDouble()
println("X="+X)
println("D="+D)
}
```

The result is X = 10, and D is 10.0 because 10 is given a Double of 10.0.

This is widening conversion→Taken from a smaller storage conversion to a larger storage conversion.

Consider example conversion in the Listing 6.

Listing 6. LearnDataConversion/App_Double_to_Int.kt

```
fun main(args: Array<String>) {
var F:Double=10.5
//Convert value of F from Double data type to Int data type
 var Y:Int = F.toInt()
println("F="+F)
println("Y="+Y)
}
```

The result of F = 10.5 and Y = 10. In this case, we loss the data, this is the case of narrowing, taken from the conversion, which has a larger storage area→on the data conversion which has smaller storage area. Narrowing is very dangerous because it causes data loss, especially problems related to minimum requirements, or bank transfer. This should be avoided.

Implicit Conversion

Kotlin also supports one case of Implicit Conversion, Kotlin interprets the data conversion to assign variables, usually by arithmetic operations, for example:

```
var t=13L+1
println(t)
```

13L is of LONG, 1 is of Int → Kotlin takes the largest data conversion as standard and assigns t → t to Long.

Let take another example in the Listing 7.

Listing 7. LearnDataConversion/App_ImplicitConversion.kt

1	fun main(args: Array<String>){	1	fun main(args: Array<String>) {
2	var x:Int=5	2	var x:Int=5
3	//get error	3	//convert x to Double
4	var d:Double =x+1	4	var d:Double =x+1.0
5	println("d=$d")	5	println("d=$d")
6	}	6	}

Unlike the Java language, Kotlin does not allow assignments or operations with incorrect numeric data types. With Kotlin we have to implement the correct data type. In command line number 4, calling d=x+1 will give an error because x and number 1 are of type Int and d is of type Double. However, we can adjust d=x+1.0, now 1.0 has a Double and it automatically converts x to Double to perform the math.

We have presented how to converse data in Kotlin, this lesson is very important. We need to make sure that the conversion rule is chosen properly. And certainly, in the programming process we must encounter frequent cases of conversing.

You can download the Source code at the link: https://github.com/thanhtd32/kotlin/tree/main/LearnDataConversion.

Important Operators

Each programming language has a set of key operators that allow us to generate expressions in code to solve some of the problems involved, and these operators are also used by Kotlin Overrides as methods. (We can use pure operators and also by using methods.)

- Unary operators
- Basic arithmetic operators
- Assignment operators
- Comparison Operators
- Logic operators
- Increment and Decrement Operators
- Operator precedence:

Now we go into single details

Unary Operators

The unary operators show in the Table 1.

Table 1. Unary operators

Operators	Description	Method	For Example
+	Positive numbers	a.unaryPlus()	var a:Int =-8 var b=a.unaryPlus()
–	Negative numbers	a.unaryMinus()	var a:Int =-8 var b=a.unaryMinus()

Listing 8 shows how to use the unary operators.

Listing 8. LearnImportantOperators/App_Unary_Operators.kt

```
1   fun main(args: Array<String>) {
2   var a:Int=-8
3   var b=a.unaryPlus()
4   var c=a.unaryMinus()
5   println("a="+a)
6   println("b="+b)
7   println("c="+c)
8   }
```

Running the above code, we will have the following results

```
a=-8
b=-8
c=8
```

Note that unaryPlus and unaryMinus do not change the internal value of the variable, but it returns a value, which requires a variable to store this value.

Basic Arithmetic Operators

Like other programming languages, Kotlin also supports the basic arithmetic operators shown in Table 2.

Table 2. Basic arithmetic operators

Operators	Description	Method	For Example
+	Plus	a.plus(b)	8 + 5 → 13 8.plus(5) →13
−	Minus	a.minus(b)	8-5 →3 8.minus(5) →3
*	Multiply	times	8*5 →40 8.times(5) →40
/	Divide	div	8/5 → 1 8.div(5) → 1
%	Divide with a remainder	rem	8% 5 → 3 8.rem(5) →3

The examples for basic arithmetic operators are shown in the Listing 9.

Listing 9. LearnImportantOperators/App_Basic_Arithmetic_Operators.kt

```
1   fun main(args: Array<String>) {
2   var a:Int=8
3   var b:Int=5
4   println("Plus method 1:"+a+"+"+b+"="+(a+b))
5   println("Plus method 2:"+a+"+"+b+"="+(a.plus(b)))
6   println("Minus method 1:"+a+"-"+b+"="+(a-b))
7   println("Minus method 2:"+a+"-"+b+"="+(a.minus(b)))
8   println("Multiply method 1:"+a+"*"+b+"="+(a*b))
9   println("Multiply method 2:"+a+"*"+b+"="+(a.times(b)))
10  println("Divide method 1:"+a+"/"+b+"="+(a/b))
11  println("Divide method 2:"+a+"/"+b+"="+(a.div(b)))
12  println("Find remainders method 1:"+a+"%"+b+"="+(a%b))
13  println("Find remainders method 2:"+a+"/"+b+"="+(a.rem(b)))
14  println(8.plus(9))
15  }
16
```

Running the above code, we will have the following results:

```
Plus method 1:8+5=13
Plus method 2:8+5=13
Minus method 1:8-5=3
Minus method 2:8-5=3
Multiply method 1:8*5=40
Multiply method 2:8*5=40
Divide method 1:8/5=1
Divide method 2:8/5=1
Find remainders method 1:8%5=3
Find remainders method 2:8/5=3
17
```

Assignment Operators

Kotlin also uses assignment operators like other programming languages, the usage of which is shown in Table 3.

Table 3. Assignment operators

Operators	Description	For Example	Equivalent To
=	Assigns the right value to the variable to the left of the equals sign	x=5	
+=	Plus and assign	x=2 x+=5 →x=7	x=x+5
-=	Minus and assign	x=2 x-=5 →x=-3	x=x-5
*=	Multiply and assign	x=2 x*=5 →x=10	x=x*5
/=	Divide and assign	x=7 x/=5 →x=1	x=x/5
%=	Divide with a remainder	x=7 x%=5 →x=2	x=x%5

Example for assignment operators is shown in the Listing 10.

Listing 10. LearnImportantOperators/App_Assignment_Operators.kt

```
1    fun main(args: Array<String>) {
2    var x:Int=5
3    x+=2
4    println("x="+x)
5    x-=2
6    println("x="+x)
7    x*=2
8    println("x="+x)
9    x/=2
10   println("x="+x)
11   x=7
12   x%=3
13   println("x="+x)
14   }
```

Running the above code, we will have the following results

```
x=7
x=5
x=10
x=5
x=1
```

Comparison Operators

Kotlin language supports comparison operators, they are shown in the Table 4.

Table 4. Comparison operators

Operators	Description	Method	For Example
==	Equality operator	a.equals(b)	5 == 5 → True
!=	In equality operator	!a.equals(b)	5 != 5 → False
<	Less than operator	a.compareTo(b) < 0	5 < 5 → False
<=	Less than or equal operator	a.compareTo(b) <= 0	5 <= 5 → True
>	Greater than operator	a.compareTo(b) > 0	5 > 5.5 → False
>=	Greater than or equal operator	a.compareTo(b) >= 0	113>= 5 → True

The Listing 11 shows how to use the comparison operators.

Listing 11. LearnImportantOperators/App_Comparison_Operators.kt

```
1    fun main(args: Array<String>) {
2    var a:Int=8
3    var b:Int=5
4    println(a==b)//false
5    println(a.equals(b))//false
6    println(!a.equals(b))//true
7    println(a.compareTo(b))//1
8    println(3.compareTo(3))//0
9    println(3.compareTo(5))//-1
10   println(5.compareTo(3))//1
11   }
```

a.equals(b) returns true if a and b are equal, false if a and b are different.
a.compareTo(b) returns 0 if a and b are equal, returns >0 if a>b, and returns <0 if a<b.

Running the above code, we will have the following results

```
false
false
true
1
0
-1
1
```

Logic Operators

Kotlin support logic operators && and ‖, the details are shown in the Table 5.

Table 5. Logic operators

Operators	Description	Method	For Example
&&	AND operator: If both conditions are True then the result will be True	a.and(b)	x=false y=true x&&y→false
‖	OR operator: If one condition is True, it is True; if all conditions are False, it is False	a.or(b)	x=false y=true x‖y→true

The examples logic operators are shown in the Listing 12.

Listing 12. LearnImportantOperators/App_Logic_Operators.kt

```
1    fun main(args: Array<String>) {
2    var x: Boolean = true
3    var y: Boolean = false
4    var z: Boolean = false
5    println("x=" + x)//x=true
6    println("y=" + y)//y=false
7    println("z=" + z)//z=false
8    println("x&&y=" + (x && y))//x&&y=false
9    println("x.and(y)=" + x.and(y))//x.and(y)=false
10   println("x || y =" + (x || y))//x || y =true
11   println("x.or(y)=" + x.or(y))//x.or(y)=true
12   println("x || z =" + (x || z))//x || z =true
13   println("x.or(z)=" + x.or(z))//x.or(z)=true
14   println("x && z =" + (x && z))//x && z =false
15   println("x.and(z)=" + x.and(z))//x.and(z)=false
16   println("y || z =" + (y || z))//y || z =false
17   println("y.or(z)=" + y.or(z))//y.or(z)=false
18   println("y && z =" + (y && z))//y && z =false
19   println("y.and(z)=" + y.and(z))//y.and(z)=false
20   println("x && y && z =" + (x && y && z))//x && y && z =false
21   println("x.and(y).and(z)=" + x.and(y).and(z))
22   //x.and(y).and(z)=false
23   println("x|| y||z =" + (x || y || z))//x|| y||z =true
24   println("x.or(y).or(z)=" + x.or(y).or(z))//x.or(y).or(z)=true
25   }
```

Running the above code, we will have the following results

```
x=true
y=false
z=false
x&&y=false
x.and(y)=false
x || y =true
x.or(y)=true
x || z =true
x.or(z)=true
x && z =false
x.and(z)=false
y || z =false
y.or(z)=false
y && z =false
y.and(z)=false
x && y && z =false
x.and(y).and(z)=false
x|| y||z =true
x.or(y).or(z)=true
```

Increment and Decrement Operators

Increment and decrement operator details are shown in the Table 6.

Table 6. Increment and decrement operators

Operators	Description	Method	For Example
++	Increase the internal variable by one unit	a.inc()	x=5 x++ →x=6
--	Decreases the internal variable by one unit	a.dec()	x=5 x-- →x=4

Note that the inc () and dec () functions themselves will not change (increase or decrease) the inner value of the variable, we need another variable to store the changed value.

With this incremental and descending operator, putting ++ or - in front of and behind the variable has a different meaning in a complex expression, usually it will work in principle (there are some case-sensitive. We do not consider this rule, mainly because of Testing Problem:

- **Step 1:** Prioritize to process the prefix (the ++ or --)
- **Step 2:** Calculates the remaining operations in the expression
- **Step 3:** Assign the value in step 2 to the result storage variable to the left of the '=' sign
- **Step 4:** Process the Postfix (the ++ or --)

Example for increment and decrement is shown in the Listing 13.

Listing 13. LearnImportantOperators/App_Increment_Decrement_Operators.kt

```
1   fun main(args: Array<String>) {
2   var a:Int=5
3   var b:Int=8
4   var c:Int=2
5   a--
6   b++
7   var z=a++ + ++b - --c + 7
8   println("a="+a)
9   println("b="+b)
10  println("c="+c)
11  println("z="+z)
12  }
```

Explain the execution of the above program as follows:

- Line 2, 3, 4 initializes values for variables a=5, b=8 and c=2.
- Line 5 reduces a by 1, so a = 4
- Line 6 increments b by 1, so b = 9
- Line 7 works according to the following principle:
  - **Step 1:** Implement prefixes, including ++b and --c, which means increment b by 1 value, decrement c by 1 value. Now b=10 and c=1.
  - **Step 2:** Perform the remaining operations to the right of the equal sign of the expression z. Now we have the result 4+10-1+7 this operation has a value of 20.
  - **Step 3:** Assign the results found in step 2 to the variable z to the left of the = sign, now z=20.
  - **Step 4:** Perform the postfix, that means, it does a++, increment a by 1 value, so a=5.

Running the above code, we will have the following results as the same we explained:

```
a=5
b=10
c=1
z=20
```

However, we should use parentheses to delimit operator precedence, avoid self-trapping when programming, and also ensure the clarity of expressions.

Operator Precedence

Kotlin has a constraint in the order precedence of the operators and it is shown in the Table 7. However, it is best that you manipulate it by using parentheses () to make it clearer. The table below refers to the priority from high to low (however, please use the parentheses () to specify).

Table 7. Operator precedence

Priority	Operators	Description
1	* / %	Multiplication, division, extraction
2	+ –	Plus and minus operator
3	<= < > >=	Comparison Operators
4	<> == !=	Comparison Operators
5	= %= /= -= += *=	Assignment Operators
6	&&, ‖	Logic Operators

We have given you a brief introduction about operators, please read it and examples carefully.

Download source code here: https://github.com/thanhtd32/kotlin/tree/main/LearnImportantOperators.

User Input

In this lesson, the book will show how to input data from the keyboard.

For Kotlin, to input data from the keyboard, we use the readLine() function, which is located in the default library kotlin.io

The readLine () function will returns a string of data entered from the keyboard or null if no data is available.

From this result string we can converse the data type of any type, we wish to match the value entered.

Listing 14. LearnInputData/App_InputData.kt

```
1    fun main(args: Array<String>) {
2    println("What is your name?")
3    var name:String?= readLine()
4    println("Welcome to!!!")
5    println(name)
6    }
```

Example to enter a string is shown in the Listing 14.
Run the program and put your name:

```
What is your name?
Tran Duy Thanh
```

```
Welcome to!!!
Tran Duy Thanh
```

Did you notice that I have declared String? The data type is null able, which is a new way of declaring it in Kotlin. It is the same for Int? and Double?, etc.

With some formatting in the Kotlin, we always pass the data type to the original format. String in Kotlin is supported by a set of methods, it is shown in the Table 8.

Table 8. Convert string to numeric

Function	Description	For Example
toBoolean()	Convert the string to Boolean	"true".toBoolean()
toByte()	Convert the string to Byte	"3".toByte()
toShort()	Convert the string to Short	"30".toShort()
toInt()	Convert the string to Int	"15".toInt()
toLong()	Convert the string to Long	"100".toLong()
toFloat()	Convert the string to Float	"15.5".toFloat()
toDouble()	Convert the string to Double	"15.5".toDouble()

Coding example for converting string to numerics is shown in the Listing 15.

Listing 15. LearnInputData/App_StringConvertMethod.kt

```
1
2
3
4     fun main(args: Array<String>) {
5     var x1:Boolean="true".toBoolean()
6     println(x1)
7     var x2:Byte="3".toByte()
8     println(x2)
9     var x3:Short="30".toShort()
10    println(x3)
11    var x4:Int="15".toInt()
12    println(x4)
13    var x5:Long="100".toLong()
14    println(x5)
15    var x6:Float="15.5".toFloat()
16    println(x6)
17    var x7:Double="15.5".toDouble()
18    println(x7)
19    }
20
21
22
```

48

Running the above program, we will have the following results:

```
true
3
30
15
100
15.5
15.5
```

For example, write a program to solve the first-degree equation, this one will apply the readLine () input from the key to solve the first-degree equation, however the book will explain how the If and Else works in the next lesson, Listing 16 shows details of the coding.

Listing 16. LearnInputData/App_First_Degree_Equation.kt

```
1    fun main(args: Array<String>) {
2    var a:Double=0.0
3    var b:Double=0.0
4    println("Input a:")
5    var s= readLine()
6    if(s!=null)
7    a=s.toDouble()
8    println("Input b:")
9    s= readLine()
10   if(s!=null)
11   b=s.toDouble()
12   if(a==0.0 && b==0.0)
13   {
14   println("Infinite!!!")
15   }
16   else if(a==0.0 && b!=0.0)
17   {
18   println("Unknown")
19   }
20   else
21   {
22   var x=-b/a
23   println("x="+x)
24   }
25   }
```

Running the above code, we will have the following results. Table 9 shows some test cases.

Table 9. Test cases for first-degree equation

Test Case 1	Test Case 2	Test Case 3
Input a: 3 Input b: 6 x=-2.0	Input a: 0 Input b: 0 Infinite!!!	Input a: 0 Input b: 5 Unknown!!!

This is the end of the lesson. Please try to best to read the lesson and examples.

Here is the link to download the code for this lesson: https://github.com/thanhtd32/kotlin/tree/main/LearnInputData.

Knowledge about data types, how to declare variables, operators, readers can learn more in the books by Dmitry Jemerov et al. (2017) and Dawn Griffiths and David Griffiths (2019) and Andrew Bailey et al. (2021).

Exercises

1. What are the built-in data types in Kotlin?
2. Why do we have to know the data types?
3. What is the syntax for declaring variables in Kotlin?
4. Do the following commands give an error? Explain why or why not.

```
var d:Double
d=10
```

5. Do the following commands give an error? Explain why or why not.

```
var f:Float
f=9.5
```

6. How to declare a string on multiple lines?
7. What is the difference between var and val?
8. What is the Data type conversion?
9. Explain the Implicit conversion and Explicit Conversion.
10. What is the difference betwen widening conversion and Narrowing conversion?
11. How to cast data in Kotlin by using the built-Method?
12. Present and give examples of Unary operators.
13. Present and give examples of Basic arithmetic operators.

14. Present and give examples of Assignment operators.
15. Present and give examples of Comparison Operators.
16. Present and give examples of Logic operators.
17. Present and give examples of Increment and Decrement Operators.
18. What are the results when run the following statements?

```
var x: Boolean = true
var y: Boolean = false
var z: Boolean = true
println(x.and(y))
println(x.or(y))
println(x.or(y).and(y))
println(!x.or(y).and(y))
```

19. What are the results when run the following statements?

```
var a:Int=4
var b:Int=7
var c:Int=3
var z=a++ + ++b - --c + 2
println("a="+a)
println("b="+b)
println("c="+c)
println("z="+z)
```

20. How to input data from command line in Kotlin?
21. What is the difference between String? and String in Kotlin?
22. Enter the radius of the circle. Calculate and print the circumference and area of the corresponding circle.
23. Write the program to calculate the Area of the Triangle.
    The area of the triangle is calculated by the formula: $S(ABC) = 1/2*a*h$.

Figure 3.

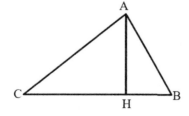

      ◦   Where a is the length of the base side in the figure is side BC.

      ◦   h is the height from the top to the bottom edge, in the figure is AH.

24. ASCII character

Write a program to input a character: Print the ASCII code of that character and prints its next character.

25. Write a program to reverse a positive integer exactly 3 digits, Eg: if we Input a value is 456 then output is 654.

REFERENCES

Bailey, Greenhalgh, & Skeen. (2021), *Kotlin Programming: The Big Nerd Ranch Guide* (2nd ed.). Big Nerd Ranch, LLC.

Dmitry & Svetlana. (2017). *Kotlin in Action.* Manning.

Griffiths, D., & Griffiths, D. (2019). *Head First Kotlin. O'Reilly Media.*

Chapter 3
Conditional Execution

ABSTRACT

Almost every programming language has to use conditional constructs to handle the business of the software. Basically, the operating mechanism of these conditional structures is the same, but with the Kotlin programming language, it has added a lot of extended and very convenient features, it helps programmers more optimal options in the process of processing business. This chapter will present conditional constructs about simple if statement, if/ else statement, nested conditionals, expression and block form {}, and when structure. The when structure has been greatly improved in Kotlin, it provides a lot of use cases so that programmers can easily handle business tasks more optimally, such as when with if/else statement, group multiple conditions. For each conditional structure, this chapter provides simple examples and detailed explanations to help readers understand the working mechanism of the conditional structure and apply them to specific business handling. At the end of the chapter, there is a list of exercises to help readers improve programming skills on conditional structures.

CONDITIONAL EXECUTION

Almost programming language has to use conditional constructs to handle the business of the software. Basically, the operating mechanism of these conditional structures is the same, but with the Kotlin programming language, it has added a lot of extended and very convenient features, it helps programmers more optimal options in the process of processing business.

DOI: 10.4018/978-1-6684-6687-2.ch003

This chapter will present conditional constructs about simple if statement, if/else statement, nested conditionals, expression and block form { }, and when structure. The when structure has been greatly improved in Kotlin, it provides a lot of use cases so that programmers can easily handle business tasks more optimally, such as when with if/ else statement, group multiple conditions. For each conditional structure, this chapter provides simple examples and detailed explanations to help readers understand the working mechanism of the conditional structure and apply them to specific business handling. At the end of the chapter, there is a list of exercises to help readers improve programming skills on conditional structures.

The Simple if Statement

The syntax of the if structure.

```
if (<expression>)
{
    <statement>
}
```

The "if" statement is only concerned with the correct condition, when <expression> in "if" true, it will execute the <statement> statement inside the "if".

The Figure 1 shows the Flow Chart of if simple if statement.

Figure 1. The flow chart of simple if statement

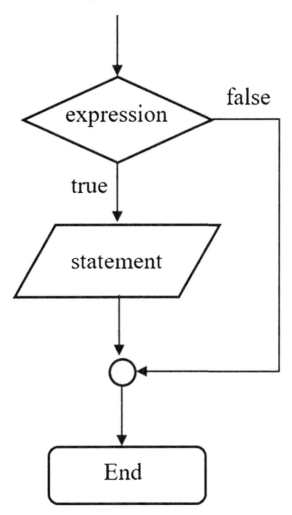

For example, We write a program to show the Student learning outcomes. If the Score> = 65 then write Pass (don't care Score<65). Listing 1 shows how to use the if statement.

Listing 1. LearnIfElse/App_If.kt

```
1   fun main(args: Array<String>) {
2   var score: Double = 75.0;
3   if (score >= 65) {
4   println("Pass")
5   }
6   }
```

The above program code only checks the condition score>=65, command at line 2 assigns score = 75.0, so the result will output "Pass". If we change the score=50.0, the program will not output any results.

The If/Else Statement

The syntax of the if else statement.

```
if (<expression>)
{
  <statement 1>
}
else
{
  <statement 2>
}
```

The "if else" statement is concerned with true and false conditions. If <expression> is true then the content <statement 1> of if will be executed, if <expression> is false then the else statement <statement 2> will be executed. This is one of the most commonly used statements in the conditional check process.

Figure 2 shows the Flow Chart of the if/else statement.

Figure 2. The flow chart of if/else statement

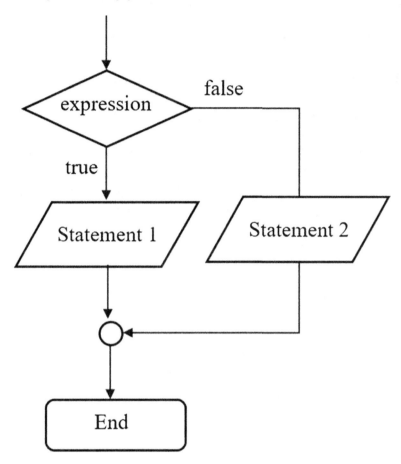

For example, We write a program to show the Student learning outcomes. If the Score> = 65 then print "Pass" and if the Score<65 then print "Fail". The code is shown in the Listing 2.

Listing 2. LearnIfElse/App_IfElse.kt

```
1   fun main(args: Array<String>) {
2   var score: Double = 75.0;
3   if (score >= 65) {
4   println("Pass")
5   }
6   else
7   {
8   println("Fail")
9   }
10  }
```

The above program code only checks the condition score>=65, command at line 2 assigns score = 75.0, so the result will output "Pass". If we change the score=50.0, the program will output "Fail".

Nested Conditionals

In fact, when dealing with problems, we have to use many nested if else, with many complex conditions.

We edit the example above: Enter the score in the range [0...100], if score >=65, then output "Pass". If score <= 65, then output "Fail". And If user enters the value is out of range [0...100] or nothing, then print incorrect information. Listing 3 shows the details of the coding.

Listing 3. LearnIfElse/App_NestedIfElse.kt

```
1    fun main(args: Array<String>) {
2    var score:Double=0.0;
3    println("Enter Score:")
4    var s:String?= readLine()
5    if(s.isNullOrBlank()==false)
6    {
7    score=s.toDouble()
8    if(score>=0 && score<=100)
9    {
10   if (score >= 65)
11   {
12   println("Pass")
13   }
14   else
15   {
16   println("Fail")
17   }
18   }
19   else
20   {
21   println("You must enter value in [0...100]")
22   }
23   }
24   else
25   {
26   println("Please Enter value")
27   }
28   }
```

Run the program and do some test cases.

Table 1. Test cases of the nested conditional

Test Case 1	Test Case 2	Test Case 3
Enter Score: 50 Fail	Enter Score: 90 Pass	Enter Score: Please Enter value
Test Case 4		**Test Case 5**
Enter Score: 150 You must enter value in [0...100]		Enter Score: -10 You must enter value in [0...100]

Thus, we have already learned the "if else" approach by the traditional method (as a conditional expression).

Conditional Statement as Expression

Now the book will present the new "if else" point in Kotlin that is it works as an expression that returns the result. For example, if we have 2 numbers a and b, how to find the largest number? Listing 4 shows the conditional statement as expression.

Listing 4. LearnIfElse/App_IfElseExpression.kt; App_IfElseTraditional.kt

	Written by Expression		Traditional Writing

1
2
3
4
5
6
7
8
9
10
11
	fun main(args: Array<String>)
	{
	var a:Int=10
	var b:Int=15
	var max:Int
	max=if (a>b) a else b
	println("max = "+max)
	}
		1
		2
		3
		4
		5
		6
		7
		8
		9
		10
		11
			fun main(args: Array<String>)
			{
			var a:Int=10
			var b:Int=15
			var max:Int
			if(a>b)
			max=a
			else
			max=b
			println("max = "+max)
			}

Note that when writing an if statement with return results, it is mandatory to have else (see the Written by expression).

Run the program, we have the same result: max = 15

Conditional Statement as Expression in Block Form {}

In addition, the if else expression allows you to write in block form { }, the last line in each block that returns the result, Listing 5 shows the coding.

Listing 5. LearnIfElse/App_BlockForm.kt

```
1    fun main(args: Array<String>) {
2    var a:Int=10
3    var b:Int=15
4    var max = if (a > b) {
5    println("Choose a")
6    a
7    } else {
8    println("Choose b")
9    b
10   }
11   println("max = "+max)
12   }
```

Run the program, we have the result as below:

```
Choose b
max = 15
```

The value a at the end of if, the value b at the end of else is the result returned and assigned to the max variable.

This is the end of the lesson, please pay attention to it through the examples above. Take special note of the flow chart, the way of writing in the form of the if else expression. Download source code here: https://github.com/thanhtd32/kotlin/tree/main/LearnIfElse.

When Expression

For Kotlin, the "switch" expression was replaced by the "when" expression. When operating very powerful, versatile, meet many processing cases for programmers. Hopefully with 6 types of when in this lesson, it will help you understand the operation of when, which can be applied smoothly to the other more complex.

Syntax of when

```
when(<expression>)
{
<value 1> -> <statement 1>
<value 2> -> <statement 2>
<value 3> -> <statement 3>
<value ...> -> <statement ...>
<value n> -> <statement n>
else -> <statement else>
}
```

when statement will get the value in <expression>, compare it with the <value> inside, if it matches any value, the <statement> will be executed. If all <value> do not match <expression> then else will be executed. The flowchart of when can be operated as shown in the Figure 3.

Figure 3. The flow chart of when statement

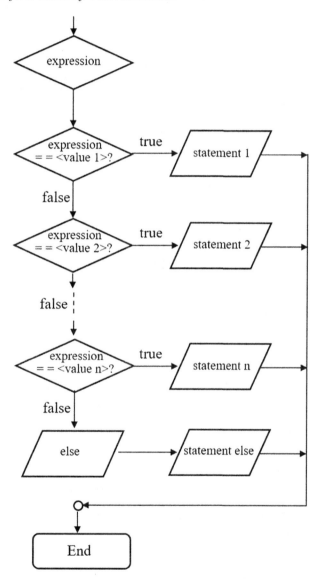

Below are examples related to the use of when expressions in different situations, which learners can easily apply in practice.

The Simple When Statement

The simple when statement is shown in this example, we ask the user to enter an integer value from 1→7, the program will output the corresponding weekdays as follows.

Table 2. The value of weekdays

Value	Weekdays
1	Sunday
2	Monday
3	Tuesday
4	Wednesday
5	Thursday
6	Friday
7	Saturday
If value is out of [1...7]	Invalid Value

The illustrative code is shown in the Listing 6.

Listing 6. LearnWhen/App_Example1.kt

```
1    fun main() {
2    var value:Int
3    println("Please enter a value[1..7]:")
4    value= readLine()!!.toInt()
5    when(value)
6    {
7    1 -> println("Sunday")
8    2 -> println("Monday")
9    3 -> println("Tuesday")
10   4 -> println("Wednesday")
11   5 -> println("Thursday")
12   6 -> println("Friday")
13   7 -> println("Saturday")
14   else -> println("Invalid value")
15   }
16   }
```

Run the coding and take some test cases.

Table 3. Test cases for weekdays

Test Case 1	Test Case 2	Test Case 3
Please enter a value[1..7]: 4 Wednesday	Please enter a value[1..7]: 2 Monday	Please enter a value[1..7]: 9 Invalid value

In the above test cases, we enter 4 programs that will output "Wednesday", enter 2 programs will output "Monday", enter 9 programs will report the error "Invalid value".

The When with If/Else Statement

We can use if/else or another statement in when expression. Write a program that allows you to enter two numbers a, b, and one operation +, -, *, /. Print the output result corresponding to the operation, see the Listing 7.

Listing 7. LearnWhen/App_Example2.kt

```
1    fun main(args: Array<String>) {
2    var a:Double=0.0;
3    var b:Double=0.0;
4    var op:String?
5    println("Input a:")
6    a= readLine()!!.toDouble()
7    println("Input b:")
8    b= readLine()!!.toDouble()
9    println("Enter operator(+,-,*,/):")
10   op= readLine()
11   when(op)
12   {
13   "+"-> println("$a + $b = "+(a+b))
14   "-"-> println("$a - $b = "+(a-b))
15   "*"-> println("$a * $b = "+(a*b))
16   "/"->
17   if(b==0.0)
18   println("Denominator must be different
19   from 0")
20   else
21   println("$a / $b = "+(a/b))
22   else-> println("Invalid operator")
23   }
24   }
```

Run the coding and take some test cases.

Table 4. Test cases for corresponding operation

Test Case 1	Test Case 2
Input a: 3 Input b: 5 Enter operator(+,-,*,/): + 3.0 + 5.0 = 8.0	Input a: 3 Input b: 5 Enter operator(+,-,*,/): - 3.0 - 5.0 = -2.0
Test Case 3	**Test Case 4**
Input a: 3 Input b: 5 Enter operator(+,-,*,/): * 3.0 * 5.0 = 15.0	Input a: 3 Input b: 5 Enter operator(+,-,*,/): / 3.0 / 5.0 = 0.6
Test Case 5	**Test Case 6**
Input a: 5 Input b: 0 Enter operator(+,-,*,/): / Denominator must be different from 0	Input a: 7 Input b: 8 Enter operator(+,-,*,/): ? Invalid operator

In the above program, we carry out 4 test cases corresponding to +, -, *, / operations. And 2 special cases are denominator =0 and incorrect math input.

Kotlin also allows us to group multiple conditions in the when expression if they resolve the same problem by using a comma to separate the values:

When Expression With Group Multiple Conditions

Kotlin support group multiple conditions in when expression by using comma. Let's do the example: Input a month, ask what quarter of the year this month belongs to. We all know that January, February, March is the 1st quarter; April, May, June is the second quarter; June, July, August is the third quarter; and October, November, December is the fourth quarter. Coding is shown in the Listing 8.

Listing 8. LearnWhen/App_Example3.kt

```
1    fun main(args: Array<String>) {
2    var month:Int=0
3    println("Enter month:")
4    month= readLine()!!.toInt()
5    when(month)
6    {
7    1,2,3-> println("Month "+month+" belongs to
8    quarter 1")
9    4,5,6-> println("Month "+month+" belongs to
10   quarter 2")
11   7,8,9-> println("Month "+month+" belongs to
12   quarter 3")
13   10,11,12->println("Month "+month+" belongs to
14   quarter 4")
15   clsc-> println("Month " ι month ι " is not valid")
16   }
17   }
```

Run the coding and take some test cases.

Table 5. Test cases for group multiple conditions

Test Case 1	Test Case 2
Enter month: 2 Month 2 belongs to quarter 1	Enter month: 5 Month 5 belongs to quarter 2
Test Case 3	Test Case 4
Enter month: 9 Month 9 belongs to quarter 3	Enter month: 12 Month 12 belongs to quarter 4
Test Case 5	
Enter month: 13 Month 13 is not valid	

In the above program, we carry out some test cases such as February, May, September, February. In addition, there is an invalid month that is month 13. You can conduct tests on the remaining months.

The when Kotlin's architecture is in, allowing for continuous data:

When Expression Within Conditions

Kotlin language also uses "in" conditions in when expression to check if the value is in the specified data group. Let's observe how GPA and Letter Grade are calculated based on the Table 6.

Table 6. GPA and letter grade

Percentage	Letter Grade	GPA
90-100	A	4.0
80-89	B	3.0
70-79	C	2.0
60-69	D	1.0
0-59	F	0.0

Use the when expression to calculate Letter Grade and GPA when the Percentage is known, the Listing 9 shows full coding.

Listing 9. LearnWhen/App_Example4.kt

```
1   fun main(args: Array<String>) {
2   var percentage:Int=0
3   var letterGrade:String=""
4   var gpa:Double=0.0
5   println("Enter Percentage:")
6   percentage= readLine()!!.toInt()
7   when(percentage)
8   {
9   in 90..100 ->
10  {
11  letterGrade="A"
12  gpa=4.0
13  }
14  in 80..89 ->
15  {
16  letterGrade = "B"
17  gpa = 3.0
18  }
19  in 70..79 ->
20  {
21  letterGrade="C"
22  gpa=2.0
23  }
24  in 60..69 ->
25  {
26  letterGrade="D"
27  gpa=1.0
28  }
29  in 0..59 ->
30  {
31  letterGrade="F"
32  gpa=0.0
33  }
34  !in 0..100 ->
35  println("Invalid Percentage")
36  }
37  println("Your result: $letterGrade ($gpa)")
38  }
```

Run the coding and take some test cases.

Table 7. Test cases for GPA and Letter Grade

Test Case 1	Test Case 2
Enter Percentage: 97 Your result: A (4.0)	Enter Percentage: 86 Your result: B (3.0)
Test Case 3	**Test Case 4**
Enter Percentage: 79 Your result: C (2.0)	Enter Percentage: 62 Your result: D (1.0)
Test Case 5	**Test Case 6**
Enter Percentage: 40 Your result: F (0.0)	Enter Percentage: 200 Invalid Percentage Your result: (0.0)

You can try the remaining cases to test the program.

So, if you want to test the variable belonging to a continuous data area, you can use the above syntax, we find it very interesting in this case. It can be also applied well to matching algorithms.

When Expression as Returns Results

Also, when is an expression that returns results, the flexible way of writing is shown in the Listing 10.

Listing 10. LearnWhen/App_Example5.kt

```
1   fun main(args: Array<String>) {
2   var x:Int=8
3   var result=when(x)
4   {
5   in 1..10->x+100
6   in 20..30->x-1000
7   else -> x
8   }
9   println("Result=$result")
10  }
```

Run the program, we will have result=108 Because the above writing assigns the result to the result variable, when x = 8 then the range 1...10, we have the result = 8 + 100 = 108.

Similarly, you can try changing x=25, x = 40 to see how the result changes.

When Behave as if-Else Expression

Finally, when can behave as an if-else expression, let's see the Listing 11.

Listing 11. LearnWhen/App_Example6.kt

```
1    fun main(args: Array<String>) {
2    var x:Int
3    println("Input x:")
4    x= readLine()!!.toInt()
5    when
6    {
7    x%2==0-> println("$x is the even number")
8    x%2!=0->println("$x is the odd number")
9    }
10   }
```

Run the coding and take some test cases.

Table 8. Test cases for when can behave as an if-else expression

Test Case 1	Test Case 2
Input x: 4 4 is even number	Input x: 9 9 is the odd number

This is the end of the lesson, please pay attention to learn and understand it through the examples above. Particularly grasp the flow chart, how to write in different ways.

This is the link to download the source code of this lesson:

https://github.com/thanhtd32/kotlin/tree/main/LearnWhen

Readers can read more explanations of the conditional structure in the authors' books (Jemerov et al., 2017. Griffiths & Griffiths, 2019; Bailey et al., 2021).

Exercises

1. What is the output to the screen when running the following commands?

```
var x: Int = 5
var y: Int = 6
if (x%2!=0 && y %2==0) {
    println("A")
}
else{
    println("B")
}
```

   (a) A

   (b) B

2. What is the output to the screen when running the following commands?

```
var x: Int = 5
var y: Int = 6
if (!(x%2!=0) && y %2==0) {
    println("A")
}
else{
    println("B")
}
```

   (a) A

   (b) B

3. What is the output to the screen when running the following commands?

```
var x: Int = 5
var y: Int = 6
var z:Int =8
if (z%y!=0) {
    if(x>=y){
        println("A")
    }
    else{
        println("C")
    }
}
else{
    println("B")
}
```

   (a)   A
   (b)   B
   (c)   C

4.   What is the output to the screen when running the following commands?

```
var a:Int=5
var s=if (a>7) "X" else if (a<=4) "Y" else "Z"
println(s)
```

   (a)   X
   (b)   Y
   (c)   Z

5.   What is the output to the screen when running the following commands?

```
var a:Int=10
var b:Int=15
var c:Int=20
var z = if (a > b){
    a
}
else if(b<c) {
    b
}
else{
    c
}
println(z)
```

   (a)   10
   (b)   15
   (c)   20

6.   Print digital clock. User enters any number of seconds t>=0. Calculate
     and print the digital as folling format:
     hour:minute:second AM or hour:minute:second PM
     <u>For example:</u> If user enters the seconds are 3750, then print 1:2:30 AM.
     If user enters the seconds are 51100, then print 2:11:40 PM
     The calculation formula is as follows:
     hour=(t/3600)%24
     minute=(t%3600)/60
     second=(t%3600)%60

7. Write a program to find the largest number from 3 double numbers a, b, c.

8. Solve and argue the first-degree equation: $ax + b = 0$.

9. Solve and argue quadratic equations: $ax^2+bx+c=0$.

10. What is the output to the screen when running the following commands?

```
var value=5
when(value%2)
{
    0-> println("X")
    1-> println("Y")
    2-> println("Z")
}
```

   (a) X
   (b) Y
   (c) Z

11. What is the output to the screen when running the following commands?

```
var value=5
when(value%2)
{
    0,1-> println("X")
    1,2-> println("Y")
    0,2-> println("Z")
}
```

   (a) X
   (b) Y
   (c) Z
   (d) Compiler Error

12. What is the output to the screen when running the following commands?

```
var x:Int=15
var y:Int=5
var result=when(x/y)
{
    in 1..2->x+y
    in 3..7->x-y
    else -> x
}
println(result)
```

     (a)   20

     (b)   10

     (c)   15

13. Write a program to check the set of characters, The program description is as follows:

    Input: a character comes from the keyboard.

    Check which of the following groups this character belongs to:

    − Uppercase characters: 'A' ...'Z'

    − Lowercase characters: 'a' ... 'z'

    − Alphanumeric characters: '0' ... '9'

    − Other characters.

14. Write a program to check hexadecimal numbers

    The hexadecimal system uses 16 digits including the characters: 0, 1, 2, 3, 4, 5, 6, 7, 8, 9 and A, B, C, D, E, F. The characters A, B, C, D, E, F have their respective values in the decimal system as follows:

    $A \rightarrow 10, B \rightarrow 11, C \rightarrow 12, D \rightarrow 13, E \rightarrow 14, F \rightarrow 15$

    Write a program to input the character representing one digit of the hexadecimal system and give the corresponding decimal value. In case the input character does not belong to the above characters, an error message: "Hexadecimal does not use this digit".

15. Program an Automatic coffee ordering machine software

    I ordered 2 Americano cups, 2 cafe lattes, and 1 cappuccino in front of the cash coffee machine with my friends. Americano costs 2,500 USD per cup, cafe latte costs 3,000 USD, and cappuccino costs 3,000 USD. After deciding the type of coffee and the number of cups, I invested 15,000 USD in cash and received a change of 1,000 USD. I wonder how the automatic coffee ordered calculates the total amount of coffee and returns the change.

REFERENCES

Bailey, Greenhalgh, & Skeen. (2021), *Kotlin Programming: The Big Nerd Ranch Guide* (2nd ed.). Big Nerd Ranch, LLC.

Dmitry & Svetlana. (2017). *Kotlin in Action.* Manning.

Griffiths, D., & Griffiths, D. (2019). *Head First Kotlin. O'Reilly Media.*

Chapter 4
Loop Executions

ABSTRACT

Similar to the conditional structure, in all software, programmers have to use loop structures to handle repetitive tasks according to certain rules. When dealing with list data such as character strings, numeric arrays, list of objects, etc. then loops will be used. Kotlin provides loop controls such as for, while, do while and abnormal loop termination. The loop executions are greatly improved, such as for loops that are divided many types such as closed range, half-open range, step and downTo navigation. And these kinds cover most of the loop handling cases, making it easy for programmers to use them optimally. This chapter also demonstrates how to handle break statement and continue statement in abnormal loop termination, these are very important statements in loop handling. This chapter also provides complete code and detailed explanations for each loop, making it easy for learners to understand and practice loops. At the end of the chapter, there are exercises to help readers practice programming skills for loops and consolidate the knowledge in previous chapters.

LOOP EXECUTIONS

Similar to the conditional structure, in all software, programmers have to use loop structures to handle repetitive tasks according to certain rules. When dealing with list data such as character strings, numeric arrays, list of objects, etc. then loops will be used. Kotlin provides loop controls such as for, while, do while and abnormal loop termination. The loop executions

DOI: 10.4018/978-1-6684-6687-2.ch004

are greatly improved, such as for loops that are divided many types such as closed range, half-open range, step and downTo navigation. And these kinds cover most of the loop handling cases, making it easy for programmers to use them optimally. This chapter also demonstrates how to handle break statement and continue statement in abnormal loop termination, these are very important statements in loop handling. This chapter also provides complete code and detailed explanations for each loop, making it easy for learners to understand and practice loops. At the end of the chapter, there are exercises to help readers practice programming skills for loops and consolidate the knowledge in previous chapters.

For Loop Execution

Kotlin provides about 5+ ways of working with a very wide range of "for" loop. These techniques will detail you through theoretical as well as illustrative illustrations, hopefully you will understand and master the For Loop in Kotlin.

For – Closed Range

The for – closed range, this way use to browse all the values in the list, the syntax as below:

```
for (i in a..b)
{
    Processing variable i
}
```

With the syntax above, variable i is an actually loop variable, which automatically increments from a to b. You can substitute the variable i for any variable name.

Listing 1, we write a program to calculate the factorial of a positive integer n:

Listing 1. LearnFor/App_for_closed_range.kt

1	fun main(args: Array<String>) {
2	var factorial:Int=1
3	val n:Int=5
4	for (i in 1..n)
5	{
6	factorial *= i
7	}
8	*println*("$n!=$factorial")
9	}

In the above statement, i variable will run sequentially from 1 to n (with n = 5). Each time you run it, there will multiply i for variable factorial. When the loop is finished, we will have factorial of n.

Details of the process of factorial calculation in the above algorithm is show in the Table 1.

Table 1. Details of the process of factorial calculation

Iterations	Value of i Variable	Value of Factorial Variable
0		factorial =1
1	1	factorial *=i → factorial=1*1=1
2	2	factorial *=i → factorial =1*2=2
3	3	factorial *=i → factorial =2*3=6
4	4	factorial *=i → factorial =6*4=24
5	5	factorial *=i → factorial =24*5=120

Then command runs: println("$n!=$factorial")
We have the result: 5!=120

For – Half-Open Range

for – half-open range - Browse almost all the values in the list, syntax as below:

```
for (i in a until b)
{
  Processing variable i
}
```

With the syntax above, variable i is an actually loop variable, which automatically increments from a to near b (excluding b). You can substitute the variable i for any variable name

The Listing 2, we write a program that computes sum from 1 until positive integer n.

Listing 2. LearnFor/App_for_half_open_range.kt

```
1    fun main(args: Array<String>) {
2    var sum:Int=0
3    val n:Int=5
4    for (i in 1 until n)
5    {
6    sum += i
7    }
8    println("Sum=$sum")
9    }
```

Details of the sum calculation is shown in the Table 2.

Table 2. Details of the sum calculation

Repeat	Value of i Variable	Value of Sum Variable
0		sum=0
1	1	sum+=i=>sum=0+1=1
2	2	sum+=i=>sum=1+2=3
3	3	sum+=i=>sum=3+3=6
4	4	sum+=i=>sum=6+4=10

Note that the loop only runs to 4, because the syntax for until is run to nearly equal. Therefore, until n is close to n, if n = 5 → i only run to 4.

Then command runs: println("Sum=$sum")
We have the result: Sum=10

1.1.3 For – Step Navigation

for – step navigation use the step to iterate the value, syntax as below:

```
for (i in a .. b step x)
{
    Processing variable i
}
```

With the syntax above, variable i is an actually loop variable, it automatically increments from a to b, but each time it is incremented by x units. You can substitute the variable i for any variable name

The Listing 3, we write a program that calculates the sum of even numbers less than or equal to positive integers n.

Listing 3. LearnFor/App_for_step_navigation.kt

1
2
3
4
5
6
7
8
	fun main(args: Array<String>) {
	var sum:Int=0
	var n:Int=10
	for (i in 2 .. n *step* 2)
	sum+=i
	println("Sum of even numbers=$sum")
	}

Details of the process of calculating the sum of even numbers is shown in the Table 3.

Table 3. Details calculating sum of even numbers

Iterations	Value of i Variable	Value of Sum Variable
0		sum=0
1	2	sum+=i =>sum=0+2=2
2	4	sum+=i =>sum=2+4=6
3	6	sum+=i =>sum=6+6=12
4	8	sum+=i =>sum=12+8=20
5	10	sum+=i =>sum=20+10=30

The program runs every time i increments by 2 units, the initialization i runs from 2 so it automatically increments into even numbers, if it meets 10, it executes and ends the loop.

Then command runs: println("Sum of even numbers = $sum")

We have the result: Sum of even numbers = 30

For – DownTo Navigation

for – downTo navigation, we use for loop with downTo keyword to increase the variable when run for statement.

```
for (i in b downTo a)
{
  Processing variable i
}
```

With the syntax above, variable i is an actually loop variable, it automatically decreases from b to a, but each time it decreases 1 unit. You can substitute the variable i for any variable name

Or we can use downto and step keyword to navigation x.

```
for (i in b downTo a step x)
{
  Processing variable i
}
```

With the syntax above, variable i is an actually loop variable, it automatically decrements from a to b, but each time it is decremented by x units. You can substitute the variable i for any variable name

The Listing 4, we use for loop with downTo navigation to write the Greatest common divisor (GCD) for any two numbers.

Listing 4. LearnFor/App_for_downTo.kt

```
1    fun main(args: Array<String>) {
2    var a:Int
3    var b:Int
4    println("Input a:")
5    a= readLine()!!.toInt()
6    println("Input b:")
7    b= readLine()!!.toInt()
8    var gcd=1
9    var min=if (a>b) b else a
10   for (i in min downTo 1)
11   {
12   if(a%i==0 && b%i==0)
13   {
14   gcd=i
15   break
16   }
17   }
18   println("GCD of $a and $b is $gcd")
19   }
```

Details of the process of finding the largest common divisor is shown in the Table 4.

Assume that the user inputs a=9, b=6. gcd has an initial value of 1

At line statement 9, We proceed to calculate min = 6 (we have to find min because with 2 numbers it may only be divisible by smaller numbers).

Table 4. Details processing of GCD algorithms

Iterations	Value of i Variable	Value of GCD Variable
0		a=9, b=6, gcd=1, min=6
1	6	if (a%i==0 && b%i==0) ← if (9%6==0 && 6%6==0) → unsatisfactory
2	5	if (a%i==0 && b%i==0) ←if (9%5==0 && 6%5==0) →unsatisfactory
3	4	if (a%i==0 && b%i==0) ←if (9%4==0 && 6%4==0) →unsatisfactory
4	3	if (a%i==0 && b%i==0) ←if (9%3==0 && 6%3==0) →satisfactory ←We have gcd=i←gcd=3 And then the break is executed→ end the for loop

To the 4th iteration, then both a and b are divisible by i (i = 3), so if the if statement is executed, then gcd = 3 and the break command stops the loop.

Then command runs:

```
println("GCD of $a and $b is $gcd")
```

We have the result: GCD of 9 and 6 is 3

For – Set Object Loop

for – Set object loop, When we want to traverse each item in a collection, the syntax is as follows:

```
for (item in collection)
{
    Process item
}
```

The for structure will browse each object in a set object.

The Listing 5 prints the name of the list programming language, books variable is an array, next lesson the book will introduce the array.

Listing 5. LearnFor/App_for_setobject1.kt

```
1    fun main(args: Array<String>) {
2    var books= arrayOf("Kotlin","Java","C#","Python","R")
3    for (item in books)
4    println(item)
5    }
```

The above code, the program will browse each element in the book list array and export their names.

```
Kotlin
Java
C#
Python
R
```

Also, we can browse by index, from this index we can export the output the value as Listing 6.

Listing 6. LearnFor/App_for_setobject2.kt

```
1    fun main(args: Array<String>) {
2    var books= arrayOf("Kotlin","Java","C#","Python","R")
3    for (i in books.indices)
4    println("The value at index $i is [${books[i]}]")
5    }
```

The out:

```
The value at index 0 is [Kotlin]
The value at index 1 is [Java]
The value at index 2 is [C#]
The value at index 3 is [Python]
The value at index 4 is [R]
```

Finally, the Kotlin language also supports both getting the index and the value in the Listing 7.

Listing 7. LearnFor/App_for_setobject3.kt

```
1   fun main(args: Array<String>) {
2   var books= arrayOf("Kotlin","Java","C#","Python","R")
3   for ((index,value) in books.withIndex())
4   {
5   println("The value at index $index is [$value]")
6   }
7   }
```

The output when we run the program.

```
The value at index 0 is [Kotlin]
The value at index 1 is [Java]
The value at index 2 is [C#]
The value at index 3 is [Python]
The value at index 4 is [R]
```

This is the end of the lesson, please pay attention to learn and understand it through the examples above. Particularly grasp 5 ways of operation of for to be able to apply well into actual projects.

You can download source code here: https://github.com/thanhtd32/kotlin/tree/main/LearnFor.

While Loop Execution

In the previous lesson we learned how the for loop works, in this tutorial, the book will explain the while loop excution. This is also one of the most common repetition structures (loop) in any programming languagcs, the syntax is as follows:

```
while(expression)
{
  statement
}
```

The Flow chart of the while loop execution:

83

Figure 1. Flow chart of the while loop

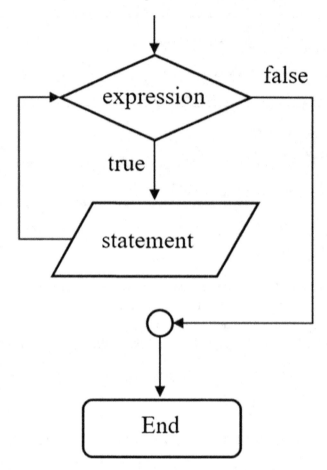

Describe the implementation step:

- **Step 1:** Expressions are defined
- **Step 2**: If the result is true then the statement executes and returns to Step 1
- **Step 3:** If the result is false, end the while loop.

Note: The while statement may not be executed at all because the expression does not match at the beginning. The Listing 8 shows the program to calculate 5 factorials.

Listing 8. LearnWhile/App_Factorials.kt

```
1    fun main(args: Array<String>) {
2    var factorial:Int=1
3    var n:Int=5
4    var i:Int = 1
5    while (i <= n)
6    {
7    factorial *= i
8    i++
9    }
10   println("$n! =$factorial")
11   }
```

Detailed explanation of running process

```
Initialize n = 5, factorial = 1, i = 1
1st:
check i <= n ↔ 1 <= 5 (true) →execute body white:
factorial = factorial*i=1*1=1
i++→i=i+1=1+1=2
2nd:
check i <= n → 2 <= 5 (true) →execute body while:
factorial = factorial *i=1*2=2
i++→i=i+1= 2+1=3
3rd:
check i <= n ↔3 <= 5 (true) →execute body while:
factorial = factorial *i=2*3=6
i++→i=i+1=3+1=4
4th:
check i <= n ↔ 4 <= 5 (true) → execute body while:
factorial = factorial *i=6*4=24
i++→i=i+1=4+1=5
5th:
check i <= n ↔ 5 <= 5 (true) → execute body while:
factorial = factorial *i=24*5=120
i++→i=i+1=5+1=6
6th:
check i <= n ↔ 6 <= 5 (false) → stop while.
```

Finishing the program, we have the factorial = 120

You can combine different loops, for example, to combine the while and for loops, the example below illustrates this combination. This is the end of the lesson, please pay attention the examples above and do extra research to have a better understanding of the lesson. Particularly grasp the way the operation of while loop to be able to apply well to his actual project.

We can download the source code at the link: https://github.com/thanhtd32/kotlin/tree/main/LearnWhile.

Do While Loop Execution

In previous lesson, we studied the while loop structure, in this lesson, we will go through a similar structure that is do ... while. The syntax of the do ... while loop:

```
do
{
    statement
}
while(expression)
```

Flow char of the do while expression.

Figure 2. Flow chart of the do...while loop

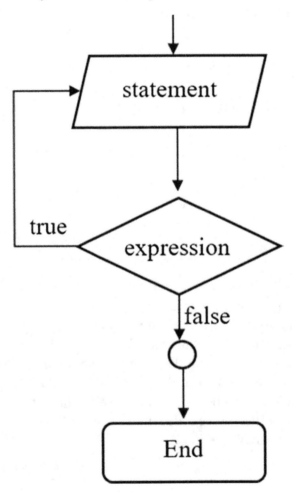

Describe the implementation step:

- **Step 1:** Statement is executed
- **Step 2:** Expression is defined.
- If expression is true then return to Step 1
- If the expression is false then end the loop
  Note: The command in do ... while is certainly executed at least once.

The Listing 9, we write a program to calculate factorial of 5

Listing 9. LearnDoWhile/App_Example1.kt

```
1    fun main(args: Array<String>) {
2    var n:Int = 5
3    var factorial:Int=1
4    var i:Int = 1
5    do
6    {
7    factorial *= i
8    i++
9    }while (i<=n)
10   println("$n! =$factorial")
11   }
```

Detailed explanation of running process

```
Initialize: n=5; factorial =1, i=1
1st:
factorial = factorial *i=1*1=1
i++ → i=i+1=1+1=2
Check i <= n ↔ 2 <= 5 (true)
2nd:
factorial = factorial *i=1*2=2
i++→i=i+1=2+1=3
Check i <= n ↔3 <= 5 (true)
3rd:
factorial = factorial *i=2*3=6
i++→i=i+1=3+1=4
Check i <= n ↔ 4 <= 5 (true)
4th:
factorial = factorial *i=6*4=24
i++→i=i+1=4+1=5
Check i <= n ↔ 5 <= 5 (true)
5th:
factorial = factorial *i=24*5=120
i++→i=i+1=5+1=6
Check i <= n ↔6 <= 5(false) → stop do while
```

Finishing the program, we have the factorial = 120

This is the end of the lesson, please pay attention the examples above and do extra research to have a better understanding of the lesson. Particularly grasp the way of operating do…while to be able to apply well to your actual projects.

The source code can be downloaded at the link: https://github.com/thanhtd32/kotlin/tree/main/LearnDoWhile.

Abnormal Loop Termination

In addition, Kotlin also provides break and continue keywords to navigate the loop. use break to exit the loop, use continue to continue execution of the loop with the next iteration.

The Break Statement

Kotlin provides the break statement to implement middle-exiting loop control logic. The break statement causes the program's execution to immediately exit from the body of the loop.

Write a program Check whether any numbers are prime numbers (prime numbers are divisible by 1 and itself, numbers 0 and 1 are not prime numbers). The programmer allows asking users whether they want to continue or not? The Listing 10 shows details of the code.

Listing 10. LearnWhileAbnormal/App_Prime.kt

```
1    fun main(args: Array<String>) {
2    var n:Int=0
3    println("Welcome to the Prime Program")
4    while (true)
5    {
6    println("Enter an integer number:")
7    n= readLine()!!.toInt()
8    var count:Int=0
9    for(i in 1..n)
10   {
11   if(n%i==0)
12   count++
13   }
14   if(count==2)
15   println("$n is prime number")
16   else
17   println("$n is not prime number")
18   print("Continue?(y/n):")
19   var s= readLine()
20   if(s=="n")
21   break
22   }
23   println("Goodbye!")
24   }
```

Run the program and enter the following values to see the result, we can repeat entering to test the values:

```
Welcome to the Prime Program
Enter an integer number:
9
9 is not prime number
Continue?(y/n):y
Enter an integer number:
5
5 is prime number
Continue?(y/n):y
Enter an integer number:
6
6 is not prime number
Continue?(y/n):n
Goodbye!
```

This is the end of the lesson, please pay attention the examples above and do extra research to have a better understanding of the lesson. Particularly grasp the way the operation of while loop to be able to apply well to his actual project.

The source code can be downloaded at the link: https://github.com/thanhtd32/kotlin/tree/main/LearnWhileAbnormal.

The Continue Statement

The continue statement is similar to the break statement, except the continue statement does not necessarily exit the loop. The continue statement skips the rest of the body of the loop and immediately checks the loop's condition.

Write a program to check whether a year is a leap year or not (leap year is divisible by 4 but not divisible by 100 or divisible by 400). The program requires users to enter the year$> = 0$, if entered incorrectly enter again until the input is correct, the end of the program allows the user to choose whether to continue or not. The Listing 11 shows the details of the code:

Listing 11. LearnDoWhileAbnormal/App_Example2.kt

```
1   fun main(args: Array<String>) {
2   var year:Int=0
3   var s:String?
4   println("Welcome to the leap year program!")
5   do
6   {
7   while (true)
8   {
9   println("Enter 1 year (>0):")
10  s= readLine()
11  if(s.isNullOrBlank())
12  continue
13  year=s.toInt()
14  if(year>0)
15  break
16  }
17  if(year%4==0&&year%100!=0 || year%400==0)
18  {
19  println("Year $year is a leap year ")
20  }
21  else
22  {
23  println("Year $year is not a leap year")
24  }
25  print("Continue?(y/n):")
26  s= readLine()
27  if(s=="n")
28  break;
29  }while (true)
30  println("Good bye!")
31  }
```

Run the program and enter the following values to see the result:

```
Welcome to the leap year program!
Enter 1 year (>0):
-5
Enter 1 year (>0):
2000
Year 2000 is a leap year
Continue?(y/n):y
Enter 1 year (>0):
1995
Year 1995 is not a leap year
Continue?(y/n):n
Good bye!
```

This is the end of the lesson, please pay attention the examples above and do extra research to have a better understanding of the lesson. Particularly grasp the way of operating do…while to be able to apply well to your actual projects.

The sourcode code can be downloaded at the link: https://github.com/thanhtd32/kotlin/tree/main/LearnDoWhileAb normal.

Readers can read more explanations of the conditional structure in the authors' books (Jemerov et al., 2017; Griffiths & Griffiths, 2019; Eckel & Isakova, 2020; Bailey et al., 2021).

Exercises

1. When do we use the Loop Executions?
2. What kind of for loop is this?

```
var n:Int=5
for (i in 1..n){
    println(i)
}
```

    (a)   for – step navigation
    (b)   for – closed range
    (c)   for – half-open range
    (d)   for – downTo navigation

3. What kind of for loop is this?

```
var n:Int=5
for (i in 1 until n){
    println(i)
}
```

   (a) for – closed range
   (b) for – downTo navigation
   (c) for – half-open range
   (d) for – step navigation

4. What kind of for loop is this?

```
var n:Int=5
for (i in 2 .. n step 2){
    println(i)
}
```

   (a) for – step navigation
   (b) for – closed range
   (c) for – half-open range
   (d) for – downTo navigation

5. What kind of for loop is this?

```
var n=5
for (i in n downTo 1){
    println(i)
}
```

   (a) for – half-open range
   (b) for – downTo navigation
   (c) for – step navigation
   (d) for – closed range

6. What is the output printed to the screen after executing the following commands?

```
var n:Int=5
var s=0
for (i in 1..n){
    if(i%2==0)
        s=s+i
}
println(s)
```

    (a) 6

    (b) 8

    (c) 9

    (d) 2

7.   What is the output printed to the screen after executing the following commands?

```
var n:Int=5
var s=0
for (i in 1..n){
    if(i%2!=0)
        s=s+i
}
println(s)
```

    (a) 6

    (b) 4

    (c) 9

    (d) 8

8.   What is the output printed to the screen after executing the following commands?

```
var n:Int=5
var s=0
for (i in 1 until n){
    if(i%2==0)
        continue
    s=s+i
}
println(s)
```

    (a) 2

    (b) 4

    (c) 1

    (d) 8

9.   What is the output printed to the screen after executing the following commands?

```
var n:Int=5
var s=0
for (i in 1 until n){
    if(i%2==0)
        break
```

```
    s=s+i
}
println(s)
```

    (a) 1

    (b) 4

    (c) 3

    (d) 8

10. What Shape is drawn when the following commands are executed?

```
for (i in 1..5){
    for (j in 1..5){
        if(j==1 || j==5 || i==j)
            print("*")
        else
            print(" ")
    }
    println()
}
```

Figure 3.

(a)	(b)	(c)
* *	* *	*****
* *	** *	* *
* *	* * *	* *
* *	* **	* *
*****	* *	* *

11. What Shape is drawn when the following commands are executed?

```
for (i in 1..5){
    for (j in 1..5){
        if(j==1 || j==5 || i==5)
            print("*")
        else
            print(" ")
    }
```

```
        println()
    }
```

Figure 4.

(a)	(b)	(c)
* *	* *	*****
* *	** *	* *
* *	* * *	* *
* *	* **	* *
*****	* *	* *

12. What Shape is drawn when the following commands are executed?

```
for (i in 1..5){
    for (j in 1..5){
        if(j==1 || j==5 || i==1)
            print("*")
        else
            print(" ")
    }
    println()
}
```

Figure 5.

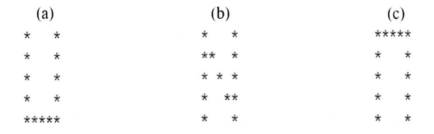

(a)	(b)	(c)
* *	* *	*****
* *	** *	* *
* *	* * *	* *
* *	* **	* *
*****	* *	* *

13. What is the output printed to the screen after executing the following commands?

```
var n:Int=5
var i:Int = 1
var s:Int=0
while (i <= n){
    s=s+i
    i++
    if(i==3)
        continue
}
println(s)
```

    (a) 4

    (b) 15

    (c) 3

    (d) 9

14. What is the output printed to the screen after executing the following commands?

```
var n:Int=5
var i:Int = 1
var s:Int=0
while (i <= n){
    s=s+i
    i++
    if(i==3)
        break
}
println(s)
```

    (a) 2

    (b) 15

    (c) 3

    (d) 7

15. What is the output printed to the screen after executing the following commands?

```
var n:Int = 5
var s:Int=1
var i:Int = 1
do{
    s=s+i
```

```
        i=i+2
    }while (i<=n)
    println(s)
```

    (a) 4

    (b) 10

    (c) 3

    (d) 7

16. What is the output printed to the screen after executing the following commands?

```
var n:Int = 5
var s:Int=1
var i:Int = 0
do{
    s=s+i
    i=i+2
}while (i<=n)
println(s)
```

    (a) 7

    (b) 10

    (c) 9

    (d) 5

17. Write a program to enter n>0 and calculate the expression S(n)

$$S\left(n\right)=1+\frac{1}{3}+\frac{1}{5}+...+\frac{1}{2n+1}$$

18. Write a program to enter n and check if n is prime or not?

19. Write a program to count the number of even digits of a positive integer n.

20. Write a program to enter n>0 and calculate the expression S(n)

$$S\left(n\right)=1+\frac{1}{3}+\frac{1}{5}+...+\frac{1}{2n+1}$$

21. Multiplication table game machine

    I want to play a multiplication table game that is easy in everyday life with a computer. In the game method, the computer creates a random multiplication table and asks the player to guess it within a set time. If the player hits it within the specified time, it is counted as the correct number, and if the calculation is incorrect or exceeds the time, it is regarded as invalid. Also, for the difficulty of multiplication tables, the 2nd and 5th stages are excluded.

22. Multiplication table game machine (more level)

It was found that there were cases of asking the same multiplication table while playing the game. Let's modify it to eliminate the case of asking for the same multiplication table. Also, if you do not answer within a limited time, try to correct it so that it is regarded as wrong.

Readers modified the code in Exercise 21:

◦ Check duplication random number for multiplication

◦ Update the limit time about 45 second, if user answered the product is over limit time, program will set wrong answer.

REFERENCES

Bailey, Greenhalgh, & Skeen. (2021). Kotlin Programming: The Big Nerd Ranch Guide (2nd ed.). Big Nerd Ranch, LLC.

Dmitry & Svetlana. (2017). *Kotlin in Action.* Manning.

Eckel & Isakova. (2020). Atomic Kotlin. Mindview LLC.

Griffiths, D., & Griffiths, D. (2019). *Head First Kotlin. O'Reilly Media.*

Chapter 5
Exception Handling

ABSTRACT

In the process of programming, most of mistakes can be raised. And making errors while programming is inevitable. Therefore, programmers need to have ways to distinguish the types of errors and how to handle errors. This chapter will present error levels such as compiler error, runtime exception error, and exception logic error. This chapter also provides techniques for catching errors such as try catch structure and throw exception technique. Illustrative codes are presented for how to handle this error for readers to easily grasp. However, most programming tools support debugging functions, and this tool makes it easy for programmers to find errors and from there it helps programmers easily find the solutions to fix errors quickly and accurately, so this chapter presents IntelliJ IDEA's debugging tool. At the end of the chapter there are exercises to help readers improve the skills in exception handling.

EXCEPTION HANDLING

In the process of programming, most of mistakes can be raised. And making errors while programming is obvious. Therefore, programmers need to have ways to distinguish the types of errors and how to handle errors. This chapter will present error levels such as Compiler error, Runtime exception error, Exception logic error. This chapter also provides techniques for catching errors such as try catch structure, throw exception technique, and illustrative codes are presented for how to handle this error for readers to easily grasp. However, most programming tools support debugging function, readers need

DOI: 10.4018/978-1-6684-6687-2.ch005

to know how to use it, this tool makes it easy for programmers to find errors and from there it helps programmers easily find the solutions to fix errors quickly and accurately, so this chapter presents IntelliJ IDEA's debugging tool. At the end of the chapter there are exercises to help readers improve the skills in exception handling.

Why Do You Have to Handle Exceptions?

In the process of executing the software, there will be errors in the coding process that have been predicted or unpredictable.

Controlling exceptions helps the software continue to work if an error occurs or also prompts the User Problem.

When programming, we normally encounter three levels of error:

- **Compiler error** (beginners' mistakes, write the wrong code, syntax error)
- **Runtime exception error** (not master programming, there are still many errors)
- **Exception logic error** – wrong professional requirements (experienced programmers, but they have errors that are hard to fix)

And when there are errors, there are usually two behaviors with errors: Unchecked error and Checked error.

For professional programmer, we need to take care of these errors, to check carefully so that when the error occurs, the program will continue without being turned off.

Try Catch Handler

Kotlin supports us the general syntax for handling exceptions as follows

```
try
{
// write the commands here and these commands are those likely to generate errors
}
catch (e: SomeException)
{
// error handler here -> Detailed error message to know what is wrong to fix
}
finally
{
// optional finally block – Regardless of whether or not the error occurred, the block is always executed
}
```

The Listing 5.1 we write a program dividing two numbers a and b. For sample denominator = 0 to generate error.

Listing 1. LearnException/App_Example1.kt

```
1   fun main(args: Array<String>) {
2   try {
3   var a:Int=5
4   var b:Int=0
5   var c=a/b
6   println("$a/$b=$c")
7   }
8   catch (e:Exception)
9   {
10  println(e.message)
11  }
12  finally {
13  println("This is finally, 100% running, whether errors exist or not")
14  }
15  }
16
```

When running the above program, the line a / b will generate an error and it will jump to the exception, then finally will be executed:

```
/ by zero
This is finally, 100% running, whether errors exist or not
```

Throw Exception Keyword

Kotlin also supports the throw keyword to throw this error elsewhere, where it calls it to handle the error. The Listing 2 shows how to use the throw keyword.

Listing 2. LearnException/App_Example2.kt

```
1    fun divide(a:Int,b:Int):Int
2    {
3    if(b==0)
4    throw Exception("Denominator =0")
5    return a/b
6    }
7    fun main(args: Array<String>) {
8    divide(5,0)
9    println("Good Bye!")
10   }
```

When running the program in Example 2, it will issue an error message: Denominator = 0 and turn off the software when it is running, not allow the "Good Bye!" to appear. For now, we have not used try...catch to checked error:

```
Exception in thread "main" java.lang.Exception: Denominator =0
        at App_Example2Kt.divide(App_Example2.kt:4)
        at App_Example2Kt.main(App_Example2.kt:8)
```

In the Listing 3, we modify the above code so that when the error occurs, the program will continue to operate.

Listing 3. LearnException/App_Example2.kt

```
1    fun divide(a:Int,b:Int):Int
2    {
3    if(b==0)
4    throw Exception("Denominator =0")
5    return a/b
6    }
7    fun main(args: Array<String>) {
8    try {
9    divide(5, 0)
10   }
11   catch (e:Exception)
12   {
13   println(e.message)
14   }
15   println("Good Bye!")
16   }
17
```

When try ... catch, despite the error, the program will continue to execute the remaining commands (avoid turning off the software), the program on the run will have the result:

```
Denominator =0
Good Bye!
```

This is the end of the lesson, please pay attention the examples above and do extra research to have a better understanding of the lesson. Especially understand how the operation of try…catch...finally ... throw to be able to apply well to actual projects.

The source code can be downloaded at the link: https://github.com/thanhtd32/kotlin/tree/main/LearnException.

How to Debug Kotlin

In this lesson, the book will show how to handle exceptions to control bugs in the runtime process However, in order to fix every step that the program performs to find difficult errors such as Logic errors, we must use the Debug tool, IntelliJ IDEA software has a built-in Debug tool to help us easily fix.

According to our experience, we have to spend more time fixing bugs than writing new code.

With any Debug tool, we usually have three main operations:

- How to set break point?
- How to debug each line?
- How to view the value of a variable while debugging?

Now the book will go into details of each operation in the IntelliJ IDEA tool for you to Debug, assuming we have a command to solve the second-degree equation in the Listing 4 (we are intentionally wrong in logic), our task is to find out the logic errors by using the Debug tool:

Listing 4. LearnDebugTool/App_Second_Degree_Equation.kt

```
1   fun main(args: Array<String>) {
2   var a:Double=0.0
3   var b:Double=0.0
4   var c:Double=0.0
5   println("Welcome to Second-Degree Equation!")
6   println("Input a:")
7   a= readLine()!!.toDouble()
8   println("Input b:")
9   b=readLine()!!.toDouble()
10  println("Input c:")
11  c=readLine()!!.toDouble()
12  if(a==0.0)
13  {
14  if(b==0.0 && c==0.0)
15  println("Infinite solutions")
16  else if(b==0.0 && c!=0.0)
17  println("No solutions")
18  else
19  println("X="+(-b/c))
20  }
21  else
22  {
23  val delta:Double=Math.pow(b,2.0)-4*a*c
24  if(delta<0)
25  println("No solutions")
26  else if(delta==0.0)
27  {
28  var x:Double=-b/(2*a)
29  println("Double root x1=x2=$x")
30  }
31  else
32  {
33  var x1:Double=(b-Math.sqrt(delta))/(2*a)
34  var x2:Double=(b+Math.sqrt(delta))/(2*a)
35  println("x1=$x1")
36  println("x2=$x2")
37  }
38  }
39  }
```

Looking at the command above, have you found any logic errors?
We have 2 cases to test the Logic error above as follows

Case 1: $0x^2+5x+2=0$ 1.

If true then the result should be x = -0.4, but when run up the result is x = -2.5. This is the first wrong logic.

2.Case 2: $x^2+5x-6 =0$

If it is true then the result would be: x1=-6, x2= 1. But the result above is x1 = -1.0, x2 = 6.0 here is the second Logic error

So how to debug it? Usually, we have to Debug in each line to test (of course, we will hard encounter such trivial algorithms in reality, here is just the typical example of solving the second order equation to who you the debugging method).

Now we go into the details:

Step 1: To stop checking the command at any point, make a break point in that line (this step is called set Break Point):

For example, if you want to set Break Point at command line 19 and the command line 33 then click next to the number of lines where the red arrow points to it, it will appear as a dot of that color, want to remove it then Press again:

Figure 1. Set break point to debug

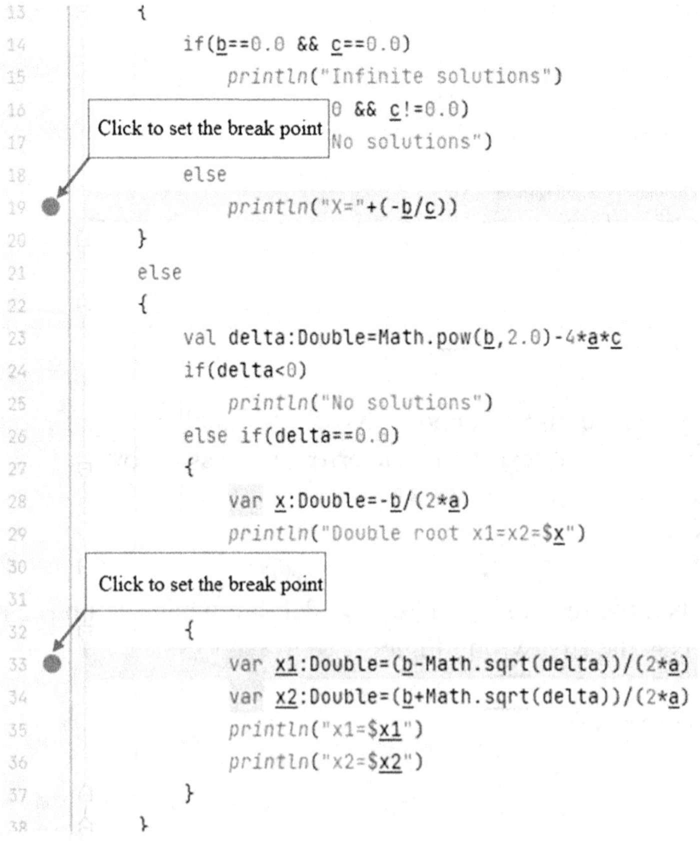

When a line with a red dot appears, the breakpoint is set successfully.

Step 2: Run Debug in each line

Go to the Run menu / select Debug App_debug.kt (which is the file that we wrote the main command to Debug)

Figure 2. Choose debug

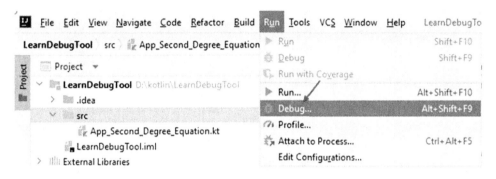

The program executes and we enter the values for the variables:

```
Connected to the target VM, address: '127.0.0.1:51099',
    transport: 'socket'
Welcome to Second-Degree Equation!
Input a:
0
Input b:
5
Input c:
2
```

A = 0, b = 5 and c = 2 ==> Now, the program will automatically launch the Debugger tab next to the Console tab and move the command pointer to line 19 that we have set Break Point:

Figure 3. The stop break point

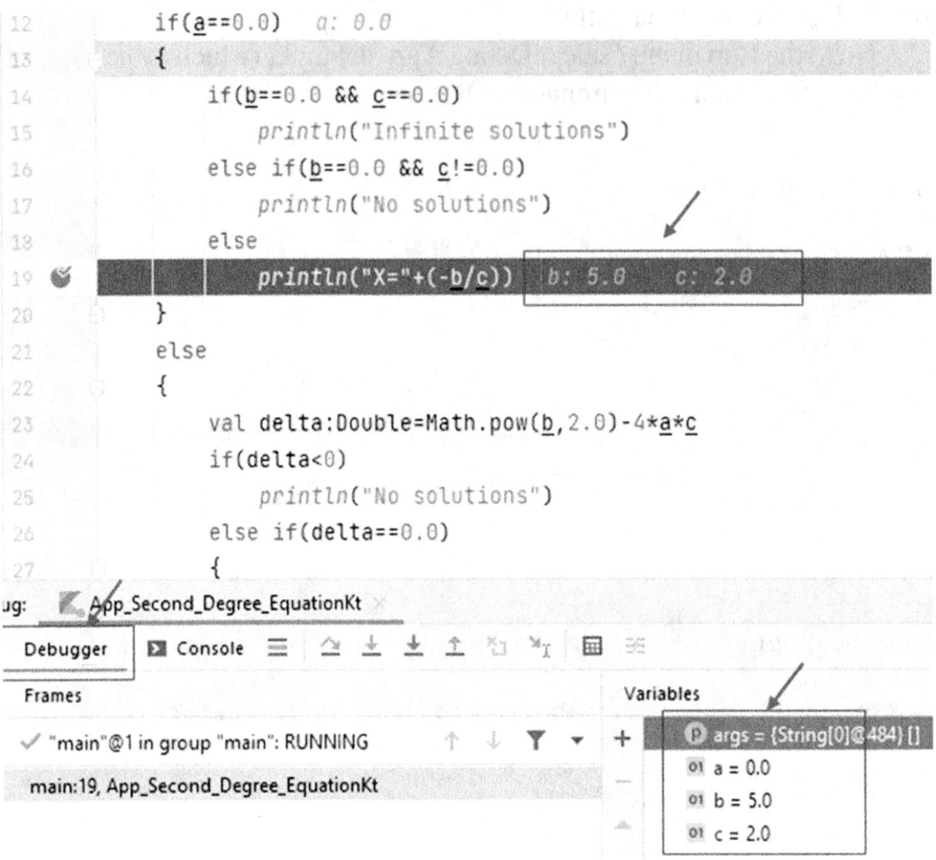

```
12        if(a==0.0)    a: 0.0
13        {
14            if(b==0.0 && c==0.0)
15                println("Infinite solutions")
16            else if(b==0.0 && c!=0.0)
17                println("No solutions")
18            else
19                println("X="+(-b/c))   b: 5.0    c: 2.0
20        }
21        else
22        {
23            val delta:Double=Math.pow(b,2.0)-4*a*c
24            if(delta<0)
25                println("No solutions")
26            else if(delta==0.0)
27                {
```

ug: App_Second_Degree_EquationKt

Debugger | Console ≡ 📥 📤 🔼 📥 ❎ ❎ | ⊞ ❌

Frames | Variables

✓ "main"@1 in group "main": RUNNING ↑ ↓ ▼ ▾ +   args = {String[0]@484} []

main:19, App_Second_Degree_EquationKt

oi a = 0.0
oi b = 5.0
oi c = 2.0

At the top of the screen, we can see the value of the variables right in the debug line.

And the tool in Debug mode allows you to use the keys F7, F8, F9 to navigate the Debug process:

Figure 4. Debugging actions

F7 is going inside the invoked method, F8 is over invoked, F9 is going back to normal mode. And there are other shortcuts you can test.

Step 3: How to view the value of a variable while debugging

To see more values of the variables during debugging, IntelliJ IDEA also provides the Add to Watches function (highlight any -> right click -> select Add to Watches):

Figure 5. Add to watches

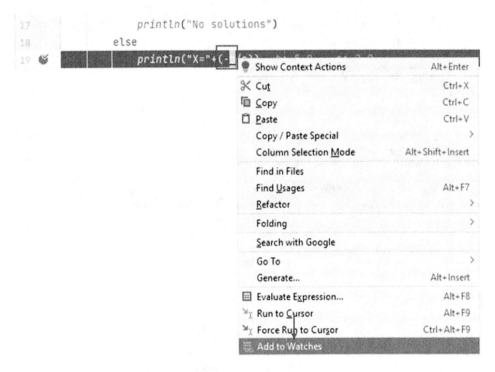

After selecting Add to Watches -> this variable will be displayed in the Variables screen:

Figure 6. View variables in the debugger

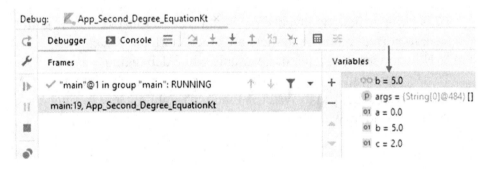

Press F8 to run, then see the result:

Figure 7. Console output the data

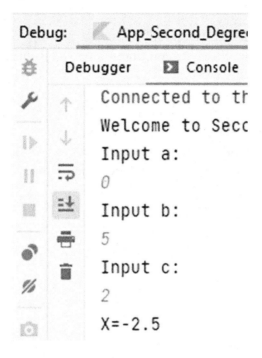

Because of the Logic error, we know the result is certainly wrong, and we need to fix the command (in fact it is much harder, sometimes you have to F7, F8 all day, and you still don't find the bugs).

Similarly, you test the second case that if have two distinct false solutions.

This is the end of the lesson, please pay attention to the examples above and do extra research to have a better understanding of the lesson. You need to master Debug Tools, debug keys as well as Add to Watches to apply to your actual projects.

You can download the wrong source code for this lesson here: https://github.com/thanhtd32/kotlin/tree/main/LearnDebugTool.

Readers can read more explanations of the conditional structure in the authors' books (Jemerov et al., 2017; Griffiths & Griffiths, 2019; Eckel & Isakova. 2020; Bailey et al., 2021).

Exercises

1. Why have to handle exception?
2. What is the difference between Compiler error, Runtime exception error and Exception logic error?
3. What is the benefit of try catch handler?
4. What is finally keyword used for?
5. What is the benefit of throw exception keyword?
6. What are the benefits of the Debug tool?
7. What is the result after executing the code below?

```
fun main(args: Array<String>) {
    var x
    var y
    x=5
    y=x+1
    println("x=$x")
    println("y=$y")
}
```

   (a) Compiler error
   (b) x=5 and y=6
   (c) Runtime exception error
   (d) Exception logic error

8. What is the result after executing the code below?

```
fun main(args: Array<String>) {
    var a=5
    var b=2
    var c=b/a
    var x=1/c+b
    println("x=$x")
}
```

   (a) Compiler error
   (b) Runtime exception error
   (c) x=2
   (d) Exception logic error

9.   What is the result after executing the code below?

Let's observe the Point and the Result on the Table

Point	Result
60→100	Pass
<60	Fail

```kotlin
fun main(args: Array<String>) {
    var point:Double
    println("Input point:")
    point= readLine()!!.toDouble()
    if(point>60)
        println("Pass")
    else
        println("Fail")
}
```

Assume that the user enters point=60
(a) Pass, but the program is Runtime exception error
(b) Fail, but the program is Runtime exception error

10. What is the result after executing the code below?

```kotlin
fun main(args: Array<String>) {
    var x:Int=0
    var z:Int=5
    try{
        z=3/x
        println(z)
    }
    catch (e:Exception){
        println("error")
    }
    finally {
        println("z=$z")
    }
}
```

(a) error, z=5
(b) error
(c) z=5

11. TOEIC Score Analyzer

I am trying to analyze the TOEIC score to find out the English proficiency of college students. I want to know the frequency band with the most frequent frequency and the score band with the smallest frequency by calculating the frequency for each score band.

However, there may be cases where the frequency of each group is the same. Let's modify it so that we can see all the scores with the same frequency. Also, let's find the average by adding a function to find the average of the TOEIC students acquired.

The program should provide these functions:

° List all Toiec Score for each Student acquired: Score-Frequency-Frequency rate

° List all Score with range complex for Student acquired: Base Score-Frequency- Frequency rate

° See all the scores with the same max frequency.

° See all the scores with the same min frequency.

° A function to find the average of the TOEIC students acquired.

The handle exception must be put in the coding in case user enter an invalid value (such as negative score, string value, etc.)

REFERENCES

Bailey, Greenhalgh, & Skeen. (2021). Kotlin Programming: The Big Nerd Ranch Guide (2nd ed.). Big Nerd Ranch, LLC.

Dmitry & Svetlana. (2017). *Kotlin in Action.* Manning.

Eckel &Isakova. (2020). Atomic Kotlin. Mindview LLC.

Griffiths, D., & Griffiths, D. (2019). *Head First Kotlin. O'Reilly Media.*

Chapter 6
Commonly Important Libraries

ABSTRACT

Every programming language has a set of libraries that will help programmers quickly solve certain tasks, and programmers must certainly use it because programmers either cannot write some libraries or it takes a long time; so programmers must know how to use them. These libraries may be in the JVM or KotlinJavaRuntime or in any other external library. In this chapter, the book will present some commonly used libraries, such as numeric data processing library, date processing library, math processing library, random number processing library, and string processing library. And there are many other processing libraries—readers can do more research about those libraries. At the end of the chapter there are exercises to help readers improve the skills in important libraries commonly.

COMMONLY IMPORTANT LIBRARIES

Every programming language has a set of libraries that will help programmers quickly solve certain tasks, and programmers must certainly use it because programmers cannot write some libraries or it spends long time, so programmers must know how to use it. These libraries may be in the JVM or KotlinJavaRuntime or in any other external library:

DOI: 10.4018/978-1-6684-6687-2.ch006

Figure 1. KotlinJavaRuntime

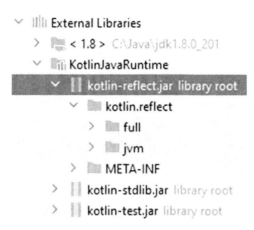

In this chapter, the book will present some commonly used libraries

- Numeric Data Processing Library
- Date processing library
- Math processing library
- Random number processing library
- String processing library

And there are many other processing libraries, readers can more research about those libraries. At the end of the chapter there are exercises to help readers improve the skills in important libraries commonly.

Numeric Data Processing Library

To format decimal digits for real numbers, you can use the following format, syntax "%.nf" with n is the number of decimals to format, The Listing 1 shows how to use the decimal format.

Listing 1. LearnLibrariesCommonly/App_NumericFormat.kt

```
1   fun main(args: Array<String>) {
2   var d:Double=10.0/3.0
3   println(d)
4   println("%.2f".format(d))
5   }
```

The output is unformatted or formatted in decimal format:

```
3.3333333333333335
3.33
```

"% .2f" is the decimal number, We choose 2 that means 2 decimal numbers, you can choose as you wish.

You can use the DecimalFormat library located in the JVM to format the number, the example below illustrates the decimal grouping separator in the Listing 2.

Listing 2. LearnLibrariesCommonly/App_DecimalFormat.kt

```
1    import java.text.DecimalFormat
2    import java.text.DecimalFormatSymbols
3    import java.util.Locale
4    fun main(args: Array<String>) {
5    var x:Int=986553823
6    var dcf=DecimalFormat("#,###")
7    var dcfs= DecimalFormatSymbols(Locale.getDefault())
8    dcfs.groupingSeparator=','
9    dcf.decimalFormatSymbols=dcfs
10   println(x)
11   println(dcf.format(x))
12   }
13
```

Results when running the program:

```
986553823
986,553,823
```

Notice the import command above is IntelliJ IDEA itself, just type Control + Space when using the library, it will automatically appear. Kotlin makes it easy to invoke libraries in the JVM to help Java programmers to switch languages.

Date Processing Library

When dealing with the day of the year we usually use 3 libraries:

- Date
- Calendar

- SimpleDateFormat

These libraries are in the package:

import java.util.Date
import java.util.Calendar
import java.text.SimpleDateFormat
  - Get current date:
var cal=Calendar.getInstance()
  - Take each criterion
var year=cal.get(Calendar.YEAR)
var month=cal.get(Calendar.MONTH)
var day=cal.get(Calendar.DAY_OF_MONTH)
  - Change the date parameter:
cal.set(Calendar.*YEAR, 1990);*
cal.set(Calendar.MONTH,2)
cal.set(Calendar.DAY_OF_MONTH,20)
  - Get Date object:
var date=cal.time
  - Format date as dd/MM/YYYY
var date=cal.time
var sdf=SimpleDateFormat("dd/MM/yyyy");
println(sdf.format(date))

The example for Date Format is shown in the Listing 3.
Results when running the program:

```
Year=2021
Month=7
Day=16
16/08/2021
16/08/2021 03:36:51 PM
```

Note month is always running from 0-> 11, so when the number 4 is May (we can see SimpleDateFormat output month).

hh:mm:ss aaa is the hour format: minutes: seconds, aaa is AM or PM. If you want to format 24h to replace hh to HH

Listing 3. LearnLibrariesCommonly/App_DateFormat.kt

```
1    import java.util.Date
2    import java.util.Calendar
3    import java.text.SimpleDateFormat
4    fun main(args: Array<String>) {
5        //Get the Calendar object (current date)
6        var cal:Calendar=Calendar.getInstance()
7        //Get year from cal object
8        var year:Int=cal.get(Calendar.YEAR)
9        //Get month from cal object
10       var month:Int=cal.get(Calendar.MONTH)
11       //Get day of the month from cal object
12       var day:Int=cal.get(Calendar.DAY_OF_MONTH)
13       println("Year=$year")
14       println("Month=$month")
15       println("Day=$day")
16       //Get DateTime from cal object
17       var date:Date=cal.time
18       //Create SimpleDateFormat object
19       var sdf=SimpleDateFormat("dd/MM/yyyy")
20       //print date with format
21       println(sdf.format(date))
22       var sdf2=SimpleDateFormat("dd/MM/yyyy hh:mm:ss aaa")
23       println(sdf2.format(date))
24   }
25
26
```

Math Processing Library

For math processing we use the Math library contained in the java.lang package. Some common Math methods is shown in the Table 1.

Table 1. Math methods

Method Name	Description
PI	Returns the PI value
abs(a)	Returns the absolute value of a
max(a,b)	Returns the maximum value between a and b
min(a,b)	Returns the smallest value between a and b
sqrt(a)	Returns the square root of a
pow(x,y)	Powers x
sin(radian)	Calculate sin, radian = Math.PI * angle / 180
cos(radian)	Calculate cos
tan(radian)	Calculate tan

The example for math library, the coding is shown in the Listing 4.

Listing 4. LearnLibrariesCommonly/App_Math.kt

```
1   fun main(args: Array<String>) {
2   println("PI number="+Math.PI)
3   println("Absolute value of -4="+Math.abs(-4))
4   println("number "+Math.max(9,2)+" is greater number")
5   println("Square root of 25="+Math.sqrt(25.0))
6   println("3 power of 4 ="+Math.pow(3.0,4.0))
7   var angle=45
8   var rad=Math.PI*angle/180
9   println("sin($angle)="+Math.sin(rad))
10  println("cos($angle)="+Math.cos(rad))
11  println("tan($angle)="+Math.tan(rad))
12  println("cotan($angle)="+
13  Math.cos(rad)/Math.sin(rad))
14  }
```

Results when running the program:

```
PI number=3.141592653589793
Absolute value of -4=4
number 9 is greater number
Square root of 25=5.0
3 power of 4 =81.0
sin(45)=0.7071067811865475
cos(45)=0.7071067811865476
tan(45)=0.9999999999999999
cotan(45)=1.0000000000000002
```

Random Number Processing Library

To deal with random numbers we use the Random class in the import java. util. Random package

```
var rd=Random()
var x=rd.nextInt(n);
```

Returns random numbers from [0 ... n-1]

For example:

❖ To generate a random number in [0....100] we call the command rd.nextInt(101)

❖ To generate a random number in [-100 ...100] we call the command -100+rd.nextInt(201)

❖ To generate a random number in [-100 ... -50] we call the command -100+rd.nextInt(51)

❖ rd.nextDouble () returns random number [0 ... 1]

Example:

Write the game "Guess the number". The computer will issue a random number [0...100], requiring the player to guess this number, allowing for 7 wrong guesses (more than 7 times the game over). If player guessed wrong, let the player know that the number of player's guess is smaller or larger than the number of players.

And after the game ends (WIN or LOST). Program should ask if the player wants to play again. The source code is shown in the Listing 5.

Listing 5. LearnLibrariesCommonly/App_Random.kt

```
1    import java.util.Random
2    fun main(args: Array<String>) {
3    while (true) {
4    play()
5    println("Do you want to play again?(y/n):")
6    val tl = readLine()
7    if (tl.equals("n", ignoreCase = true))
8    break
9    }
10   println("Good bye!")
11   }
12   fun play()
13   {
14   var rd = Random()
15   var numberofProgram = rd.nextInt(101)
16   println("Program picked a value in [0...100] Please guess!")
17   var numberofPeople: Int=0
18   var numberofGuesses = 0
19   do {
20   println("What number do you guess?:")
21   var s=readLine()
22   if(s!=null)
23   numberofPeople = s.toInt()
24   numberofGuesses++
25   println("You guess the $numberofGuesses times")
26   if (numberofPeople == numberofProgram) {
27   println("Congratulations!!!")
28   println("You are right!!")
29   println("Number of program is $numberofProgram")
30   break
31   }
32   if (numberofPeople < numberofProgram) {
33   println("You are wrong!!!")
34   println("Number of program> your number")
35   } else {
36   println("You are wrong!!!")
37   println("Number of program<your number")
38   }
39   if (numberofGuesses == 7) {
40   println("You are Game Over!!!")
41   println("Because you are wrong 7 times!")
42   break
43   }
44   } while (numberofGuesses <= 7)
45   }
46
47
48
49
```

Results when running the program:

```
Program picked a value in [0...100] Please guess!
What number do you guess?:
50
You guess the 1 times
```

```
You are wrong!!!
Number of program> your number
What number do you guess?:
75
You guess the 2 times
You are wrong!!!
Number of program<your number
What number do you guess?:
65
You guess the 3 times
You are wrong!!!
Number of program<your number
What number do you guess?:
57
You guess the 4 times
You are wrong!!!
Number of program> your number
What number do you guess?:
61
You guess the 5 times
You are wrong!!!
Number of program> your number
What number do you guess?:
63
You guess the 6 times
You are wrong!!!
Number of program<your number
What number do you guess?:
62
You guess the 7 times
Congratulations!!!
You are right, number of program is 62
Do you want to play again?(y/n):
n
Good bye!
```

1.5 String Processing Library

We often use the StringBuilder class (located in kotlin.text) to process the string

- **StringBuilder**(): By default, a StringBuilder object can hold 16 characters
- **StringBuilder(int capacity):** Creates a StringBuilder object that holds the character capacity

- **StringBuilder(String s):** Creates a StringBuilder object that retrieves information from string s

Commonly Used Methods:

- append () - append string
- insert () - insert string
- delete() – delete string
- reverse() – reserve string

The examples how to use the StringBuilder is shown in the Listing 6.

Listing 6. LearnLibrariesCommonly/App_StringBuilder.kt

```
1   fun main(args: Array<String>) {
2   //Create StringBuilder object
3   var sb= StringBuilder("Hello Kotlin")
4   //Hello Kotlin
5   println(sb.toString())
6   //append a string to last original string
7   sb.append(" Language")
8   //Hello Kotlin Language
9   println(sb.toString())
10  //insert say at the first string
11  sb.insert(0,"Say ")
12  //Say Hello Kotlin Language
13  println(sb.toString())
14  //delete a string from index 3 to 9
15  sb.delete(3,9)
16  //Say Kotlin Language
17  println(sb.toString())
18  //reverse the original string
19  sb.reverse()
20  //egaugnaL niltoK yaS
21  println(sb.toString())
22  }
```

Results when running the program:

```
Hello Kotlin
Hello Kotlin Language
Say Hello Kotlin Language
Say Kotlin Language
egaugnaL niltoK yaS
```

Especially when concatenated as read from File, read from internet with long content, we should use StringBuilder to append instead of +. Because the use of the + sign of processing speed will be very slow.

This is the end of the lesson, please pay attention the examples above and do extra research to have a better understanding of the lesson. Especially understand how the libraries work to be able to apply well to actual projects.

The source code can be downloaded at the link: https://github.com/thanhtd32/kotlin/tree/main/LearnLibraries Commonly.

Readers can read more explanations of the conditional structure in the authors' books (Jemerov et al., 2017. Griffiths & Griffiths, 2019; Eckel & Isakova, 2020; Bailey et al., 2021).

Exercises

1. What is the output to the screen when running the following commands?

```
var a=5
var b=3
var c:Double=(a+b)/3.0
println("%.2f".format(c))
```

   (a) 2.67
   (b) 2.66
   (c) 2.70

2. What is the output to the screen when running the following commands?

```
var x:Int=1000000
var dcf= DecimalFormat("#,###")
var dcfs= DecimalFormatSymbols(Locale.getDefault())
dcfs.groupingSeparator=','
dcf.decimalFormatSymbols=dcfs
println(dcf.format(x))
```

   (a) 1000000
   (b) 1,00,00,00
   (c) 1,000,000

3.   What is the output to the screen when running the following commands?

```
var cal:Calendar=Calendar.getInstance()
cal.set(Calendar.DATE,9)
cal.set(Calendar.MONTH,3)
cal.set(Calendar.YEAR,2021)
var sdf= SimpleDateFormat("dd/MM/yyyy")
println(sdf.format(cal.time))
```

  (a)   03/09/2021
  (b)   04/09/2021
  (c)   09/03/2021
  (d)   09/04/2021

4.   What is the output to the screen when running the following commands?

```
var x=Math.sqrt(Math.abs(-4).toDouble())
println(x)
```

  (a)   2.0
  (b)   2
  (c)   Compiler Error
  (d)   Runtime Error

5.   How to random a number in [-100 … -50]? rd is a variable of Random
  (a)   -100-rd.nextInt(50)
  (b)   -100+rd.nextInt(50)
  (c)   -100+rd.nextInt(51)
  (d)   -100-rd.nextInt(51)

6.   How to random a number in [-100 … 100]? rd is a variable of Random
  (a)   -100-rd.nextInt(201)
  (b)   -100-rd.nextInt(200)
  (c)   -100+rd.nextInt(200)
  (d)   -100+rd.nextInt(201)

7.   What is the difference between using StringBuilder to concatenate strings and using + operator to concatenate strings?

8.   Write a program to enter x>0, n>0 and calculate the expression S(x, n)

$$S\left(x,n\right) = x + x^2 + x^3 + \ldots + x^n$$

9.   Write a program to enter x>0, n>0 and calculate the expression S(x, n)

$$S(x, n) = x^2 + x^4 + x^6 + \ldots + x^{2n}$$

10. Write a program to enter x>0, n>0 and calculate the expression S(x, n)

$$S(x, n) = x + \frac{x^2}{2} + \frac{x^3}{3} + \ldots + \frac{x^n}{n}$$

11. Write a program to enter x>0, n>0 and calculate the expression S(x, n)

$$S(x, n) = x + \frac{x^2}{1+2} + \frac{x^3}{1+2+3} + \ldots + \frac{x^n}{1+2+3+\ldots+n}$$

12. Write a program to enter n>=1 and calculate the expression S(n)

$$S(n) = \sqrt{n + \sqrt{(n-1) + \sqrt{(n-2) + \ldots + \sqrt{2 + \sqrt{1}}}}}$$

13. GPA management
    Using libraries related to Numeric, Date, Math and String processing library to write GPA management software.
    ◦ Input data: Student ID, Student Name, Date of Birth, Percent Grade
    ◦ Output data: The input data is displayed in a table and including GPA Letter

The conversion table between Percent Grade and Letter Grade is as follows:

Table 2.

Percent Grade	GPA letter
97-100	A+
93-96	A
90-92	A-
87-89	B+
83-86	B
80-82	B-
77-79	C+
73-76	C
70-72	C-
67-69	D+
65-66	D
Below 65	E/F

The results after inputting and displaying data after processing are similar to the following table:

Table 3.

#	Student ID	Student Name	Date of Birth	Percent Grade	GPA
1	ST1	Tom	01/01/2004	97	A+
2	ST2	John	02/02/2004	85	B
3	ST3	Peter	01/03/2004	90	A-

REFERENCES

Bailey, Greenhalgh, & Skeen. (2021). *Kotlin Programming: The Big Nerd Ranch Guide* (2nd ed.). Big Nerd Ranch, LLC.

Eckel & Isakova. (2020). *Atomic Kotlin. Mindview LLC.*

Dmitry & Svetlana. (2017). *Kotlin in Action.* Manning.

Griffiths, D., & Griffiths, D. (2019). *Head First Kotlin. O'Reilly Media.*

Chapter 7
String Processing

ABSTRACT

In all programming languages, string processing is extremely important. This chapter will present how to declare strings and summarize the commonly used functions of strings, such as indexOf, lastIndexOf, contains, substring, replace, trim, compare, plus, split, upper case and lowercase functions, etc. Each function has sample code along with detailed explanations that make it easy for readers to understand how to use basic string functions. In this chapter, the book will present some of the most commonly used functions in the string. At the end of the chapter there are exercises to help readers improve the skills in string processing.

STRING PROCESSING

In all programming languages, string processing is extremely important, almost all of which are related to string processing. This chapter will present how to declare strings and summarize the commonly used functions of strings, such as indexOf, lastIndexOf, contains, substring, replace, trim, compare, plus, split, upper case and lowercase functions, etc. Each function has sample code along with detailed explanations that make it easy for readers to understand how to use basic string functions.

All detailed information about the string in Kotlin is presented here https://kotlinlang.org/api/latest/jvm/stdlib/kotlin/-string/, please take a quick look. In this chapter, the book will present some of the most commonly used

DOI: 10.4018/978-1-6684-6687-2.ch007

functions in the string. At the end of the chapter there are exercises to help readers improve the skills in string processing.

String Declaration and Function Summary

To declare the string in Kotlin we use:

```
var s:String= "Kotlin"
```

> or

```
var s:String?= "Kotlin"
```

The Table 1 shows the properties and methods string in Kotlin (you can see more at https://kotlinlang.org/api/latest/jvm/stdlib/kotlin/-string/).

Table 1. String properties and methods

Property Name/Method	Description
length	the property returns the length of the string
indexOf(string)	Returns the first location found, if not found returns -1
lastIndexOf(string)	lastIndexOf returns the last found location
contains	Check whether Contains are in the string s?
subString(index)	Extract the whole right of the string from index
subString(startIndex,endIndex)	Extract between strings between start and end index(exclusive)
replace (old string, new string)	Convert entire old string to new string
replaceFirst(old string, new string)	Convert old strings to new strings, but apply only to the first strings
trimStart	Removes the excess whitespace on the left
trimEnd	Removes the excess whitespace on the right
trim	Removes the excess whitespace on the right and left
compareTo(string s2)	Compare two sequences, distinguish UPPERCASE and lowercase =0 when s1=s2 >0 when s1>s2 <0 when s1<s2
compareTo(s2, ignoreCase = true)	Compare two sequences, no distinguish UPPERCASE and lowercase =0 when s1=s2 >0 when s1>s2 <0 when s1<s2
plus(string x)	Append the string x to the original string
split(spilt string)	Extract the original string into List <String>
uppercase	Convert string to UPPERCASE
lowercase	Convert string to lowercase

Now, we will go into details of each function.

IndexOf

IndexOf function returns the first position found, if not found returns -1. The Listing 1 shows how to use this function.

Listing 1. LearnStringProcessing/App_IndexOf.kt

```
1   fun main(args: Array<String>) {
2     var s:String="Hello Kotlin"
3     var i = 0
4     // Return i = 4
5     i = s.indexOf("o")
6     println(i)
7   }
```

It is obvious that the character/string **o** appears twice, but Kotlin only cares about the first result, so the result = 4 will be output to the screen (the starting location counts from 0).

If we change s.indexOf("a"), we will get the -1. Because of there is no **a** string in the string.

LastIndexOf

lastIndexOf function returns the last location found, if not found returns -1. The Listing 2 shows how to use this function.

Listing 2. LearnStringProcessing/App_LastIndexOf.kt

```
1   fun main(args: Array<String>) {
2     var s:String="Hello Kotlin"
3     var i = 0
4     // Return i = 7
5     i = s.lastIndexOf("o")
6     println(i)
7   }
```

We see output 7 is the last position of character / string o.

Contains

Contains function checks whether the contains exists in the original string or not. The Listing 3 shows how to use this function.

Listing 3. LearnStringProcessing/App_Contains.kt

```
1   fun main(args: Array<String>) {
2   var s:String = "Hello Kotlin !"
3   var s2="Kotlin"
4   if(s.contains(s2))
5   {
6   println("Exist [$s2]")
7   }
8   else
9   {
10  println("Doesn't exist [$s2]")
11  }
12  }
```

The results show that the output "Exist [Kotlin]". The contains function is used a lot to check the existence of the contains.

SubString

subString(index): Extract the whole right of the string from index.

subString(startIndex, endIndex): Extract between strings between start and end index(exclusive).

Listing 4. LearnStringProcessing/App_SubString.kt

```
1
2   fun main(args: Array<String>) {
3   val s = "Hello Kotlin Language"
4   println("Original string:")
5   println(s)
6   //get all the right string from startIndex=6
7   val s2 = s.substring(6)
8   println("The string from startIndex=6:")
9   //s2=Kotlin Language
10  println(s2)
11  //get child string from startIndex=6, endIndex=12(exclusive)
12  val s3 = s.substring(6, 12)
13  println("The string from startIndex=6, endIndex=12(exclusive):")
14  //s3=Kotlin
15  println(s3)
16  }
17
18
```

The code how to use these functions is shown in the Listing 4.
Results when running the program:

```
Original string:
Hello Kotlin Language
The string from startIndex=6:
Kotlin Language
The string from startIndex=6, endIndex=12(exclusive):
Kotlin
```

In order to substring to the right of the string, use the substring with 1 parameter, in order to substring to the middle of the string, use the substring with 2 parameters.

Replace

replace function converts old string to new string and we can use ignorecase. The Listing 5 shows how to use this function.

Listing 5. LearnStringProcessing/App_Replace.kt

```
1    fun main(args: Array<String>) {
2    var s = "Hello Kotlin Language"
3    println("The original string:")
4    println(s)
5    //change kotlin to Python (ignorecase)
6    s = s.replace("KOTLIN", "Python",true)
7    println("The replacing string:")
8    println(s)
9    }
```

In the above example, in the replace function, the third argument is true, which means the change is case-insensitive.
Results when running the program:

```
The original string:
Hello Kotlin Language
The replacing string:
Hello Python Language
```

ReplaceFirst

replaceFirst function converts old strings to new strings, but apply only to the first string. The Listing 6 shows how to use this function.

Listing 6. LearnStringProcessing/App_ReplaceFirst.kt

```
1    fun main(args: Array<String>) {
2    var s = "Hello Kotlin Language, and Hello Python Language"
3    println("The original string:")
4    println(s)
5    //oldValue: "Hello"
6    //newVale: "Hi"
7    //true is ignorecase
8    s = s.replaceFirst("Hello", "Hi",true)
9    println("The string after replacing first:")
10   println(s)
11   }
12
```

Results when running the program:

```
The original string:
Hello Kotlin Language, and Hello Python Language
The string after replacing first:
Hi Kotlin Language, and Hello Python Language
```

Although the original string has two "Hello" contains, the program only applies to the first one.

Trim

Functions to remove whitespace: trimEnd(), trimStart(), trim()

- trimStart() function removes the excess whitespace on the left
- trimEnd() function removes the excess whitespace on the right
- trim() function removes the excess whitespace on the right and left

The Listing 7 shows how to use these functions.

Listing 7. LearnStringProcessing/App_Trim.kt

```
1   fun main(args: Array<String>) {
2   var s:String= " Tran Duy Thanh "
3   println("The Original string:")
4   println("[$s]")
5   println("->The length of the string:${s.length}")
6   println("--------------------------------")
7   //remove the whitespace string from start
8   var s2=s.trimStart()
9   println("The string after calls the trimStart:")
10  println("[$s2]")
11  println("->The length of the string:${s2.length}")
12  println("--------------------------------")
13  //remove the whitespace string from end
14  var s3=s.trimEnd()
15  println("The string after calls the trimEnd:")
16  println("[$s3]")
17  println("->The length of the string:${s3.length}")
18  println("--------------------------------")
19  //remove the whitespace string start and end
20  var s4=s.trim()
21  println("The string after calls the trim:")
22  println("[$s4]")
23  println("->The length of the string:${s4.length}")
24  }
25
```

Results when running the program:

```
The Original string:
[    Tran Duy Thanh        ]
->The length of the string:24
--------------------------------
The string after calls the trimStart:
[Tran Duy Thanh        ]
->The length of the string:20
--------------------------------
The string after calls the trimEnd:
[    Tran Duy Thanh]
->The length of the string:18
--------------------------------
The string after calls the trim:
[Tran Duy Thanh]
->The length of the string:14
```

CompareTo

s1.compareTo(string s2) compares two string, distinguish UPPERCASE and
lowercase, it returns a value:
- ◦ =0 if s1=s2
- ◦ >0 if s1>s2
- ◦ <0 if s1<s2

s1.compareTo(s2, ignoreCase = true) compares two string, no distinguish
UPPERCASE and lowercase
- ◦ =0 if s1=s2
- ◦ >0 if s1>s2
- ◦ <0 if s1<s2

The Listing 8 shows how to the use compareTo function.

Listing 8. LearnStringProcessing/App_CompareTo.kt

```
1    fun main(args: Array<String>) {
2    var s1 = "KOTLIN"
3    var s2 = "Kotlin"
4    println("s1=$s1")
5    println("s2=$s2")
6    var x = s1.compareTo(s2, ignoreCase = true)
7    println("compareTo return $x when ignoreCase true")
8    var y = s1.compareTo(s2, ignoreCase = false)
9    println("compareTo return $y when ignoreCase false")
10   }
```

Results when running the program:

```
s1=KOTLIN
s2=Kotlin
compareTo return 0 when ignoreCase true
compareTo return -32 when ignoreCase false
```

in this example, If the comparison is not case-sensitive (ignoreCase =
true) then the result is 0, and if it is case-sensitive (ignoreCase = false) then
the result is< 0 (-32).

Plus

plus(string x) appends the string x to the original string. The Listing 9 shows how to use this function.

Listing 9. LearnStringProcessing/App_plus.kt

```
1   fun main(args: Array<String>) {
2   var s:String="Kotlin"
3   s=s.plus(" is")
4   s=s.plus(" a")
5   s=s.plus(" new")
6   s=s.plus(" programming")
7   s=s.plus(" Language")
8   println(s)
9   }
```

Results when running the program:

```
Kotlin a new programming Language
```

The plus function above pluses string, but it does not change the original string that returns a new string, so we have to save this new address. You can use the + sign (but do not use this sign too many times when you add strings, especially when read from files or the internet). Also, you can use StringBuilder to process string.

Split

The split(spilt string) function extracts the original string into List <String>. The Listing 10 shows how to use this function.

Listing 10. LearnStringProcessing/App_Split.kt

```
1   fun main(args: Array<String>) {
2     //the string with format: ID;FullName;Email
3     var s:String="123;Tran Duy Thanh;thanhtd@uel.edu.vn"
4     //split by ; character
5     //The elements are stored in the List
6     var arr:List<String> = s.split(";")
7     println("Number of elements="+arr.size)
8     //Get ID
9     var id=arr[0]
10    //Get Name
11    var fullName=arr[1]
12    //Get Email
13    var email=arr[2]
14    //print the informations:
15    println("ID=$id")
16    println("Full Name=$fullName")
17    println("Email=$email")
18
19  }
```

Results when running the program:

```
Number of elements=3
ID=123
Full Name=Tran Duy Thanh
Email=thanhtd@uel.edu.vn
```

String-splitting function is very important, as we will meet it in almost all software development process. Input is a regular string, and we must analyze it to spilt strings and then model it into structured data (usually OOP).

Uppercase and Lowercase

uppercase() method converts string to UPPERCASE

Listing 11. LearnStringProcessing/App_UperAndLowerCase.kt

```
1   fun main(args: Array<String>) {
2     var s:String="Tran Duy Thanh"
3     println("The original string:")
4     println(s)
5     var s2=s.uppercase()
6     println("The uppercase string:")
7     println(s2)
8     var s3=s.lowercase()
9     println("The lowercase string:")
10    println(s3)
11  }
```

lowercase() method converts string to lowercase

The Listing 11 shows how to use these functions.
    Results when running the program:

```
The original string:
Tran Duy Thanh
The uppercase string:
TRAN DUY THANH
The lowercase string:
tran duy thanh
```

Now, the Book will do a string optimization program: For any string, optimize the string as described: The string has no whitespace, the words separated by a whitespace, the first characters of the words are UPPERCASE.
    For example:

Listing 12. LearnStringProcessing/app_optimize_string.kt

```
1   fun optimize(s: String): String {
2   var sToiTuu = s
3   sToiTuu = sToiTuu.trim()
4   val arrWord = sToiTuu.split(" ");
5   sToiTuu = ""
6   for (word in arrWord) {
7   var newWord = word.lowercase()
8   if (newWord.length > 0) {
9   newWord = newWord.replaceFirst((newWord[0] + ""),
10  (newWord[0] + "").uppercase())
11  sToiTuu += newWord + " "
12  }
13  }
14  return sToiTuu.trim()
15  }
16  fun main(args: Array<String>) {
17  var s1 = " TRAN dUY THanh "
18  println("The original string:")
19  println(s1)
20  //call optimize string method
21   var s2 = optimize(s1)
22  println("The optimization string:")
23  println(s2)
24  println("--------------------------")
25  var s3 = " I am kotlin LANGUAGE "
26  println("The original string:")
27  println(s3)
28  //call optimize string method
29   var s4 = optimize(s3)
30  println("The optimization string:")
31  println(s4)
32  }
```

Input: "TRAN duY THAnh"
Output: "Tran Duy Thanh"

We can use regular expressions, but the purpose of this example is to practice using the learned string functions. The Listing 12 use string method to optimize string.

Results when running the program:

```
The original string:
   TRAN          dUY     THanh
The optimization string:
Tran Duy Thanh
--------------------------
The original string:
    I       am       kotlin         LANGUAGE
The optimization string:
I Am Kotlin Language
```

This is the end of the lesson, please pay attention the examples above and do extra research to have a better understanding of the lesson. Especially understand how the libraries work to be able to apply well to actual projects.

Readers need to read many examples of how to handle strings from Kotlin, since in this lesson the book has listed some of the most commonly used methods, but there are countless other useful methods. Download source code here: https://github.com/thanhtd32/kotlin/tree/main/LearnStringProcessing.

Readers can read more explanations of the conditional structure in the authors' books (Jemerov et al., 2017; Griffiths & Griffiths, 2019; Eckel & Isakova, 2020; Bailey et al., 2021).

Exercises

1. How to declare a String that can understand null value?
    (a) var s:String= null
    (b) var s:String?= null
2. What is the output to the screen when running the following commands?

```
var s="Hello Kotlin Language"
println(s.substring(6,12))
```

    (a) Hello
    (b) Kotlin
    (c) Language
3. How to extract string "Language"?

```
var s="Hello Kotlin Language"
```

    (a) s.substring(13)
    (b) s.substring(13,8)
    (c) s.substring(14)
    (d) s.substring(14,8)
4. What is the output to the screen when running the following commands?

```
var s = "EUREKA EUREKA EUREKA"
s = s.replaceFirst("eureka", "Hello",false)
println(s)
```

    (a) Hello EUREKA EUREKA
    (b) EUREKA EUREKA EUREKA
    (c) Hello eureka eureka
    (d) EUREKA EUREKA Hello
5. What is the output to the screen when running the following commands?

```
var s = "EUREKA EUREKA EUREKA"
s = s.replaceFirst("eureka", "Hello",true)
println(s)
```

    (a) Hello EUREKA EUREKA
    (b) EUREKA EUREKA EUREKA
    (c) Hello eureka eureka
    (d) EUREKA EUREKA Hello

6. What is the output to the screen when running the following commands?

```
var s1="D:/music/hello.mp3"
var s2=s1.substring(s1.lastIndexOf("/")+1)
println(s2)
```

    (a) hello.mp3
    (b) hello
    (c) music
    (d) mp3

7. What is the output to the screen when running the following commands?

```
var s1="D:/music/hello.mp3"
var s2=s1.substring(
    s1.indexOf("/")+1,
    s1.lastIndexOf("/"))
println(s2)
```

    (a) hello.mp3
    (b) hello
    (c) music
    (d) mp3

8. Write a program to check if a string is symmetric?
Eg, "radar" is a symmetric string, "hello" is not a symmetric string

9. Write a program to check if an email is valid or not?

10. What is the output to the screen when running the following commands?

```
var s:String="Kotlin"
s=s.plus(" Programming")
s=s.plus(" Language")
println(s)
```

    (a) Kotlin Programming Language
    (b) KotlinProgrammingLanguage
    (c) Kotlin

11. What is the output to the screen when running the following commands?

```
var s:String="Kotlin"
s.plus(" Programming")
s.plus(" Language")
println(s)
```

    (a)   Kotlin Programming Language

    (b)   KotlinProgrammingLanguage

    (c)   Kotlin

12. Write a function named NegativeNumberInStrings(String str). This function takes any string as an argument. Write program to output negative integers in a string. Eg: If input the string "abc-5xyz-12k9l--p", the function must output 2 negative integers that are -5 and -12

REFERENCES

Bailey, Greenhalgh, & Skeen. (2021). Kotlin Programming: The Big Nerd Ranch Guide (2nd ed.). Big Nerd Ranch, LLC.

Eckel & Isakova. (2020). Atomic Kotlin. Mindview LLC.

Griffiths, D., & Griffiths, D. (2019). *Head First Kotlin. O'Reilly Media.*

Jemerov, D. & Isakova, S. (2017). *Kotlin in Action.* Manning.

Chapter 8

Array Processing

ABSTRACT

Array is one of the very important data in software processing, it will be used to store data in the form of a list. Almost all programming languages support array processing, and so does the Kotlin language. However, with Kotlin, arrays are a very powerful data type, which overcome many disadvantages compared to other programming languages such as C++, C#, Java, etc. The book has briefly mentioned some of the array types that are built-in in Kotlin, such as: CharArray, BooleanArray, ByteArray, ShortArray, IntArray, LongArray, FloatArray, and DoubleArray. Depending on the purpose of use, programmers can choose different types of arrays; to help readers easily understand how to declare and use one-dimensional arrays in Kotlin, the book will use IntArray to illustrate in the examples below. Other types of arrays Readers can infer. At the end of the chapter, there are exercises to help readers improve programming skills to handle arrays.

ARRAY PROCESSING

Array is one of the very important data in software processing, it will be used to store data in the form of a list. Almost programming languages support array processing, and so does the Kotlin language. However, with Kotlin, arrays are a very powerful data type, which overcomes many disadvantages compared to other programming languages such as C++, C#, Java, etc.

In chapter data type, the book has briefly mentioned some of the array types that are built-in in Kotlin, such as: CharArray, BooleanArray, ByteArray,

DOI: 10.4018/978-1-6684-6687-2.ch008

ShortArray, IntArray, LongArray, FloatArray, DoubleArray. Depending on the purpose of use, programmers can choose different types of arrays, to help Readers easily understand how to declare and use one-dimensional arrays in Kotlin, the book will use IntArray to illustrate in the examples below, other types of arrays Readers can infer. At the end of the chapter, there are exercises to help readers improve programming skills to handle arrays.

One-Dimensional Array Processing

Syntax

To declare and allocate array we do the following:

```
var M:IntArray= IntArray(n) or var M = IntArray(n)
```

Where n is the maximum storage element of the array.

M is an array of storage types Int (storage of up to n elements). We can also say that M is an object of type IntArray. Similar to other programming languages, the array also saves the index from 0, allowing access to the elements through the index, The example below shows an array M with 8 elements:

Figure 1. Structure of a one-dimensional array

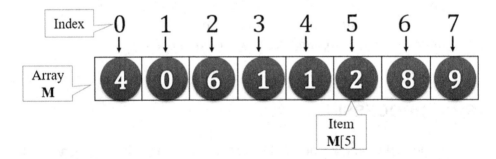

But readers need to keep in mind that element retrieval is just a tiny function in Kotlin's array, since with the array in Kotlin there are many methods, it is an object built with countless efficient methods: min, max, average, sum, search, sort ...

We can initialize an array in Kotlin with values by syntax, eg:

```
var M= intArrayOf(10, 20, 12, 40, 8)
```

The above example, we initialize an array in Kotlin with values 10, 20, 21, 40, 8

Using Functions

The list some common attributes and methods of Arrays are shown in the Table 1 (of course there are many other methods, when you find them, you study more):

Table 1. Attributes and methods of Arrays

Property/Method Name	Description
size	Attribute returns the actual size of the array
[i]	Indexer allows access and change of values at location i of the array
count/count{ }	Count/ conditional count
min()	The function returns the smallest number in the array
max()	The function returns the largest number in the array
sum()	The function returns the sum of the array
average()	The function returns the average of the array
sort()	Sort array ascendingly
sortDescending()	Sort array descendingly
filter{ }	Search / filter list in array
reverse()	Reverse array
contains()	Check whether the array contains any elements

For example, the M array declaration can hold up to 10 elements:

```
var M:IntArray= IntArray(10)
```

Enter the value for each element in the M array:

```
M[0]=100
M[1]=20
...
M[9]=-5
```

Because array M can hold 10 elements, Indexers will run from 0 to 9
To get a value at an index (index =2):

```
var x:Int=M[2]
```

To access the elements in the array we can access by location as follows:

```
for (i in M.indices)
    print("${M[i]}\t")
```

or acessing in the following way:

```
for (i in M)
    print("$i\t")
```

Other functions in the array are also easy to implement. A detailed example of creating an M array has 10 elements with random values is shown in the Listing 1.
Results after running the program:

```
List of elements in the array by value:
44    27    6    62    15    84    69    18    61    81
List of elements in the array: by index:
44    27    6    62    15    84    69    18    61    81
MAX=84
MIN=6
SUM=467
AVERAGE=46.7
Even number=5
Odd number=5
List of array elements in ascending order:
6    15    18    27    44    61    62    69    81    84
List of array elements in descending order:
84    81    69    62    61    44    27    18    15    6
Even number:
84    62    44    18    6
Odd number:
81    69    61    27    15
List of array elements > 50:
84    81    69    62    61
```

Listing 1. LearnOneDimensionalArray/App_Array.kt

```
1    import java.util.*
2
3    fun main(args: Array<String>) {
4        //Declares array M with 10 elements of type Int
5        var M:IntArray= IntArray(10)
6
7        var rd=Random()
8        for(i in M.indices)
9            M[i]=rd.nextInt(100)
10       println("List of elements in the array by value:")
11       for (i in M)
12           print("$i\t")
13       println()
14       println("List of elements in the array: by index:")
15       for (i in M.indices)
16           print("${M[i]}\t")
17       println()
18       //Largest number
19       println("MAX=${M.maxOrNull()}")
20       //smallest number
21       println("MIN=${M.minOrNull()}")
22       //Sum of array
23       println("SUM=${M.sum()}")
24       //average of array
25       println("AVERAGE=${M.average()}")
26       //count even number
27       println("Even number=${M.count { x->x%2==0 }}")
28       //count odd number
29       println("Odd number=${M.count { x->x%2==1 }}")
30       //Sort up ascending
31       M.sort()
32       println("List of array elements in ascending order:")
33       for (i in M)
34           print("$i\t")
35       println()
36       //sort up descending
37       M.sortDescending()
38       println("List of array elements in descending order:")
39       for (i in M)
40           print("$i\t")
41       println()
42       //filter  even number in array
43       var evenNumbers= M.filter { x->x%2==0 }
44       println("Even number:")
45       for (i in evenNumbers)
46           print("$i\t")
47       println()
```

continued on following page

151

Listing 1. Continued

```
48      //filter odd number in array
49      var oddNumbers= M.filter { x->x%2==1 }
50      println("Odd number:")
51      for (i in oddNumbers)
52          print("$i\t")
53      println()
54      var k=50
55      //filter  number >50 in array
56      var dsTim=M.filter { x->x>k }
57      println("List of array elements > $k:")
58      for (i in dsTim)
59          print("$i\t")
60      println()
61  }
```

This is the end of the lesson, please pay attention the examples above and do extra research to have a better understanding of the lesson. Especially understand how the libraries work to be able to apply well to actual projects.

The source code can be downloaded at the link: https://github.com/thanhtd32/kotlin/tree/main/LearnOneDimens ionalArray.

Two-Dimensional Array Processing

In previous lesson, we have already studied one-dimensional array/ In this lesson, the book will show you how to declare and use two-dimensional arrays of Kotlin.

Syntax

Syntax of two-dimensional array declaration in Kotlin:

```
var M:Array<Data_Type_Array> = Array(Number_of_Rows,{Data_type_
Array(Number_of_Columns)})
```

The following example declares a two-dimensional array named M with 10 rows and 5 columns, the data elements in M are of type Int:

```
var M:Array<IntArray> = Array(10,{IntArray(5)})
```

The row and column indices also run from 0 to n-1
You can imagine the data structure of 2-dimensional arrays as follows:

Figure 2. Structure of a two-dimensional array

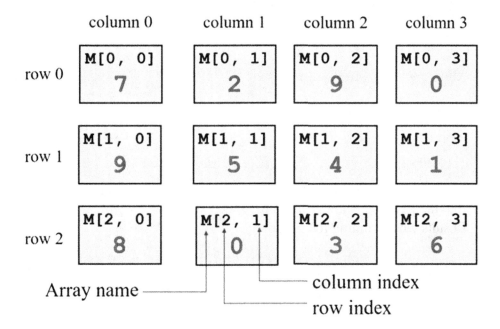

The two-dimensional array in Kotlin also has an extremely robust set of methods.

Using Functions

To input elements in a 2-dimensional array M, do the following:

```
var rd:Random = Random()
for(i in M.indices)
{
    for(j in M[i].indices)
    {
        M[i][j]=rd.nextInt(100)
    }
}
```

We use two iterative browsing for loop (indices). External loop is browsing by line; inner loop is browsing by column. Each time we browse, we have M [i] [j] as the element in the i th row and the j th column. We update the data for this element.

To output the data of the elements in the array to the screen we do the following:

```
for(i in M.indices)
{
    for(j in M[i].indices)
    {
      print("${M[i][j]}\t")
    }
    println()
}
```

Examples for some of the two-dimensional array processing functions in Kotlin, the Listing 2 shows the code.

Results when running the program:

```
Two-dimentional Array after input data:
59      15      25      89      52
33      17      49      71      76
57      96      36      56      78
64      90      80      75      78
 3       0      94      51      19
27      87      75      81      89
Two-dimentional Array after input data - way 2:
59      15      25      89      52
33      17      49      71      76
57      96      36      56      78
64      90      80      75      78
 3       0      94      51      19
27      87      75      81      89
Array at row 1:
33      17      49      71      76
```

This is the end of the lesson, please pay attention the examples above and do extra research to have a better understanding of the lesson. You need to check out many other methods in the 2-dimensional array to be able to apply well to your actual project.

The source code can be downloaded at the link: https://github.com/thanhtd32/kotlin/tree/main/LearnTwoDiment ionalArray.

Listing 2. LearnTwoDimentionalArray/App_2DArray.kt

```
1    import java.util.*
2
3    fun main(args: Array<String>) {
4        var M:Array<IntArray> = Array(6,{IntArray(5)})
5        var rd:Random = Random()
6        for(i in M.indices)
7        {
8            for(j in M[i].indices)
9            {
10               M[i][j]=rd.nextInt(100)
11           }
12       }
13       println("Two-dimentional Array after input data:")
14       for(i in M.indices)
15       {
16           for(j in M[i].indices)
17           {
18               print("${M[i][j]}\t")
19           }
20           println()
21       }
22       println("Two-dimentional Array after input data -
23   way 2:")
24
25       for(row in M)
26       {
27           for(item in row)
28           {
29               print("$item \t")
30           }
31           println()
32       }
33       println("Array at row 1:")
34       var M1=M[1]
35       for (i in M1.indices)
36           print("${M1[i]}\t")
37       println()
38   }
```

Readers can read more explanations of the conditional structure in the authors' books (Dmitry Jemerov, et al. 2017), and (Dawn Griffiths, David Griffiths. 2019), and (Bruce Eckel and Svetlana Isakova. 2020) and the book (Andrew Bailey, et al. 2021).

Exercises

1. How to declare an array of type int with 5 elements? multiple options
    (a) var M:IntArray= IntArray(5)
    (b) var M[5]
    (c) var M= IntArray(5)
    (d) var Int M[5]
2. How to initialize an array in Kotlin with values, such as 5, 8, 2
    (a) var M= Int[]{5,8,2}
    (b) var M= intArrayOf(5,8,2)
    (c) var M= IntArray{5,8,2}
    (d) var M= Int{5,8,2}
3. What is the result after executing the code below?

```
var M= doubleArrayOf(1.5,2.0,3.8,4.5)
var x=M.count { i->i>3 }
println(x)
```

    (a) 3
    (b) 2
    (c) 0
    (d) 5
4. What is the result after executing the code below?

```
var M= intArrayOf(10,20,15,40,30)
var x=M.count { i->i%2==0 }
println(x)
```

    (a) 4
    (b) 2
    (c) 5
    (d) 1
5. What is the result after executing the code below?

```
var M= intArrayOf(10,20,15,40,30)
var x=M.count { i->i%2!=0 }
println(x)
```

    (a) 4
    (b) 2

    (c) 5

    (d) 1

6.   What is the result after executing the code below?

```
var M= intArrayOf(10,20,15,40,30)
var x=M.filter { i->i>=20 }
println(x)
```

    (a) [20, 40, 30]

    (b) [30, 40, 20]

    (c) [10, 15]

    (d) [15, 10]

7.   What is the result after executing the code below?

```
var M= intArrayOf(10,20,15,40,30)
var x=M.filter { i->i>=20 }.sorted()
println(x)
```

    (a) [40, 30, 20]

    (b) [20, 30, 40]

    (c) [10, 15]

    (d) [15, 10]

8.   How to declare a 2-dimensional array of type Int with 3 rows and 4 columns?

    (a) var M:Array<IntArray> = Array(3,{IntArray(4)})

    (b) var M = IntArray(3,{IntArray(4)})

    (c) var M:IntArray = IntArray(3,{IntArray(4)})

    (d) var M = Array (4,{IntArray(3)})

9.   Write a program to plus 2 matrices

10.   Write a program to input an array of Int numbers. Please print it out screen

    ◦   Line 1: includes odd numbers, how many odd numbers in total.

    ◦   Line 2: includes even numbers, how many even numbers in total.

    ◦   Line 3: contains prime numbers.

    ◦   Line 4: contains numbers that are not prime.

11.   Book Search Machine

I have a book I want to buy, so I visited the website of an internet bookstore. If there is a book, I first searched for the book using the information of the name of the book I wanted to buy, the author, and the publisher's name, and then tried to order the book. I'm curious about how internet bookstores provide book search functionality.

The computer running the Internet bookstore must do the following to provide the ability to find books:

- Receive user input, such as the name of the book to be searched or the name of the author, and keywords
- Saving book information as a dictionary
- Find the desired book in the dictionary where book information is stored.

You have to think about how to present the information so that the user can enter it easily:

- Thinking about what information to present to the user in order to receive information from the book
- Thinking about how to print out the found book information

Array of the books example:

Title	Author	Publisher	Price ($)	Publication Year
Android app development	Thanh Tran	VNU	25	2017
Python	Thanh Tran	VNU	23	2019
JavaScript	Pham Dieu	SSS	38	2018
HTML5	Man Nhi	HCM	33	2012
Kotlin	Thanh Tra	IGI Global	24	2023
C language	Man Nhi	SSS	29	2010
Programming linguistics	Pham Dieu	HCM	41	2009

REFERENCES

Bailey, Greenhalgh, & Skeen. (2021). Kotlin Programming: The Big Nerd Ranch Guide (2nd ed.). Big Nerd Ranch, LLC.

Eckel & Isakova. (2020). Atomic Kotlin. Mindview LLC.

Griffiths, D., & Griffiths, D. (2019). *Head First Kotlin. O'Reilly Media.*

Jemerov, D., & Isakova, S. (2017). *Kotlin in Action.* Manning.

Chapter 9
Collections

ABSTRACT

Similar to other programming languages, arrays and collections are indispensable data types in the process of processing list data. In the previous chapter presented about arrays, there are some benefits of arrays, but in some cases, arrays do not meet requirements and are difficult to implement. Usually, the data has no change in quantity, no deleting or changing the position of data, then it is appropriate to use an array, but when it comes to cases where the data changes continuously, or the number of elements is not known in advance, or the position in the list can be shuffled, using arrays is no longer optimal, so collections are more optimal. This chapter will present hierarchical collections so that readers have an overview of collections, and then Mutable and Immutable collection are presented. The chapter also provides code and detailed explanation to help readers easily grasp the working mechanism, as well as be able to implement the collection in practice. At the end of the chapter, there are exercises to help readers improve collection processing programming skills.

COLLECTIONS

Similar to other programming languages, arrays and collections are indispensable data types in the process of processing list data. In the previous chapter presented about arrays, and there are some benefits of arrays, but in some cases, arrays do not meet and difficult to implement. Usually, the data has no change in quantity, no deleting or changing the position of data, then

DOI: 10.4018/978-1-6684-6687-2.ch009

it is appropriate to use an array, but when it comes to cases where the data changes continuously, or the number of elements is not known in advance, or the position in the list can be shuffled, using arrays is no longer optimal, so collections are more optimal. This chapter will present hierarchical collections so that readers have an overview of collections, and then Mutable and Immutable collection are presented. The chapter also provides code and detailed explanation to help readers easily grasp the working mechanism, as well as be able to implement the collection in practice. At the end of the chapter, there are exercises to help readers improve collection processing programming skills.

Hierarchical Collection

The inherited class model of collections in Kotlin / java:

Figure 1. Hierarchical collection

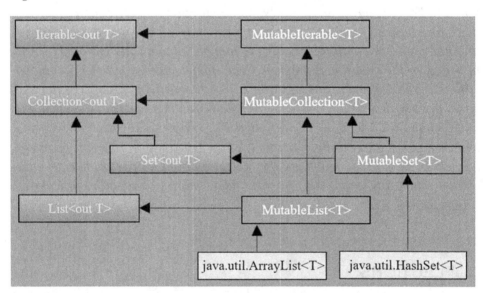

Mutable Collections is a set of classes used to store data lists and can be resized

Immutable Collections is a set of classes used to store a list of data and cannot be resized

Both of these collections are easy to create and use, they are just a little bit different in in terms of programming purpose.

Within this lesson, the book only shows about MutableList and List, please do extra research about other Collections however, with MutableList and List, we think you can handle almost all instances of archiving, interacting, displaying data in the software.

Mutable Collections

MutableList is a collection that can resize data: Can add, edit, delete ...

This collection in Kotlin do not have their own constructor constructs, but through mutableListOf()

Syntax:

```
var list:MutableList<Int> =mutableListOf()
```

The above list object is initialized with an empty list.
We can initialize with some initial data:
Example:

```
var list:MutableList<Int> =mutableListOf(5,6,1,0,4)
```

Table 1. Property and methods of the MutableList

Property/Method Name	Description
size	Attribute returns the actual size of the Collection
[i]	Indexer allows access and change of values at location i of the Collection
add()	Add an element
addAll()	Add multiple elements
removeAt()	Delete by location
remove()	Delete by object
removeIf{}	Delete by condition
clear()	Delete entire list
sort()	Sort ascendingly
sortDescending()	Sort descendingly
filter { }	Filter the data
contains()	Check whether the Collection contains any elements

The above list object is initialized with 5 elements and we can change the size, information of list.

Here are some common methods used with MutableList in the Table 1.

Please do some extra research to find out other amazing methods. The Listing 1 shows how to use the MutableList.

Listing 1(a). LearnCollection/App_MutableList.kt

```
1   fun main(args: Array<String>) {
2     var list:MutableList<Int> = mutableListOf()
3     //add one element into the list
4     list.add(10)
5     list.add(4)
6     list.add(5)
7     list.add(8)
8     //add multi elements into the list
9     list.addAll(mutableListOf(9,0,7))
10    println("Elements in MutableList - by value:")
11    for(i in list)
12    print("$i\t")
13    println()
14    println("Elements in MutableList - by index:")
15    for(i in list.indices)
16    print("${list[i]}\t")
17    println()
18    //Change the second element values to 113
19    list[2]=113
20    println("Elements in MutableList after changing:")
21    for(i in list.indices)
22    print("${list[i]}\t")
23    println()
24    //remove elements at index 3
25    list.removeAt(3)
26    println("Elements in MutableList after delete:")
27    for(i in list.indices)
28    print("${list[i]}\t")
29    println()
30    //sort ascending the list
31    list.sort()
32    println("Elements after sort ascending:")
33    for(i in list.indices)
34    print("${list[i]}\t")
35    println()
36    //sort descending the list
37    list.sortDescending()
38    println("Elements after sort descending:")
39    for(i in list.indices)
```

Results when running the program:

```
Elements in MutableList - by value:
10    4    5    8    9    0    7
Elements in MutableList - by index:
```

162

Listing 1(b). LearnCollection/App_MutableList.kt

```
40    print("${list[i]}\t")
41    println()
42    println("SUM="+list.sum())
43    println("MAX="+list.maxOrNull())
44    println("MIN="+list.minOrNull())
45    println("AVERAGE="+list.average())
46    //filter odd number
47     var oddNumbers=list.filter { x->x%2==1 }
48    println("Elements in MutableList are odd numbers:")
49    for(i in oddNumbers.indices)
50    print("${oddNumbers[i]}\t")
51    println()
52    //filter to get the prime list
53     var primes=list.filter {
54    x->
55     var count=0
56    for(i in 1..x)
57    {
58    if(x%i==0)
59    count++
60    }
61    count==2
62    }
63     println("Elements in MutableList is prime:")
64    for(i in primes.indices)
65    print("${primes[i]}\t")
66    println()
67    }
68
```

```
10      4       5       8       9       0       7
Elements in MutableList after changing:
10      4       113     8       9       0       7
Elements in MutableList after delete:
10      4       113     9       0       7
Elements in MutableList after sort ascending:
0       4       7       9       10      113
Elements in MutableList after sort descending:
113     10      9       7       4       0
SUM=143
MAX=113
MIN=0
AVERAGE=23.833333333333332
Elements in MutableList are odd numbers:
113     9       7
Elements in MutableList is prime:
113     7
```

Immutable Collections

List is a collection that only readOnly, used to display information. And of course, it will optimize memory more than MutableList. So, if you just want to display the information, you should use List.

List collection in Kotlin do not have their own constructor constructs, but through listOf() to initialize

syntax:

```
var list:List<Int> = listOf()
```

The above list object is initialized with an empty list.
We can initialize with some initial data as below:

```
var list:List<Int> = listOf(1,2,3,4)
```

The above list object is initialized with 4 elements and we cannot change the size, information of list. When we use List in our mind, we want it to be readOnly, only to display data.

Here are some common properties nad methods used with List in Table 2.

Table 2. Property and methods of the list

Property/Method Name	Description
size	Attribute returns the actual size of the Collection
[i]	Indexer allows access and change of values at location i of the Collection
sorted()	Sort ascendingly but return a different list
sortedDescending()	Sort descendingly but return a different list
filter { }	Filter the data
contains()	Check whether the Collection contains any elements

Example – Manipulation with List:

Listing 2. LearnCollection/App_List.kt

```
1    fun main(args: Array<String>) {
2    var list:List<Int> = listOf(5,6,1,9,-4,7,8,2)
3    println("Elements in List by index:")
4    for(i in list.indices)
5    print("${list[i]}\t")
6    println()
7    println("Elements in List by Item:")
8    for(i in list)
9    print("$i\t")
10   println()
11   println("Elements Sort up ascending:")
12   var list2= list.sorted()
13   for(i in list2)
14   print("$i\t")
15   println()
16   println("Elements sort up descending:")
17   var list3= list.sortedDescending()
18   for(i in list3)
19   print("$i\t")
20   println()
21   var list4=list.filter { x->x%2==0 }
22    println("Even elements(filter function):")
23   for(i in list4)
24   print("$i\t")
25   println()
26   println("SUM="+list.sum())
27   println("MAX="+list.maxOrNull())
28   println("MIN="+list.minOrNull())
29   println("AVERAGE="+list.average())
30   }
```

Results when running the program:

```
Elements in List by index:
5       6       1       9       -4      7       8       2
Elements in List by Item:
5       6       1       9       -4      7       8       2
Elements Sort up ascending:
-4      1       2       5       6       7       8       9
Elements sort up descending:
9       8       7       6       5       2       1       -4
Even elements (filter function):
6       -4      8       2
SUM=34
MAX=9
MIN=-4
AVERAGE=4.25
```

We notice that most of the List methods do not change the List internally, but it returns a new List.

We can see that the collection in Kotlin is very flexible and powerful, we can customize the processing. The filter function is a revolution in filtering data.

This is the end of the lesson, please pay attention the examples above and do extra research to have a better understanding of the lesson. Especially understand how the Collection works to be able to apply well to actual projects. The source code can be downloaded at the link: https://github.com/thanhtd32/kotlin/tree/main/LearnCollectio n.

Readers can read more explanations of the conditional structure in the authors' books (Jemerov et al., 2017; Griffiths & Griffiths, 2019; Eckel & Isakova, 2020; Bailey et al., 2021).

Exercises

1. What is the difference between array and collection?
2. What is the difference between Mutable Collection and Immutable Collection?
3. How to initialize a MutableList in Kotlin with values, such as 4, 3,8?
   (a) var list=mutableListOf(4,3,8)
   (b) var list = listOf(4,3,8)
   (c) var list=mutableListOf{4,3,8}
   (d) var list = [4,3,8]
4. How to initialize a ImmutableList in Kotlin with values, such as 4, 3,8?
   (a) var list=mutableListOf(4,3,8)
   (b) var list = listOf(4,3,8)
   (c) var list=mutableListOf{4,3,8}
   (d) var list = [4,3,8]
5. What is the result after executing the code below?

```
var list=mutableListOf(4,3,8,2,5)
println(list.filter { i->!(i%2!=0)})
```

   (a) [4, 8, 2]
   (b) [3, 5]
   (c) Compiler error

6. What is the result after executing the code below?

```
var list= listOf(10,6,7)
list.add(5)
println(list)
```

    (a) [5]
    (b) [10, 6, 7, 5]
    (c) Compiler error

7. What is the result after executing the code below?

```
var list= mutableListOf(10,6,7)
list.add(5)
println(list)
```

    (a) [5]
    (b) [10, 6, 7, 5]
    (c) Compiler error

8. What is the result after executing the code below?

```
var list= mutableListOf(9,2,4)
list.sort()
println(list)
```

    (a) [2, 4, 9]
    (b) [9, 2, 4]
    (c) [9, 4, 2]

9. What is the result after executing the code below?

```
var list= listOf(9,2,4)
list.sorted()
println(list)
```

    (a) [2, 4, 9]
    (b) [9, 2, 4]
    (c) [9, 4, 2]

10. Improving the Book Search Machine project in previous chapter

The program uses an endless loop and collection to let the user choose from 5 options as shown below:

```
do
{
    println("Enter/Search for Books:")
    println("1. Book input")
    println("2. Search by book name")
    println("3. Search by author name")
    println("4. Search by publisher name")
    println("5. End")
    println("select(1,2,3,4,5):")
    var choice= readln()
    println(choice)
    //process choice
}while (true)
```

If you select No. 1, you can enter title, author name, publisher name, price, and publication year as follows:

- title>>
- Author's name>>
- Publisher>>
- price>>
- Publication year>>

Corresponding to the options, the program will process search by book name (1), search by author name (3), search by publisher name (4) and exit the software (5).

REFERENCES

Bailey, Greenhalgh, & Skeen. (2021). Kotlin Programming: The Big Nerd Ranch Guide (2nd ed.). Big Nerd Ranch, LLC.

Eckel & Isakova. (2020). Atomic Kotlin. Mindview LLC.

Griffiths, D., & Griffiths, D. (2019). *Head First Kotlin. O'Reilly Media.*

Jemerov, D., & Isakova, S. (2017). *Kotlin in Action.* Manning.

Chapter 10
Object–Oriented Programming in Kotlin

ABSTRACT

Object-oriented programming (OOP) is a programming technique that allows programmers to abstract objects in reality and create those objects in code, this programming technique is based on the concept of classes and objects. Objects include properties and methods, properties are information, specific characteristics of each object; Methods are operations that an object is capable of performing. A class is a data type that includes many predefined properties and methods. Each class acts as a unit of combined methods and properties. Kotlin is like other programming languages that support object-oriented programming. OOP is a general concept; programming language is just one of the tools to implement that concept. This means that if readers already understand OOP, then C #, Java, Kotlin, etc. will share this concept for implementation. The chapter provides illustrative and detailed explanations to help readers easily understand OOP. And at the end of the chapter, there are exercises to help readers practice and improve OOP skills as well as review the knowledge in previous chapters.

DOI: 10.4018/978-1-6684-6687-2.ch010

OBJECT-ORIENTED PROGRAMMING CONCEPTS

In this lesson, the book will go over some of the concepts related to OOP, then we'll get familiar with an example of OOP installation using Kotlin.

Some Features of OOP

- Focus on data instead of functions.
- The program is divided into independent objects.
- Data structures are designed to be specific to objects.
- Data is hidden, enclosed.
- Objects communicate with each other through functions.
- The program is designed in the bottom-up approach: *Bottom-up approach is often used to build large, complex software The idea of this approach is that it comes from a number of small available components, combining them to create a larger functional component that continues to incorporate more components ... until the program can solve the problem.*

Some Benefits of OOP

- There is no risk of data being altered freely in the program.
- When changing the data structure of an object, there is no need to change the source code of other objects.
- We can reuse source code, and save resources.
- In line with large and complex software projects.

Some Examples for Real Object

The concept of object in object-oriented programming is like a real object in the real world.

Each object has its own attributes and behaviors:

- The attribute describes the characteristics of the object.
- Behavior is the method of object operation, referred to as method.

Example 1: Fraction object

The characteristics of Fractions (Attributes) are:

- Numerator
- Denominator

Operations on fractions (method)

- Add, subtract, multiply, divide
- Simplify
- Inverse

Example 2: Car object
The characteristics of car (Attributes) are:

- Brand
- Color
- Number of wheels
- Number of doors

Operations on cars (method)

- Run forward
- Run backward
- Stop

Objects with similar properties (attributes and methods) are grouped into a class that distinguishes them from others and is easy to manage.
A class is a classification of objects or types of objects.

Example 3:

- Toyota, Honda, Porsche belongs to car class.
- pit bull, hounds, bulldog belong to dog class.
- Heineken, Budweiser, Hanoi beer... belong to beer class

Class is an abstract concept, referring to a set of objects present in the system.
Class has attributes and methods:

- The attributes of the class correspond to the attributes of the object.
- The methods of the class correspond to the methods of the object.

A Class can have one of the following capabilities:

- Does not have any attributes or methods
- Has attributes but no methods
- Has methods but no attributes
- Has both attributes and methods, which is the most popular case
- Has relationships with other classes

Package

A set of classes and interfaces is organized into a management unit in the form of namespaces called package.

The benefit of the package is that the organization reorganizes the information system class in the project in a scientific way, which helps to keep track of project maintenance.

Abstraction

Case 1:

Class is an abstract concept. The object is a specific instance of the class.

The Figure 1 shows example for an abstraction.

Figure 1. Abstraction

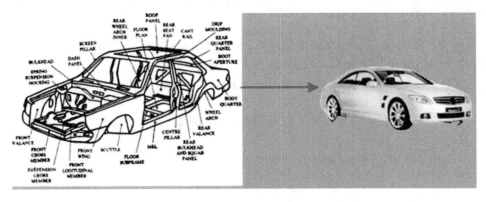

- The design of the Car is class.
- The car made from the design is the object.

Case 2:

From the similar objects: Abstraction into a class, it only provides the necessary attributes and methods of the object in the program, the Figure 2 shows this case.

Figure 2. Abstraction

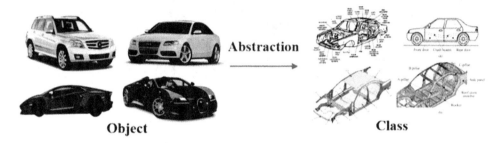

In Biology, we have Birds class, mammals' class, herbivores class. That is the abstraction, the self-aggregation of abstract objects into classes.

Encapsulation

- Each class is built to perform a specific function group of that class.
- All manipulation of the data element from one object to another must be performed by the method of the object itself.
- The packaging attribute enables the object's information marker by combining information and methods related to the information in the object.

The Figure 3 shows the example for encapsulation.

Figure 3. Encapsulation

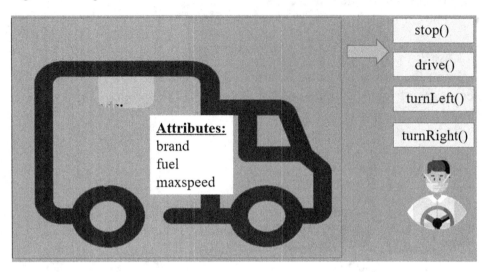

Inheritance

- Allow building a new class based on the definitions of an existing class.
- Existing classes are called super classes, new classes are called subclasses
- The subclass inherits all components of the superclass, which can extend inheritance components and add new components.

Example of inheritance is shown in the Figure 4.

Dog and Cat have some properties of animals, so they both inherit from Animal class.

Example of inheritance in Employee is show in the Figure 5.

The above illustrates the Employee inheritance model. Manager and WorkerBee both have Employee properties. In WorkerBee are further classified SalesPerson and Engineer.

Figure 4. Inheritance: Animal

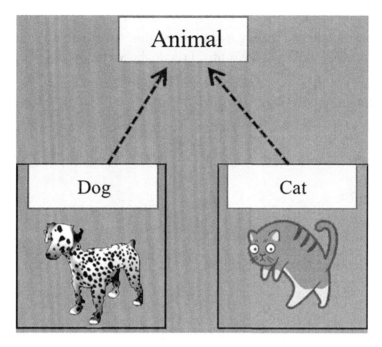

Figure 5. Inheritance: Employee

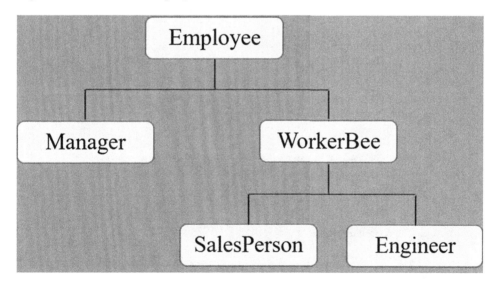

Create a Class in Kotlin Language

Here is an example of creating a class in Kotlin, we create a Project Kotlin named LearnOOP and add a Kotlin Class as shown below:

Figure 6. Choose Kotlin class

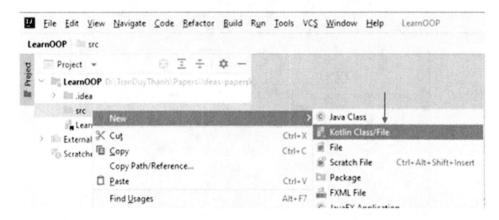

Right-click on src and choose New and then select Kotlin Class/File menu item:

Figure 7. Create Triangle Kotlin class

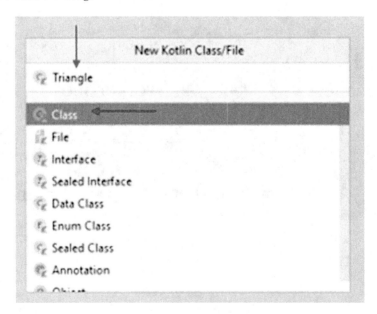

On the New Kotlin Class/File screen, select Kind as Class, name the class Triangle and press Enter to create the Triangle class

The first result when creating a class in Kotlin:

Figure 8.Triangle Kotlin class

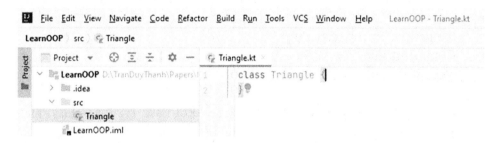

Code for Triangle (please follow these steps, the book will explain the components in the following lessons). The Triangle class details is shown in the Listing 1.

Listing 1. LearnOOP/Triangle

```
1
2    class Triangle {
3      var slide1:Double=1.0
4      var slide2:Double=1.0
5      var slide3:Double=1.0
6    constructor() constructor(slide1:Double,slide2:Double,slide3:Double)
7    {
8    this.slide1=slide1
9    this.slide2=slide2
10   this.slide3=slide3
11   }
12   fun perimeter():Double
13   {
14   return slide1+slide2+slide3
15   }
16   fun area():Double
17   {
18   var p=perimeter()/2
19   return Math.sqrt(p*(p-slide1)*(p-slide2)*(p-slide3))
20   }
21   }
22
```

The above code creates a detailed Triangle class as follows:

- Command lines 2 to 4 create 3 attributes slide1, slide2, slide3 which are initialized to the default value of 1.0.
- Command line 5 creates default constructor
- Command lines 6 to 11 create a constructor with full arguments for Triangle, when initializing objects using this constructor, the program will simultaneously initialize values for properties slide1, slide2, slide3.
- Command line 12 to command line 15 creates a method to calculate the perimeter of a triangle
- Command lines 16 to 20 create a method to calculate the area of a triangle.

We continue to create a Kotlin file AppTest.kt to use Triangle class, The Listing 2 shows code how to use the Triangle class.

Listing 2. LearnOOP/AppTest.kt

```
1   fun main(args: Array<String>) {
2     var t1=Triangle(4.0,5.0,6.0)
3     println("Information about triangle 1:")
4     println("Perimeter="+t1.perimeter())
5     println("Area="+t1.area())
6     var t2=Triangle()
7     t2.slide1=7.5
8     t2.slide2=10.3
9     t2.slide3=15.5
10    println("Information about triangle 2:")
11    println("Perimeter="+t2.perimeter())
12    println("Area="+t2.area())
13  }
14
```

The above code creates 2 Triangle objects t1 and t2.

In command line 2, the t1 object uses a constructor with arguments, when creating the object, we pass the input values at the same time. Now we don't need to call the methods to change the value of the attributes.

In command line 7, the t2 object uses the default constructor with no arguments, now the values of the properties have not been assigned, so command lines 8 to 10 are used to assign values to properties.

To output the perimeter and area of the triangle, we call the perimeter() and area() methods, respectively.

Run the program and observe the results:

```
Information about triangle 1:
Perimeter=15.0
Area=9.921567416492215
Information about triangle 2:
Perimeter=33.3
Area=33.354424275499014
```

This is the end of the lesson, please pay attention the examples above and do extra research to have a better understanding of the lesson. In the next lessons, the Book will go into details about each of the classes in Kotlin

The source code can be downloaded at the link. https://github.com/thanhtd32/kotlin/tree/main/LearnOOP.

Structure Details of the Class

In previous lesson, the book has introduced some of the characteristics of OOP with an example of creating class and using class in Kotlin. In this lesson, the book will go into detailed explanation of each component in the process of creating a class.

Regular structure of a class:

- Class name
- Constructors
- Attributes
- Getter/setter
- Methods

Declare Class Name For Kotlin

To create a class we use the class keyword as in other programming languages:

```
class Student {
}
```

Unlike other languages, Kotlin allows only one class name to be declared without any other elements, the declaration is as follows:

```
class Student
```

Class name should be set according to the following rules: First letter of the words must be Uppercase; name does not contain any white space.

Kotlin supports two types of constructors (special functions, which default to initializing objects for memory allocation) which are primary constructor and secondary constructors.

Declare Primary Constructor

```
class Student constructor(code:Int,name:String){
}
```

Above, the constructor is a keyword, inside it has two arguments, which means that the Student class has a Primary Constructor with two arguments.

If the primary constructor does not contain annotations and modifiers (private, protected, public), then the constructor keyword can be removed from the declaration, which means that we can declare the following:

```
class Student (code:Int,name:String){
}
```

It is important to note that the primary constructor can not contain any code. If you want to initialize the variables using the primary constructor, you must use the init{}, the Listing 3 shows how to create the Student class and the primary constructor.

Listing 3. LearnPrimaryConstructor/Student

1	class Student (code:Int,name:String){
2	init {
3	*println*("This is primary constructor")
4	*println*("Code=$code ; Name =$name")
5	}
6	}

Continue to create a Kotlin file TestStudent.kt to use Student class, the Listing 4 shows how to use the Student class with primary constructor.

Listing 4. LearnPrimaryConstructor/TestStudent.kt

```
1   fun main(args: Array<String>) {
2   //Create an object with name john
3   var john=Student(100,"John Barrot")
4   //Create an object with name peter
5   //Specify the data type
6   var peter:Student=Student(200,"Peter Christal")
7   }
```

Run the program, we get the results as follows:

```
This is primary constructor
Code=100 ; Name =John Barrot
This is primary constructor
Code=200 ; Name =Peter Christal
```

When declaring var john =Student(100, "John Barrot") it will automatically find the primary constructor and jump to the init block itself. Likewise when we declare var peter:Student =Student(200, "Peter Christal"), However, in this case, we specify the data type from the beginning for the peter object variable.

And we do not use the keyword new to allocate memory like C # or java ...

Here is the link of the code, you can download: https://github.com/thanhtd32/kotlin/tree/main/LearnPrimaryConstructor.

Declare Secondary Constructor

We also use the constructor keyword to declare the secondary constructor in kotlin, the example code is shown in the Listing 5.

Listing 5. LearnSecondaryConstructor/Student

```
1
2   class Student {
3   constructor()
4   {
5   println("This is secondary constructor without arguments")
6   }
7   constructor(code:Int,name:String)
8   {
9   println("This is secondary constructor with 2 arguments")
10  println("Code=$code ; Name =$name")
11  }
12  }
13
```

The Listing 6 shows how to use the secondary constructors.

Listing 6. LearnSecondaryConstructor/TestStudent.kt

```
1    fun main(args: Array<String>) {
2    //call secondary constructor without arguments
3    var tom=Student()
4    //call secondary constructor with 2 arguments
5    var kitty=Student(100,"Kitty Solidate")
6    }
7
```

When running the statements, we have the following messages:

```
This is secondary constructor without arguments
This is secondary constructor with 2 arguments
Code=100 ; Name =Kitty Solidate
```

Declaring Class Attributes

Attributes are what belong to the object, e.g., 1 Student has the following information: Student code, name, year of birth ... then these informations are the attributes of Student object.

Kotlin, like other languages, provides a number of Visibility Modifiers (private, protected, public, default) for the following properties:

Table 1. Visibility modifiers

Modifiers	Class	Package	Subclass	Outer Class
public	Yes	Yes	Yes	Yes
protected	Yes	Yes	Yes	No
No modifier – default	Yes	Yes	Yes	No
private	Yes	No	No	No

The Listing 7 shows how to declare the attributes in the class.

Listing 7. LearnAttribute/Student

```
1
2    class Student {
3    //Declare 2 attributes for Student with default modifier
4    var code:Int=0
5    var name:String=""
6    constructor()
7    {
8    println("This is secondary constructor without arguments")
9    }
10   constructor(code:Int,name:String)
11   {
12   println("This is secondary constructor 2 arguments")
13   this.code=code
14   this.name=name
15   }
16   }
17
18
```

As stated above, the two attributes code and name, which are default modifiers, do not specify in the same package any object that can access these attributes. The Listing 8 shows how to use the Student class and it's attributes.

Listing 8. LearnAttribute/TestStudent.kt

```
1    fun main(args: Array<String>) {
2    //create lucy object with default constructor
3    var lucy=Student()
4    //access attributes and assign the value
5    lucy.code=500
6    lucy.name="Lucy Brian"
7    println("Information of Lucy:")
8    println("Code =${lucy.code}")
9    println("Name=${lucy.name}")
10   println("--------------------")
11   //create crystal object with secondary constructor
12   var crystal=Student(600,"Crystal Brian")
13   println("Information of Crystal:")
14   println("Code =${crystal.code}")
15   println("Name=${crystal.name}")
16   }
17
```

When running the statements, we have the following messages:

```
This is secondary constructor without arguments
Information of Lucy:
Code =500
```

```
Name=Lucy Brian
--------------------
This is secondary constructor 2 arguments
Information of Crystal:
Code =600
Name=Crystal Brian
```

The code for this example you can download at the link below: https://github.com/thanhtd32/kotlin/tree/main/LearnAttribute.

For encapsulation, the attributes should declare private, when the declaration property should be private. At this point the objects cannot be traced directly to the given attributes, but through the getter / setter. The Listing 9 shows private visibility modifier.

Listing 9. LearnAttribute/Student

```
1    class Student {
2      private var code:Int=0
3      private var name:String=""
4    }
```

When declaring a Modifier to be private, we cannot get the object's access properties, i.e., the declaration as below will be error, please see the Listing 10.

Listing 10. LearnAttribute/TestStudent.kt

```
1
2    fun main(args: Array<String>) {
3      var tom=Student()
4      tom.code=100
5      tom.name="Tom"
6    }
```

Declare the Properties of the Class

If the properties in the class that for default and access in the same package or attribute to the modifier are public, then we do not need to declare the getter / setter.

Kotlin's getter / setter declarations are different from Java, C #, and other languages. Syntax for declaring getter / setter:

```
var <propertyName>[: <PropertyType>] [= <property_initializer>]
[<getter>]
[<setter>]
```

getter is used to access the value of the attribute in the property, the setter is used to change the value of the attribute in the property.

The Listing 11 shows how to create Properties for Attributes.

Listing 11. LearnGetterSetter/Student

1	class Student {
2	//declare attributies
3	private var code:Int=0
4	private var name:String=""
5	//declare Code property for code attribute
6	public var Code:Int
7	get()
8	{
9	//retrieve the data of the attribute
10	return this.code
11	}
12	set(value)
13	{
14	//change attribute data
15	this.code=value
16	}
17	//declare Name property for name attribute
18	public var Name:String
19	get()
20	{
21	return this.name
22	}
23	set(value)
24	{
25	this.name=value
26	}
27	constructor()
28	{
29	}
30	constructor(code:Int,name:String)
31	{
32	this.code=code
33	this.name=name
34	}
35	}

In the coding above, we have two Getter / Setter Code and Name. External objects will not be able to access the code and the name attributes that are only accessed through the Getter / Setter Code and Name. The keyword get and set above the IntelliJ IDEA software also suggests available for us, just type the first letter is it hint and then press Enter itself appears. With set you notice that the value is the default parameter, which is the parameter that receives the input value from the outside (i.e., changes the attribute information for the object). The Listing 12 shows how to use the Student class and the Properties.

Listing 12. LearnGetterSetter/TestStudent.kt

```
1   fun main(args: Array<String>) {
2   //Declare tom Student object
3   var tom=Student()
4   //call Code Property (set)
5   tom.Code=100
6   //call Name Property (get)
7   tom.Name="Tom Hoping"
8   println("The Information:")
9   //call Code Property(get)
10  println("Code = ${tom.Code}")
11  //call Name Property(get)
12  println("Name = ${tom.Name}")
13  println("----------------")
14  //We can use the constructor
15  var jerry=Student(200,"Jerry Cherry")
16  //call Code Property(get)
17  println("Code = ${jerry.Code}")
18  //call Name Property(get)
19  println("Name = ${jerry.Name}")
20
21  }
```

Results for running the above commands:

```
The Information:
Code = 100
Name = Tom Hoping
-----------------
Code = 200
Name = Jerry Cherry
```

You can download the reference code here: https://github.com/thanhtd32/kotlin/tree/main/LearnGetterSetter.

There are many cases to correct the way to write get and set above, when the specific case you find out.

More Declare the Properties

In addition, we can use the following way to declare properties, the Listing 13 shows how to create the properties with another way.

Listing 13. LearnPropertyAnotherWay/Student

```
1    class Student {
2      var Code:Int=0
3      get() = field
4      set(value) {field=value}
5      var Name:String=""
6      get() = field
7      set(value) {field=value}
8    }
```

In the example above, we do not declare the attribute code and name, but always use the property Code and Name, the key field keyword represents the property. The value variable passed to change the value of the attribute, we can change another name, but we should keep the variable name as value.

We create the main function to test how to use the above Student class, see the Listing 14.

Listing 14. LearnPropertyAnotherWay/TestStudent.kt

```
1    fun main(args: Array<String>) {
2      //We can use the constructor
3      var daisy=Student()
4      //call set term of Code property
5      daisy.Code=900
6      //call set term of Name property
7      daisy.Name="Daisy Newman"
8      //call get term of Code property
9      println("Code = ${daisy.Code}")
10     //call get term of Name property
11     println("Name = ${daisy.Name}")
12   }
```

Run the statements and see the results:

```
Code = 900
Name = Daisy Newman
```

Declare Class Methods

The method is called behavior, the business process on the object. This is the set of the strength of the object. Kotlin uses the fun keyword to declare methods. These methods may have a return value or not.

The following Listing 15 shows the example how to add two methods (returns a String value and returns no value at all).

Listing 15. LearnDeclareMethod/Student

```
class Student {
private var code:Int=0
private var name:String=""
public var Code:Int
get()
{
return this.code
}
set(value)
{
code=value
}
public var Name:String
get()
{
return name
}
set(value)
{
name=value
}
constructor()
{
}
constructor(code:Int,name:String)
{
this.code=code
this.name=name
}
fun printInfor()
{
println("Details Of Information:")
println("Code= "+code)
println("Name= "+name)
}
fun details():String
{
var s="Details of Information:"
s=s.plus("\nCode="+code)
s=s.plus("\n")
s=s.plus("Name="+name)
return s
}
}
```

In the Student class, printInfor() and details() methods are added. The printInfor() method does not return a value, merely outputs the data of the attributes. While the details() method returns a string type, the data of the attributes will be appended to the string and return the result to details().

The following example demonstrates how to use the two functions in the Listing 16.

Listing 16. LearnDeclareMethod/TestStudent.kt

```
1   fun main(args: Array<String>) {
2       var st=Student()
3       st.Code=300
4       st.Name="Jonh Weird"
5       println("Information by Property:")
6       println("Code:"+st.Code)
7       println("Name:"+st.Name)
8       println("-----Call the method printInfor()------")
9       st.printInfor()
10      println("-------Call the method detail()--------")
11      var detail=st.details()
12      println(detail)
13  }
14
```

Results when running the program:

```
Information by Property:
Code:300
Name:Jonh Weird
--------Call the method printInfor()---------
Details Of Information:
Code= 300
Name= Jonh Weird
--------Call the method detail()---------
Details of Information:
Code=300
Name=Jonh Weird
```

Kotlin language, like C # and Java language, it supports a special method called toString () that automatically prints information when the object is exported to the screen. To create this method is very simple, in the class just enter the key word to the software itself show tostring function for us, please see the Figure 9.

Figure 9. Create toString() method

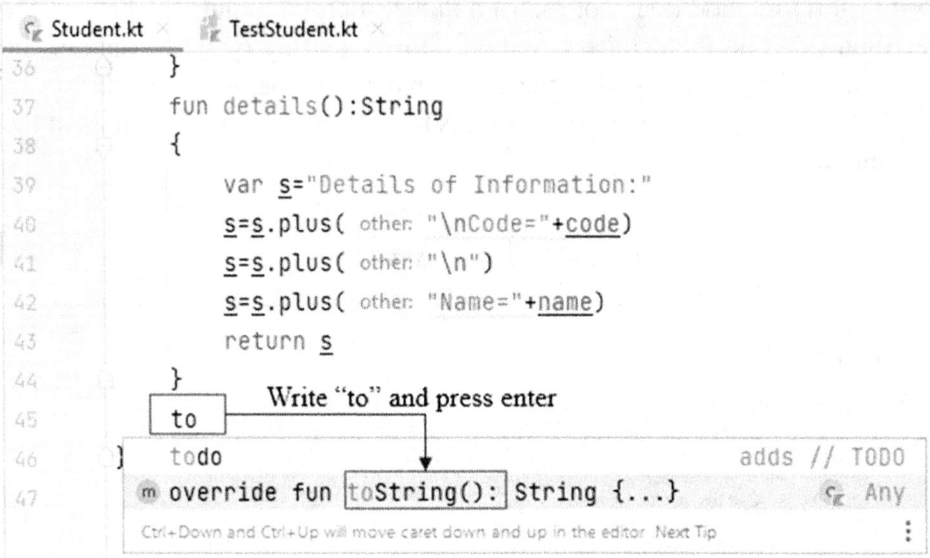

It will automatically create the following function:

```
override fun toString(): String {
    return super.toString()
}
```

The toString() function is very special and useful, we often use this function to output the internal data of the attribute when the object is output to the screen, the Listring 17 shows how to create coding for toString() method.

Listing 17. LearnDeclareMethod/Student/toString()

1	override fun toString(): String {
2	var s="Details of Information:"
3	s=s.plus("\nCode="+code)
4	s=s.plus("\n")
5	s=s.plus("Name="+name)
6	return s
7	}

Below is the completed code of Student class with toString() function in the Listing 18.

Listing 18. LearnDeclareMethod/Student

```
1    Class Student {
2    private var code:Int=0
3    private var name:String=""
4    public var Code:Int
5    get()
6    {
7    return this.code
8    }
9    set(value)
10   {
11   code=value
12   }
13   public var Name:String
14   get()
15   {
16   return name
17   }
18   set(value)
19   {
20   name=value
21   }
22   constructor()
23   {
24   }
25   constructor(code:Int,name:String)
26   {
27   this.code=code
28   this.name=name
29   }
30   fun printInfor()
31   {
32   println("Details Of Information:")
33   println("Code= "+code)
34   println("Name= "+name)
35   }
36   fun details():String
37   {
38   var s="Details of Information:"
39   s=s.plus("\nCode="+code)
40   s=s.plus("\n")
41   s=s.plus("Name="+name)
42   return s
43   }
44   override fun toString(): String {
45   var s="Details of Information:"
46   s=s.plus("\nCode="+code)
47   s=s.plus("\n")
48   s=s.plus("Name="+name)
49   return s
50   }
51   }
52
```

In the main function, just print the object that automatically invokes the toString() function, which is very beneficial. Objects contain a lot of information and relationships, and toString () is just to help us export some of the information we need to hide more information while still ensuring the nature of the object, let's see the Listing 19.

Listing 19. LearnDeclareMethod/TestStudent.kt

```
1
2     fun main(args: Array<String>) {
3     var st=Student()
4     st.Code=300
5     st.Name="Jonh Weird"
6     println("Information by Property:")
7     println("Code:"+st.Code)
8     println("Name:"+st.Name)
9     println("------Call the method printInfor()-----")
10    st.printInfor()
11    println("--------Call the method detail()-------")
12    var detail=st.details()
13    println(detail)
14    println("-----------Call toString()-------------")
15    println(st)
16    }
17
```

Results when running the program:

```
Information by Property:
Code:300
Name:Jonh Weird
--------Call the method printInfor()---------
Details Of Information:
Code= 300
Name= Jonh Weird
--------Call the method detail()---------
Details of Information:
Code=300
Name=Jonh Weird
-----------Call toString()--------------
Details of Information:
Code=300
Name=Jonh Weird
```

The book has already presented the structure of a class in Kotlin, including rules for creating:

- Class name
- Constructors
- Attributes
- Getter/setter
- Methods

You pay attention to learn, practice again and try to understand it through the examples above. In the next lessons, the book will continue introducing OOP in Kotlin (method types, overloading method, reference this), please pay proper attention.

The source code can be downloaded at the link: https://github.com/thanhtd32/kotlin/tree/main/LearnDeclareMethod.

Types of Methods

In previous lesson, the book has presented the rules for creating classes, constructors, properties, getter / setter, methods... In this lesson, the boook will continue introducing the Method types, those are Service method and Support method.

Service Method is a public method that provides access to objects.
Support Method is a private method used to support Service methods. External objects cannot be accessed through the Support Method.

Let's go back to the example of the Triangle class, see the Listing 20, in this Listing, we add service methods area(), perimeter() and support method halfPerimeter().

The coding above, you observe the halfPerimeter() method is support method because it is private, this method will support other Service methods such as area().

For outer class, we can only access methods that are Service Method, we cannot access the Support Method, the Listing 21 shows how to use the service methods.

Results when running the program:

```
Area and Perimeter of the ta1:
Area =9.921567416492215
Perimeter = 15.0
-------------
Area and Perimeter of the ta2:
```

Listing 20. LearnTypeOfMethod/Triangle

```
1
2     class Triangle {
3       public var Slide1:Double=1.0
4       get() {return field}
5       set(value) {field=value}
6       public var Slide2:Double=1.0
7       get() {return field}
8       set(value) {field=value}
9       public var Slide3:Double=1.0
10      get() {return field}
11      set(value) {field=value}
12      constructor()
13      constructor(slide1:Double,slide2:Double,slide3:Double)
14      {
15      Slide1=slide1
16      Slide2=slide2
17      Slide3=slide3
18      }
19      //This is service method
20      public fun perimeter():Double
21      {
22      return Slide1+Slide2+Slide3
23      }
24      //This is support method
25      private fun halfPerimeter(): Double {
26      return perimeter() / 2
27      }
28      //This is service method
29      public fun area():Double
30      {
31      var p=halfPerimeter()
32      return Math.sqrt(p*(p-Slide1)*(p-Slide2)*(p-Slide3))
33      }
34      }
35
```

Listing 21. LearnTypeOfMethod/TestTriangle.kt

```
1     fun main(args: Array<String>) {
2       var ta1= Triangle()
3       ta1.Slide1=4.0
4       ta1.Slide2=5.0
5       ta1.Slide3=6.0
6       var area=ta1.area()
7       var perimeter=ta1.perimeter()
8       //var ahalf=ta1.halfPerimeter()
9       //this command above will be errored
10      //because halfPerimeter() cannot access
11      println("Area and Perimeter of the ta1:")
12      println("Area =$area")
13      println("Perimeter = $perimeter")
14      println("------------")
15      var ta2=Triangle(7.0,8.0,9.0)
16      println("Area and Perimeter of the ta2:")
17      println("Area =${ta2.area()}")
18      println("Perimeter = ${ta2.perimeter()}")
19      }
20
```

```
Area =26.832815729997478
Perimeter = 24.0
```

This Reference

This Reference is very important reference in Kotlin programming languages. C#, Java programming language... also uses reference this. To understand reference this, we need to go from the concept of Instance variable and local variable.

Instance variable are attributes, declared variables inside the class. All functions in the class are accessible.

Local variable are variables declared in function or function arguments. Only this function can access its local variable variables, the arguments in the function are usually defaulted by readOnly (val)

Figure 10 illustrates two types of variables.

Figure 10. Instance variable and local variable

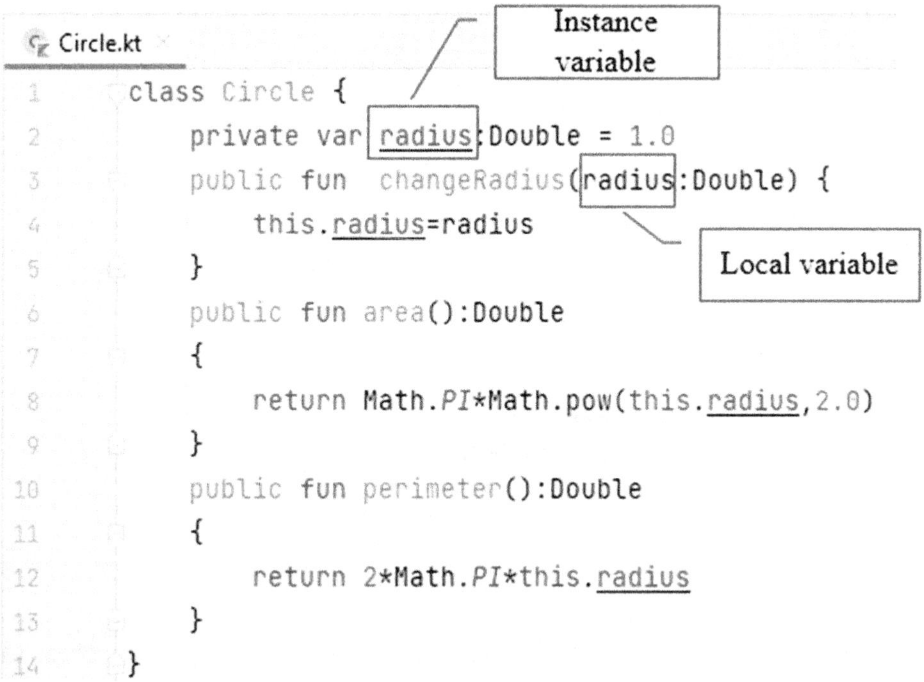
Circle.kt
Instance variable
Local variable
class Circle {
private var radius:Double = 1.0
public fun changeRadius(radius:Double) {
this.radius=radius
}
public fun area():Double
{
return Math.PI*Math.pow(this.radius,2.0)
}
public fun perimeter():Double
{
return 2*Math.PI*this.radius
}
}

Obviously, the variable radius in command line 2 is instance variable. The variable radius in line 3 is local variables (the same name).

When we are familiar with OOP rules, we can use tools to create constructors, functions. We will often encounter the cases where instance variables and local variables have the same name. So how to distinguish these variables? For example, we observe command line 4 above:

this.radius=radius

We have the following important note:

If at a command line at the same time access to instance variables and local variables (with the same name), the program will prioritize access to local variables.

This means that if the command line 4 deletes the keyword this, it becomes:

Figure 11. Error reference

```
Circle.kt
1    class Circle {
2        private var radius:Double = 1.0
3        public fun   changeRadius(radius:Double) {
4            radius=radius
5        }
6        public fun area():Double
7        {
8            return Math.PI*Math.pow(this.radius,2.0)
9        }
10       public fun perimeter():Double
11       {
12           return 2*Math.PI*this.radius
13       }
14   }
```

As mentioned in the Figure 11, if at a location where the same access to instance variable and local variable the same name, the program will prefer to handle local variale. That is, it will reference the local variable. As shown above, the book draws 2 variables from the line 4 and point to the variable line 6, So obviously it generates an error (the first one is the wrong reference, the second is the default variable in the arguments of the function, Kotlin assumes that readOnly (val) cannot be changed.

So, in this case we must use the keyword this to indicate the program: This is the current object in the class, we must access the Instance Variable. That why we have to use the keyword this, so this reference will be as follows in the Figure 12.

Figure 12. This reference

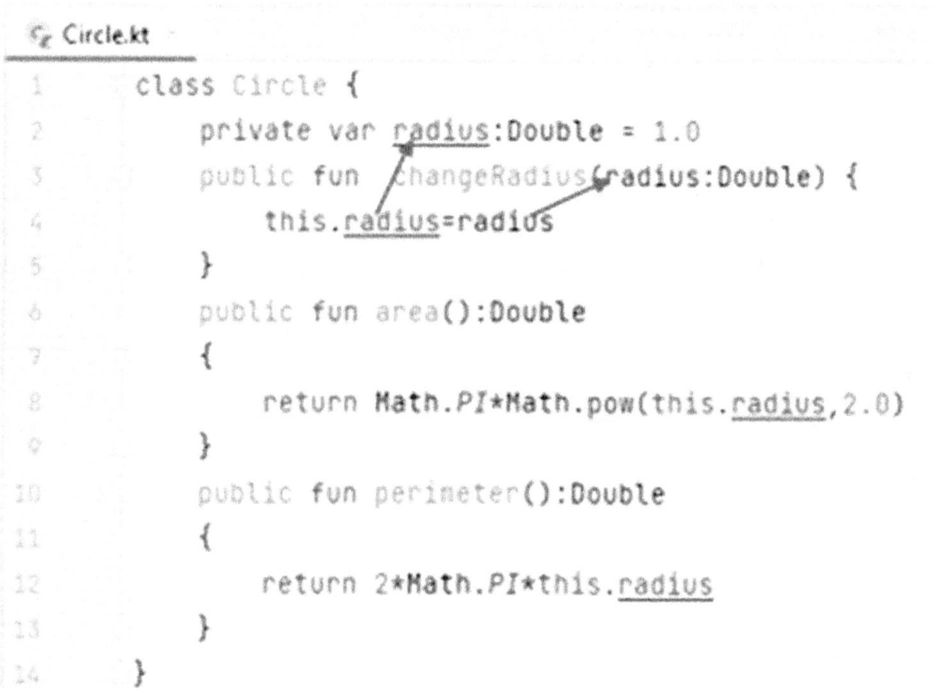

```
 Circle.kt
1       class Circle {
2           private var radius:Double = 1.0
3           public fun  changeRadius(radius:Double) {
4               this.radius=radius
5           }
6           public fun area():Double
7           {
8               return Math.PI*Math.pow(this.radius,2.0)
9           }
10          public fun perimeter():Double
11          {
12              return 2*Math.PI*this.radius
13          }
14       }
```

The code can be downloaded at the link: https://github.com/thanhtd32/kotlin/tree/main/LearnThisReference.

Overloading Method

Overloading Method is one of the most important techniques in OOP programming, Kotlin also supports this feature.

- Overloading is a feature of the same class that has many methods of the same name, but different in terms of signature.
- Signature includes: The number of arguments or data types of arguments or order of arguments.
- The return type is not included in the signature
- The benefit of overloading is the ability to reuse the method and help to call the function "flexible".
- Constructors are special instances of the Overloading Method

For example:

Listing 22. LearnOverLoadingMethod/Product

```
1   class Product {
2   public var Id:Int = 0
3   set(value) {field=value}
4   get() {return field}
5   public var Name:String = ""
6   set(value) {field=value}
7   get() {return field}
8   public var UnitPrice:Double=0.0
9   set(value) {field=value}
10  get() {return field}
11  constructor()
12  constructor(id:Int,name:String)
13  {
14  this.Id=id
15  this.Name=name
16  }
17  constructor(id:Int,name:String,unitPrice:Double)
18  {
19  this.Id=id
20  this.Name=name
21  this.UnitPrice=unitPrice
22  }
23  fun printInfor()
24  {
25  println("Id = ${this.Id}")
26  println("Name = ${this.Name}")
27  println("UnitPrice = ${this.UnitPrice}")
28  }
29  fun printInfor(id:Int,name:String,price:Double)
30  {
31  println("Id = $id")
32  println("Name = $name")
33  println("UnitPrice = $price")
34  }
35  }
```

In the example above you see the constructor, The book has created 3 constructors with different number of arguments. And there are 2 printInfor functions with different quantity of arguments (printInfor function on command line 23 has no parameters, while printInfor on command line 29 has 3 parameters). Here are two examples: Overloading Method → the methods have the same name but different Signature, please see the Figure 13.

Figure 13. Constructor overloading

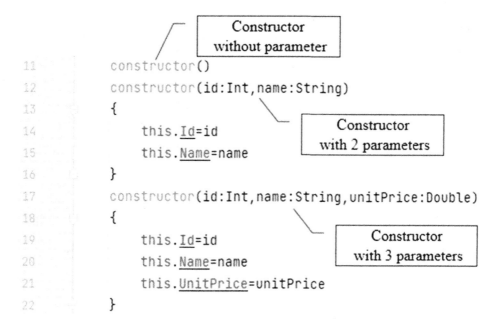

Listing 23. LearnOverLoadingMethod/TestProduct.kt

```
1    fun main(args: Array<String>) {
2    //Constructor 0 arguments is called
3    var p1=Product()
4    p1.Id=100
5    p1.Name="Coca"
6    p1.UnitPrice=2.0
7    //Constructor 2 arguments is called
8    var p2=Product(200,"Pepsi")
9    p2.UnitPrice=2.5
10   //Constructor 3 arguments is called
11   var p3=Product(300,"Sting",3.0)
12   }
```

Constructor is a special case of method overloading. Usually, the constructor with full parameters when used can replace the Property when we initialize the object, Listing 23 shows how to call the constructor overloading.

Object p1 must call properties (Id, Name, UnitPrice) to update data for attributes. The p2 object simply calls the property (UnitPrice). The p3 object does not have to update the properties because it has passed the full value of the attributes.

Continue to observe the printInfor() function overloading in the Figure 14.

Figure 14. printInfor overloading

```
23      fun printInfor()──────┌──────────────────┐
24      {                     │    printInfor     │
                              │ without parameter │
                              └──────────────────┘
25          println("Id = ${this.Id}")
26          println("Name = ${this.Name}")
27          println("UnitPrice = ${this.UnitPrice}")
28      }
29      fun printInfor(id:Int,name:String,price:Double)
30      {                     ┌──────────────────┐
                              │    printInfor     │
                              │ with 3 parameters │
                              └──────────────────┘
31          println("Id = $id")
32          println("Name = $name")
33          println("UnitPrice = $price")
34      }
```

printInfor function on command line 23 has no parameters, while printInfor on command line 29 has 3 parameters. The parameterless printInfor function outputs the values of properties through properties. The printInfor function with 3 parameters will output data based on the parameters passed into the function.

When we access these methods, we rely on the input parameters that the program automatically navigates to call the method, see the Listing 24.

Listing 24. LearnOverLoadingMethod/TestProduct.kt

```
1    fun main(args: Array<String>) {
2      //Constructor 0 arguments is called
3      var p1=Product()
4      p1.Id=100
5      p1.Name="Coca"
6      p1.UnitPrice=2.0
7      //Constructor 2 arguments is called
8      var p2=Product(200,"Pepsi")
9      p2.UnitPrice=2.5
10     //Constructor 3 arguments is called
11     var p3=Product(300,"Sting",3.0)
12     println("Details of object p1:")
13     p1.printInfor()
14     println("Details of object p2:")
15     p2.printInfor()
16     println("Details of object p3:")
17     p3.printInfor()
18     println("Details of object p3:")
19     p3.printInfor(p3.Id,p3.Name,p3.UnitPrice)
20   }
21
```

Run the statements and see the results:

```
Details of object p1:
Id = 100
Name = Coca
UnitPrice = 2.0
Details of object p2:
Id = 200
Name = Pepsi
UnitPrice = 2.5
Details of object p3:
Id = 300
Name = Sting
UnitPrice = 3.0
Details of object p3:
Id = 300
Name = Sting
UnitPrice = 3.0
```

Of course, during the coding process we will use a lot of overloading for its huge benefit, this lesson will help you know how to install the overloading technique, you can apply thi into actual projects.

Kotlin also supports a special Overloading Method called vararg (also known as Parameter list). This is a special case of Overloading Method (the signature is the number of different arguments). When declaring vararg we can pass as many arguments to the function as well.

The Listing 25 shows how to declare and use the parameter list:

Listing 25. LearnOverLoadingMethod/TestParameterList.kt

```
fun countOfEvenNumber(vararg numbers: Int):Int {
    var n=numbers.count { x->x%2==0 }
    return n
}
fun main(args: Array<String>) {
    var n1=countOfEvenNumber(1,2,3,4)
    println("Even numbers=$n1")
    var n2=countOfEvenNumber(2,4,3,8,6)
    println("Even numbers=$n2")
    var n3=countOfEvenNumber()
    println("Even numbers=$n3")
    var n4=countOfEvenNumber(1,2,3,4,5,6,7,8,9,20,18)
    println("Even numbers=$n4")
}
```

On the countOfEvenNumber function is a special Overloading Method, we can pass as many arguments. Results when running the program:

```
Even numbers=2
Even numbers=4
Even numbers=0
Even numbers=6
```

The Overloading Method is a very important knowledge in Kotlin programming. You pay attention to learn, practice again and try to understand it through the examples above. The source code can be downloaded at the link: https://github.com/thanhtd32/kotlin/tree/main/LearnOverLoadingMethod.

Static Technique

Kotlin language is similar to other programming languages, it supports static writing technique through the companion keyword, the Listing 10.26 shows how to declare the static technique.

Listing 26. LearnStatic/A

```
1    class A {
2    companion object
3    {
4    fun printData()
5    {
6    println("The Print Data method")
7    }
8    var data:Int=100
9    }
10   }
```

In class A, the data attribute and the printData() method are declared in the companion block so they are static. When declared static, it will be accessed directly from the class name:

[Class name].[Method()] is also known as class method

[Class Name].[Attribute] is also known as class member.

The Listing 27 shows how to call the static method.

Listing 27. LearnStatic/TestA.kt

```
1    fun main(args: Array<String>) {
2    //call static printData() method
3    A.printData()
4    //call static data attribute
5    println(A.data)
6    }
```

The code above we do not create any object, but we use the class A itself to directly access the methods and properties, run the statement, and see the results:

```
The Print Data method
100
```

Note that static attributes are used to share memory, it is under the management of the class, not the object. So, if you write functions that change the value of an attribute, then if any object changes the value of this static attribute, all other objects will also see that change, the Listing 28 shows creating method to access the static attribute.

Listing 28. LearnStatic/A

```
1    class A {
2    companion object
3    {
4    fun printData()
5    {
6    println("The Print Data method")
7    }
8    var data:Int=100
9    }
10   fun changeData(x:Int)
11   {
12   data=x
13   }
14   fun getData():Int
15   {
16   return data
17   }
18   }
```

The code above, the book intentionally declares the function changeData(x:Int) to change the value of data, and the function getData() to get the value of data.

The Listing 29 shows how to call method to track the static variable.

Listing 29. LearnStatic/TestA.kt

```
1
2    fun main(args: Array<String>) {
3    //call static printData() method
4    A.printData()
5    //call static data attribute
6    println(A.data)
7    var a1=A()
8    a1.changeData(200)
9    println("data be called by a1:"+a1.getData())
10   var a2=A()
11   println("data be called by a2:"+a2.getData())
12   //a2 change data to 300
13   a2.changeData(300)
14   println("data be called by a1:"+a1.getData())
15   }
16
```

Run the main function and see the results:

```
The Print Data method
100
data be called by a1:200
data be called by a2:200
data be called by a1:300
```

Command line number 8, we call a1.changeData(200) at this time the data variable will be assigned the value of 200. Command line 12, we call a2.getData() now data is shared memory, so a2.getData() will return 200. Command line 14, we call a2.changeData(300) now the data variable will be assigned the value 300. Command line 15, calling a1.getData() will output 300, not 200. Readers should try other values to check the static.

The source code can be downloaded at the link: https://github.com/thanhtd32/kotlin/tree/main/LearnStatic.

More Types of Class

In previous lesson, the book has detailed the types of methods, this, overloading, parameter list, and so on. This is one of the most important techniques in object-oriented programming. In this lesson, the book will introduce about Data Classes, Nested Classes, Inner Classes, Enum Classes in Kotlin.

Data Classes

During processing, we often just need to store data without methods. Kotlin supports this function by helping us create a special class called Data Class.

The Data Class in Kotlin will automatically provide:

*   equals() / hashCode()
*   toString()
*   componentN()
*   copy()

The Listing 30 shows how to declare and use the Data Class.

Listing 30. LearnDataClasses/TestDataClass.kt

```
1   fun main(args: Array<String>) {
2   //Create a data class with name User
3   data class User(
4   var UserName:String,
5   var Password:String)
6   //create an User object
7   var user1=User(
8   UserName = "john",
9   Password = "113@114Xa")
10  println("User information of user 1:")
11  println(user1.toString())
12  println("User Name =${user1.UserName}")
13  println("Password=${user1.Password}")
14  //copy data:
15  var user2=user1.copy()
16  println("User information of user 2:")
17  println(user2.toString())
18  //copy data and change value for Property
19  var user3=user1.copy(Password ="12345678")
20  println("User information of user 3:")
21  println(user3.toString())
22  }
23
```

In command from line 3 to line 5, we see a Data Class named User created, it has two properties is UserName and Password

Command lines 7 to line 9 create a user1 object of type User. At the same time, this object is initialized with values for the Property UserName and Password.

Command line 10 to command line 13 outputs the data of the user1 object.

Command line 16 uses the copy() function to copy data in memory for the user2 object (at this time a new memory cell appears and user2 manages this memory cell, in this new memory cell the data is copied raw copy from the memory cell in the user1 object).

Command line 20 is also used to copy data in the memory cell that user1 is managing to the user3 object to manage, but the Password property is changed.

Results when running the program:

```
User information of user 1:
User(UserName=john, Password=113@114Xa)
User Name =john
Password=113@114Xa
User information of user 2:
User(UserName=john, Password=113@114Xa)
User information of user 3:
User(UserName=john, Password=12345678)
```

Source code can be downloaded here: https://github.com/thanhtd32/kotlin/tree/main/LearnDataClasses.

Nested Classes

Kotlin, like other programming languages, has the ability to allow this class to nest in other Nested classes. Note that Nested classes will not be able to access member variables in the Outer class.

The Listing 31 shows how to create the Nested class.

Listing 31. LearnNestedClass/Outer

```
class Outer {
    var name: String = "Outer"
    fun sayHelloOuter()
    {
        println("Hello Outer")
    }
    fun useNested()
    {
        var nt=Nested()
        nt.doSomething()
    }
    class Nested {
        //nested class can not access attribute or
        // function in the outer class, such as:
        // -name attribute,
        // -sayHelloOuter() function
        fun doSomething()
        {
            println("The Nested class")
        }
    }
}
```

In the above example, the doSomething() method in the nested class cannot access the name attribute or sayHelloOuter() function in Outer class

The Listting 32 shows how to invoke doSomething() function in Nested Class.

Listing 32. LearnNestedClass/TestNested.kt

```
1   fun main(args: Array<String>) {
2   //create a nested object:
3   var nt=Outer.Nested()
4   //call method:
5   nt.doSomething()
6   //create an outer object:
7   var ot=Outer()
8   //call method:
9   ot.sayHelloOuter()
10  ot.useNested()
11  }
```

Running the program, the results will be outputted as below:

```
The Nested class
Hello Outer
The Nested class
```

Source code can be downloaded here: https://github.com/thanhtd32/kotlin/tree/main/LearnNestedClass.

Inner Classes

Kotlin, like other programming languages, has the ability to allow this class to nest in another Inner class. Note that Inner classes will be able to access member variables in the Outer class, let's see the Listing 33.

The code above shows the keyword inner in front of the Inner class. But the constructor of inner class Inner can be called only with receiver of containing class, we can not access the Inner outside of the outer class.

The Listing 34 shows the main function to use the inner class.

Running the program will result in output 1 to the screen.

```
The function in the Inner class
The name from outer=Outer
Hello Outer
```

The code example for the Inner class:
https://github.com/thanhtd32/kotlin/tree/main/LearnInnerClass

Here we notice the difference between Nested Class and Inner class both declarative as well as how to access.

Listing 33. LearnInnerClass/Outer

```
1    class Outer {
2    var name: String = "Outer"
3    fun sayHelloOuter()
4    {
5    println("Hello Outer")
6    }
7    fun useInner()
8    {
9    var inn=Inner()
10   inn.doSomething()
11   }
12   inner class Inner {
13   //inner class can access attribute or
14   // function in the outer class, such as:
15   // -name attribute,
16   // -sayHelloOuter() function
17   fun doSomething()
18   {
19   println("The function in the Inner class")
20   println("The name from outer=$name")
21   sayHelloOuter()
22   }
23   }
24   }
```

Listing 34. LearnInnerClass/TestInner.kt

```
1    fun main(args: Array<String>) {
2    //cannot create an inner object:
3    //Constructor of inner class Inner can be called
4    //only with receiver of containing class
5    //var in=Outer.Inner()//can not
6    //create an outer object:
7    var ot=Outer()
8    //call method:
9    ot.useInner()
10   }
11
```

Enum Classes

Enum is also a kind of special class in Kotlin (like other C # languages, java ...)

The Figure 15 shows how to declare Enum in Kotlin is very simple, similar to other programming languages.

When creating new file, we select Kind as Enum class, Name which is the location to name Enum. For example, we define Grade and press enter, and writing the enum class as the Listing 35.

You can use this Enum as the Listing 36 by create a Student class.

Figure 15. Creating Enum class

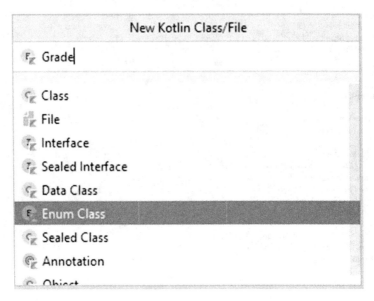

Listing 35. LearnEnum/Grade

```
1   enum class Grade {
2     A,B,C,D,F,UNKNOW
3   }
```

Listing 36. LearnEnum/Student

```
1    class Student {
2      var Code:Int=0
3      var Name:String=""
4      var GPA:Double=0.0
5      constructor()
6      constructor(code:Int,name:String,gpa:Double)
7      {
8      Code=code
9      Name=name
10     GPA=gpa
11     }
12     public fun getGrade():Grade
13     {
14     if(GPA==4.0)return Grade.A
15     if(GPA==3.0)return Grade.B
16     if(GPA==2.0)return Grade.C
17     if(GPA==1.0)return Grade.D
18     if(GPA==0.0)return Grade.F
19     return Grade.UNKNOW
20     }
21   }
```

The getGrade() function will rely on GPA to calculate the Grade for each Student.

The Listing 37 shows how to call the Student class with Enum.

Listing 37. LearnEnum/TestStudent.kt

```
fun main(args: Array<String>) {
    var st1=Student(100,"Mr John",4.0)
    println("Code=${st1.Code}")
    println("Name=${st1.Name}")
    println("GPA=${st1.GPA}")
    println("Grade=${st1.getGrade()}")
    println("----------------")
    var st2=Student()
    st2.Code=200
    st2.Name="Mr Peter"
    st2.GPA=2.0
    println("Code=${st2.Code}")
    println("Name=${st2.Name}")
    println("GPA=${st2.GPA}")
    println("Grade=${st2.getGrade()}")
}
```

Running the program will show the result:

```
Code=100
Name=Mr John
GPA=4.0
Grade=A
----------------
Code=200
Name=Mr Peter
GPA=2.0
Grade=C
```

So far, the book has covered all the special classes in Kotlin (Data Classes, Nested Classes, Inner Classes and Enum classes). Readers pay attention to learn, practice again and try to understand it through the examples above.

In the next lessons, the book will continue to talk about object-oriented programming in Kotlin (inheritance), readers pay attention to the track. The sourcecode can be downloaded at the link: https://github.com/thanhtd32/kotlin/tree/main/LearnEnum.

Class Inheritance

In this lesson, the book will present the knowledge related to the inheritance in object-oriented programming. Before going into the installation procedure of the Kotlin inheritance, The book briefs about the concept of inheritance.

What Is Inheritance?

Inheritance is the REUSE of existing code, we can extend the new code from the existing code, to improve programming efficiency. We review the concept at the beginning of the object orientation that the book mentioned:

- Allow building a new class based on the definitions of an existing class.
- Existing classes are called super classes, new classes are called subclasses
- The subclass inherits all components of the superclass, which can extend inheritance components and add new components.

Objects often share some of the same characteristics, behaviors which are grouped together. Example of inheritance is shown in te Figure 16.

Figure 16. Inheritance: Animal

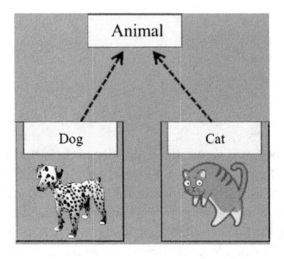

Dog and Cat have some properties of animals, so they both inherit from Animal class. Example of inheritance in Employee is shown in the Figure 17.

Figure 17. Inheritance: Employee

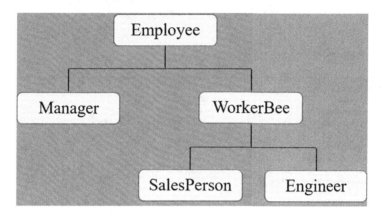

The Figure 17 illustrates the Employee inheritance model. Manager and WorkerBee both have Employee properties. In WorkerBee are further classified SalesPerson and Engineer.

In order to inherit, we need to know two concepts:

Generalize: The common features that all classes have →they are super classes

Specialize: The features that only sub-classes have →they are the subclasses

For more example: The Company has two types of employees (Official and Temporary Staff). It is clear that all employees have code, name. But official and temporary employees are different in terms of salary. Therefore, the Generalization Class is an Employee class because it has the common characteristics of official and temporary employees, while the specialized classes are: Official employees, Temporary employees.

Writing Inheritance From Class

The book will write a project in Figure 18 as shown above. In Kotlin, to write the inheritance class we take the following steps in the Listing 38. First, we create the Employee Generalization Class (superclass).

Figure 18. Inheritance: Employee

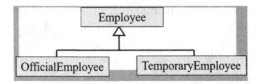

Listing 38. LearnInheritance/Employee

```
1    open abstract class Employee {
2    var Code:Int=0
3    get() {return field}
4    set(value) {field=value}
5    var Name:String=""
6    get() {return field}
7    set(value) {field=value}
8    constructor()
9    constructor(code:Int,name:String)
10   {
11   this.Code=code
12   this.Name=name
13   }
14   abstract fun calculateSalary(dayofWork:Int):Double
15   override fun toString(): String {
16   return "$Code-$Name"
17   }
18   }
```

The above superclass is an abstract class, when there is abstract method calculateSalary. The problem is how to know whether it should be declared as abstract method or not? It can be understood: All employees are paid, but at this time we do not know how to pay for employees, and do not the specific amount to play, then we declare it abstract (although we do not know who is the object of calculateSalary but make sure it must contain calculateSalary). With abstract or interface, abstract functions are like rules, templates, and require subclasses to obey (override them all).

Another thing to note is that if you want other classes to inherit from this class, then you must add the keyword open before the class declaration as the code above.

Now we create a class named OfficialEmployee inherited from Employee class as follows in the Figure 19.

Figure 19. Create the sub class OfficialEmployee

We use a colon (:) to inherit, look at the picture above we know how to write OfficialEmployee inherited from Employee (After writing the correct inheritance syntax, we move the mouse to the OfficialEmployee class and select Implement members as shown above.).

Above, Readers see it as red error, it is actually because Employee class is abstract class. Subclasses inheriting from the abstract class are forced to override the whole abstract class method of the superclass. IntelliJ IDEA supports us with this override tool. Readers move mouse to where the error, it will appear on the screen with the Implement members line as shown above, select it and press Enter, the Implement Members screen will appear as below in the Figure 20.

Figure 20. Overriding method

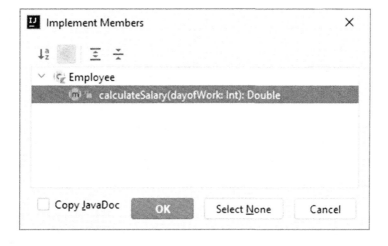

Select abstract parent methods and click OK, it will automatically generate Coding as follows in the Listing 39. (It is also called overriding method.)

Listing 39. LearnInheritance/OfficialEmployee

```
1   class OfficialEmployee:Employee {
2    override fun calculateSalary(dayofWork: Int): Double
3    {
4    TODO("Not yet implemented")
5    }
6   }
7
```

We need to add the constructors to the OfficialEmployee class.

And we assume that the official employee is paid: If dayofWork $> = 22$, the salary is 5.000$, and if it is <22 days, the salary is 5.000$- daily loss of 100$, we modify the coding as follows in the Listing 40.

Listing 40. LearnInheritance/OfficialEmployee

```
1    class OfficialEmployee:Employee {
2    constructor():super()
3    constructor(code:Int,name:String):super(code,name)
4    {
5    }
6    override fun calculateSalary(dayofWork: Int): Double
7    {
8      if(dayofWork>=22)
9      return 5000.0
10     return 5000.0-100*(22-dayofWork)
11    }
12   }
```

Listing 41. LearnInheritance/TemporaryEmployee

```
1    class TemporaryEmployee:Employee {
2    constructor():super()
3    constructor(code:Int,name:String):super(code,name)
4    {
5    }
6    override fun calculateSalary(dayofWork: Int): Double
7    {
8      return 100.0*dayofWork
9    }
10   }
```

Listing 42. LearnInheritance/TestEmployee.kt

```
1   fun main(args: Array<String>) {
2     //create an Official Employee
3     var emp1=OfficialEmployee(100,"Mr John")
4     //call the calculateSalary method
5     var salaryEmp1=emp1.calculateSalary(22)
6     println("Information of emp1:")
7     //call the toString() method
8     println(emp1)
9     println("Salary of emp1=$salaryEmp1")
10    println("-----------------------")
11    //create a Temporary Employee
12    var emp2=TemporaryEmployee(200,"Mr Peter")
13    //call the calculateSalary method
14    var salaryEmp2=emp2.calculateSalary(3)
15    println("Information of emp2:")
16    //call the toString() method
17    println(emp2)
18    println("Salary of emp2=$salaryEmp2")
19  }
```

Similarly, we create the TemporaryEmployee Class that inherits from Employee class. And the salary of the temporary employees is 100$ * the number of working days:

How to use the inheritance classes in Kotlin?

Create a Kotlin file for testing in the Listing 42.

Results when running the program:

```
Information of emp1:
100-Mr John
Salary of emp1=5000.0
-----------------------
Information of emp2:
200-Mr Peter
Salary of emp2=300.0
```

Above, the book has mentioned Override, so what is it? Overriding Method can be understood:

- In a set of blood related classes that have the same signature (different method content)
- Overriding methods help programmers define different behaviors for different objects, but they use the same method name.
- For example: Official employees and temporary employees have the method of calculating salary, however the method of salary calculation of these two objects will be different.

Readers should compare the differences between Overloading Method and Overriding Method. The source code can be downloaded here: https://github.com/thanhtd32/kotlin/tree/main/LearnInheritance.

Writing Inheritance From Interface

In Kotlin, Interface can be used to implements, Interface is not a SEND, but a set of rules (rules, rules) when subclasses implement (or inheritance), we must redefine all of these methods. Suppose we have an interface in the Listing 43.

Listing 43. MyInterface

```
1  interface MyInterface {
2  fun bar()
3  fun foo() {
4  // optional body
5  }
6  }
7
```

When subclass inherit, we can write as follows in the Listing 44.

Listing 44. Child

```
1  class Child: MyInterface {
2  override fun bar() {
3  // body
4  }
5  }
6
```

We note that, for Kotlin, inheriting from Classes is just for single inheritance like Java, C #. Inheritance from the Interface allows multiple inheritance, so it is sometimes conflicting if the interfaces that it inherits from have abstract methods with identical names. In this case, Kotlin resolves as follows in the Listing 45.

Listing 45. Multi-implements

```
1    interface A {
2      fun foo() { print("A") }
3      fun bar()
4    }
5    interface B {
6      fun foo() { print("B") }
7      fun bar() { print("bar") }
8    }
9    class C: A {
10     override fun bar() { print("bar") }
11   }
12   class D: A, B {
13     override fun foo() {
14     super<A>.foo()
15     super<B>.foo()
16   }
17     override fun bar() {
18     super<B>.bar()
19   }
20   }
```

Let's see an example of calculating the perimeter and area of circles and squares according to the inheritance model as in Figure 21.

Figure 21. Inheritance geometry model

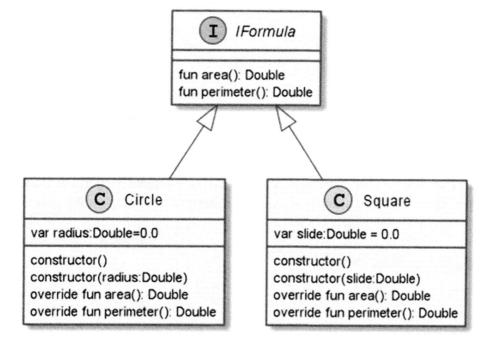

We create the IFormula interface with 2 functions, these are area() function and perimeter() function. Let's see the Listing 46.

Listing 46. LearnInheritanceInterface/IFormula

```
1   interface IFormula {
2       fun area(): Double
3       fun perimeter(): Double
4   }
```

And then we create the Square class and implements from IFormula interface. We proceed to override the methods to calculate the perimeter and area, adjust the calculation formulas accordingly. The Listing 47 shows how to create write the Square class.

Listing 47. LearnInheritanceInterface/Square

```
1    class Square:IFormula {
2        var slide:Double = 0.0
3        constructor()
4        constructor(slide:Double)
5        {
6        this.slide=slide
7        }
8        override fun area(): Double {
9        return Math.pow(slide, 2.0);
10       }
11       override fun perimeter(): Double {
12       return 2*slide;
13       }
14   }
15
```

And then we create the Circle class and implements from IFormula interface. We proceed to override the methods to calculate the perimeter and area, adjust the calculation formulas accordingly. The Listing 48 shows how to create write the Circle class.

Listing 48. LearnInheritanceInterface/Circle

```
1    class Circle:IFormula {
2     var radius:Double=0.0
3     constructor()
4     constructor(radius:Double)
5     {
6     this.radius=radius
7     }
8     override fun area(): Double {
9     return Math.PI*Math.pow(radius, 2.0);
10    }
11    override fun perimeter(): Double {
12    return 2*Math.PI*radius
13    }
14    }
15
```

Finally, we create the main function to test the program in the Listing 49.

Listing 49. LearnInheritanceInterface/TestShape.kt

```
1
2    fun main(args: Array<String>) {
3     var c = Circle(5.0)
4     System.out.println("Perimeter of the circle= ")
5     System.out.println(c.perimeter())
6     System.out.println("Area of the circle= ")
7     System.out.println(c.area())
8     var s = Square(5.0)
9     System.out.println("Perimeter of the square = ")
10    System.out.println(s.perimeter())
11    System.out.println("Area of the square=")
12    System.out.println(s.area())
13    }
14
```

The results when we run the statements:

```
Perimeter of the circle=
31.41592653589793
Area of the circle=
78.53981633974483
Perimeter of the square =
10.0
Area of the square=
25.0
```

Readers pay attention to learn, practice again and try to understand it through the examples above. In the next lessons, the book will introduce the alias and automatic garbage collection mechanism in Kotlin, please pay proper attention.

The source code can be downloaded at the link: https://github.com/thanhtd32/kotlin/tree/main/LearnInheritan ceInterface.

Alias and Automatic Garbage Collection Mechanism

In this lesson, the book will introduce more about Alias and automatic garbage collection mechanism in Kotlin.

Alias is the ability that in a memory cell there are multiple objects pointing to ($> = 2$ objects)

The automatic garbage collection mechanism automatically recovers memory when the memory is no longer managed by the object.

These two concepts are extremely important, and Readers need to make sure understanding it to be able to handle memory management issues when executing projects.

Now the book will go into details about the process of creating Alias and garbage collection in Kotlin (it is similar in other languages).

Because Kotlin runs in the JVM platform, the mechanism works the same way as Java.

Listing 50. LearnAlias/Fraction

```
1   class Fraction {
2     var Numerator:Int=1
3     get() {return field}
4     set(value) {field=value}
5     var Denominator:Int=1
6     get() {return field}
7     set(value) {field=value}
8     constructor(numerator: Int, denominator: Int) {
9     this.Numerator =numerator
10    this.Denominator = denominator
11    }
12    override fun toString(): String {
13    return "$Numerator/$Denominator"
14    }
15  }
```

In order to have a feel for Alias and automatic garbage collection mechanisms, we create a fractional class as follows in the Listing 50.

Figure 22. Different memories allocated

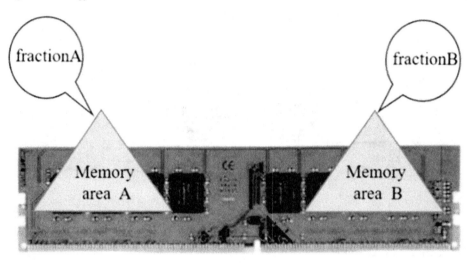

Suppose we have 2 objects fractionA, fractionB as below:

fractionA=Fraction(1,5)

fractionB=Fraction(3,7)

At this point on the memory stick, there will have two memories allocated to 2 fractional objects that are managed by 2 object variables fraction A and fraction B (Readers should imagine because you do not know what the memory box on the bar Allocated RAM), The Figure 22 shows the different memories allocated.

The above figure shows that two fractionA and fractionB objects manage two separate memory cells. i.e., fractionA manipulation on memory area A will not affect fractionB and vice versa.

Now suppose we execute the command:

```
fractionA=fractionB
```

Then the above command: The language says "Fraction A Equals Fraction B," but the computer system will work under the "The fraction A points to the memory area allocated by fraction B" In other words, "Memory area B" now has two object variables pointing to (co-management). Figure 23 shows the alias.

Figure 23. Alias

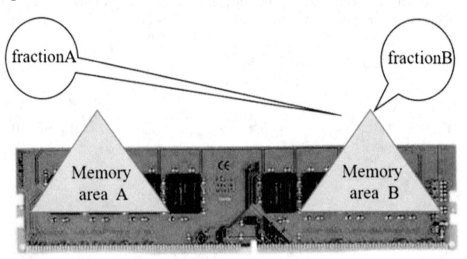

Thus, Alias appears in "memory area B". At this time, there will be two phenomena as follows:

- At "memory area B", if the fractionA changes information, it causes fractionB to change information (because both objects share a memory area).
- "Memory Area A" no longer refers to the object, the system will automatically recover memory (destroy the memory area A previously granted), this mechanism called automatic garbage collection mechanism

Figure 24. Garbage collection

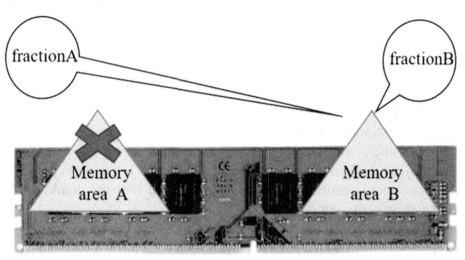

The following figure illustrates the GC (garbage collection) in the Figure 24.

Listing 51. LearnAlia/TestFraction.kt

```
1    fun main(args: Array<String>) {
2      var fractionA=Fraction(1,5)
3      println("Numerator of A="+fractionA.Numerator)
4      println("Denominator of A="+fractionA.Denominator)
5      var fractionB=Fraction(3,7)
6      println("Numerator of B="+fractionB.Numerator)
7      println("Denominator of B="+fractionB.Denominator)
8      fractionA=fractionB
9      println("-----Alias------")
10     println("Numerator of A="+fractionA.Numerator)
11     println("Denominator of A="+fractionA.Denominator)
12   }
```

In the main function we have the codes following in the Listing 51.

Command line 8 generates two phenomena: The first is the Alias (fractionA and fractionB point to a memory cell), the second is the automatic garbage collection mechanism automatically reclaim the memory allocated to the fractionA in line 2 (because at this point the fractionA has pointer over the memory of fractionB). When running the main function, what is the result?

```
Numerator of A=1
Denominator of A=5
```

```
Numerator of B=3
Denominator of B=7
-----Alias------
Numerator of A=3
Denominator of A=7
```

Why the Numerator of A is 3?

Obviously, it is declared that fractionA = Fraction (1,5), the numberator of fractionA should be 1, why it is 3?

Because the command line 8 has changed that (fractionA=fractionB), then fractionA has pointed to the memory area where fractionB is pointing. The numerator of fractionA must be 3 instead of 1 because fractionA already points to fractionB memory area.

Suppose the book changes the coding as follows in the Listing 52.

Listing 52. LearnAlias/TestFraction.kt

```
1   fun main(args: Array<String>) {
2       var fractionA=Fraction(1,5)
3       println("Numerator of A="+fractionA.Numerator)
4       println("Denominator of A="+fractionA.Denominator)
5       var fractionB=Fraction(3,7)
6       println("Numerator of B="+fractionB.Numerator)
7       println("Denominator of B="+fractionB.Denominator)
8       fractionA=fractionB
9       println("-----Alias------")
10      println("Numerator of A="+fractionA.Numerator)
11      println("Denominator of A="+fractionA.Denominator)
12      fractionA.Numerator=2
13      fractionA.Denominator=9
14      println("Numerator of B="+fractionB.Numerator)
15      println("Denominator of B="+fractionB.Denominator)
16  }
```

Command lines 12 and 13 change the numerator and denominator of fraction A(fractionA.Numerator=2 and fractionA.Denominator=9). Lines 14 and 15 output the numerator and denominator of the fraction B.

When running the main function, what is the result?

```
Numerator of A=1
Denominator of A=5
Numerator of B=3
Denominator of B=7
-----Alias------
Numerator of A=3
Denominator of A=7
```

```
Numerator of B=2
Denominator of B=9
```

Why the Numerator of B is 2 and Denominator of B is 9? Obviously, the 12th line and 13th change to fractionA.Numerator = 2 and fractionA. Denominator=9, where B does not change the numerator and denominator, why is the number B changed to A? It must be 2 for numerator and 9 for denominator. As explained above, the memory area B has fractionA and fractionB pointing to, so fractionA changes the same to fractionB and vice versa, so when fractionA.Numerator = 2 and fractionA.Denominator=9 means fractionB.Numerator = 2 and fractionB.Denominator=9.

The source code can be downloaded here: https://github.com/thanhtd32/kotlin/tree/main/LearnAlias.

Sometimes, during the implementation of the software, we need to copy the object (create an object similar to existing object but in another memory, so that we can freely change the information on the object. copy without affecting the original object). Kotlin supports our clone function in the Cloneable interface for object copying.

The book will change the Fraction class as follows in the Listing 53.

Listing 53. LearnCloneable/Fraction

```
1    class Fraction:Cloneable {
2    var Numerator:Int=1
3    get() {return field}
4    set(value) {field=value}
5    var Denominator:Int=1
6    get() {return field}
7    set(value) {field=value}
8    constructor(numerator: Int, denominator: Int) {
9    this.Numerator =numerator
10   this.Denominator = denominator
11   }
12   override fun toString(): String {
13   return "$Numerator/$Denominator"
14   }
15   fun copy():Fraction
16   {
17   var f:Fraction=clone() as Fraction
18   return f
19   }
20   }
```

We see the Fraction class inheriting from Cloneable and the book has added the copy() function to the fraction class itself. This function simply calls Cloneable's clone() command to create a new version of the object (the same data is stored in different memory cells).

Listing 54. LearnCloneable/TestFraction.kt

```
1    fun main(args: Array<String>) {
2      var fractionA=Fraction(1,5)
3      println("Numerator of A="+fractionA.Numerator)
4      println("Denominator of A="+fractionA.Denominator)
5      var fractionB=Fraction(3,7)
6      println("Numerator of B="+fractionB.Numerator)
7      println("Denominator of B="+fractionB.Denominator)
8      fractionA=fractionB
9      println("-----Alias------")
10     println("Numerator of A="+fractionA.Numerator)
11     println("Denominator of A="+fractionA.Denominator)
12     fractionA.Numerator=2
13     fractionA.Denominator=9
14     println("Numerator of B="+fractionB.Numerator)
15     println("Denominator of B="+fractionB.Denominator)
16     var fractionC=fractionA.copy()
17     fractionC.Numerator=114
18     fractionC.Denominator=113
19     println("Numerator of C="+fractionC.Numerator)
20     println("Denominator of C="+fractionC.Denominator)
21     println("Numerator of A="+fractionA.Numerator)
22     println("Denominator of A="+fractionA.Denominator)
23   }
```

In the main we revise as follows in the Listing 54.

In command line 16, We call copy() function and save to fractionC. Notice here that it created a new memory cell and let the fractionC manage it. fractionC has nothing to do with fractionA and fractionB (at this point fractionA and fractionB are still managing the memory cell B). So, when running the command above, what is the result?

```
Numerator of A=1
Denominator of A=5
Numerator of B=3
Denominator of B=7
-----Alias------
Numerator of A=3
Denominator of A=7
Numerator of B=2
Denominator of B=9
Numerator of C=114
```

```
Denominator of C=113
Numerator of A=2
Denominator of A=9
```

The book has presented the alias and Automatic Garbage Collection Mechanism in Kotlin. Please pay attention to learn, practice again and try to understand it through the examples above. In the next lessons, the book will introduce the Extension method in Kotlin. The source code can be downloaded at the link: https://github.com/thanhtd32/kotlin/tree/main/LearnCloneable.

Extensions Method

Kotlin supports Extensions Method, just like LINQ in C# Extensions Method allows you to insert a method into existing classes without having to edit the source code. The Figure 25 illustrates the extension method.

Figure 25. Extension method

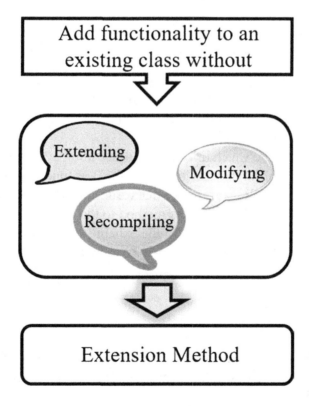

```
Syntax:
fun [Data_Type].Function_name([ arguments]):[Return_Type]
{
this keyword in this object is in [Data_Type]
}
```

When declaring as above, any [Data_Type] has a new function which is Function_Name.

Example 1: Please add the Plus function to Int data type in the Listing 55.

Listing 55. LearnExtensionMethod/TestExtensionMethod.kt

```
1    fun Int.Plus(a:Int):Int
2    {
3     return this+a
4    }
5    fun main(args: Array<String>) {
6     var t=5.Plus(9)
7     println("t=$t")
8     var x1=9
9     var x2=10
10    var x3=x1.Plus(x2)
11    println("x3=$x3")
12   }
```

Readers look at the line 1, we write Int.Plus →this is adding the Plus function to Int Data type. Command line number 3 has the keyword this, this here is the current object of type Int.

Readers continue to watch line number 6, see number 5.Plus (9). Because 5 is an integer type of Int that has just added the Plus function, so obviously 5 will have Method Plus. Readers notice that we do not know how Kotlin created the Int, but we can still add the Plus method to the Int without knowing the source code does not need to modify the existing source code.

When running the main function, we have the following result:

```
t=14
x3=19
```

Example 2: We add an extension method to check if any number is prime or not to the type of available int in Kotlin, the codes are shown in the Listing 56.

Listing 56. LearnExtensionMethod/TestExtensionMethod.kt

```
1    fun Int.CheckPrimeNumber():Boolean
2    {
3     var count=0
4     for(i in 1..this)
5     {
6     if(this%i==0)
7     count++
8     }
9     return count==2
10   }
```

So any Int has a function CheckPrimeNumber() to check if it is prime or not. The Listing 57 is the full code to use:

Listing 57. LearnExtensionMethod/TestExtensionMethod.kt

```
1    fun Int.Plus(a:Int):Int
2    {
3     return this+a
4    }
5    fun Int.CheckPrimeNumber():Boolean
6    {
7     var count=0
8     for(i in 1..this)
9     {
10    if(this%i==0)
11    count++
12    }
13    return count==2
14   }
15   fun main(args: Array<String>) {
16    var t=5.Plus(9)
17    println("t=$t")
18    var x1=9
19    var x2=10
20    var x3=x1.Plus(x2)
21    println("x3=$x3")
22    var a=7
23    if(a.CheckPrimeNumber()==true)
24    {
25    println("$a is prime")
26    }
27    else
28    {
29    println("$a is not prime")
30    }
31    var b=9
32    if(b.CheckPrimeNumber()==true)
33    {
34    println("$b is prime")
35    }
36    else
37    {
38    println("$b is not prime")
39    }
40   }
41
```

Above, we set CheckPrimeNumber () to Int. In main function CheckPrimeNumber() is automatically inserted into Int type data

When running the main function, the result is as follows:

```
t=14
x3=19
7 is prime
9 is not prime
```

Example 3: Setting the Age Function for a Written Student's Class, this class is structured as follows in the Listing 58.

Listing 58. LearnExtensionMethod/Student

```
1
2    import java.util.*
3    class Student {
4     private var code:Int=0
5     private var name:String?=null
6     private var birthday: Date?=null
7     public var Code:Int
8     get() {return code}
9     set(value) {code=value}
10    public var Name:String?
11    get()= name
12    set(value) {name=value}
13    public var Birthday:Date?
14    get() = birthday
15    set(value) {birthday=value}
16    constructor(code: Int, name: String?, birthday: Date?) {
17    this.code = code
18    this.name = name
19    this.birthday = birthday
20    }
21    }
22
23
```

So how to set the age function for this Student class? (Do not change the existing source code). We do the code as following in the Listing 59.

Listing 59. LearnExtensionMethod/TestStudentExtensionMethod.kt

```
1
2    import java.util.*
3    fun Student.Age():Int
4    {
5     var cal=Calendar.getInstance()
6     var currentYear=cal.get(Calendar.YEAR)
7     cal.time=this.Birthday
8     var yearBoy=cal.get(Calendar.YEAR)
9     return currentYear-yearBoy+1
10   }
11   fun main(args: Array<String>) {
12    var yob=Calendar.getInstance()
13    yob.set(Calendar.YEAR,1998)
14    yob.set(Calendar.MONTH,2)
15    yob.set(Calendar.DAY_OF_MONTH,15)
16    var st=Student(100,"Mr Peter",yob.time)
17    var age=st.Age()
18    println("Code of Student=${st.Code}")
19    println("Name of Student=${st.Name}")
20    println("Birthday of Student=${st.Birthday}")
21    println("Age of Student=${st.Age()}")
22   }
23
```

Above, we add the Age () function into the Student class. Based on the three examples above, Readers can apply to any projects.

When running the main function, what is the result?

```
Code of Student=100
Name of Student=Mr Peter
Birthday of Student=Sun Mar 15 15:34:13 KST 1998
Age of Student=24
```

The book has already presented the Extensions Method in Kotlin. Please pay attention to learn, practice again and try to understand it through the examples above. In the next lessons, the book will discuss the File Handling in Kotlin very important during data storage processing. The source code can be downloaded at the link: https://github.com/thanhtd32/kotlin/tree/main/LearnExtensionMethod.

Readers can read more explanations of the conditional structure in the authors' books (Jemerov et al., 2017; Griffiths & Griffiths, 2019; Eckel & Isakova, 2020; Bailey et al., 2021). Additionally, Java Object Oriented Programming book is referenced in Schild (2019).

Exercises

1. What is the difference between a class and an object?
2. What is the package?
3. What is the abstraction?
4. What is the encapsulation?
5. What is the inheritance?
6. How to create a class in Kotlin?
7. What is the difference between attributes and properties?
8. What is the benefit of Constructor?
9. What is the difference between primary constructor and secondary constructor?
10. What is the difference between an instance variable and a local variable?
11. What is the difference between support method and service method?
12. What is the "this" reference?
13. What is the overloading method?
14. What is the overriding method?
15. Presenting the working mechanism of static technique.
16. Explain the benefits of using Data class in kotlin.
17. How does Nested Class work?
18. How does Inner Class work?
19. What is the difference between Class and Enum?
20. What is the difference between Class and Interface?
21. What is the alias and automatic garbage collection mechanism? and how does it work in Kotlin?
22. How to create the Extensions Method?

23. What is the result after executing the code below?

Code

```
class A {
 var x:Int=0
 var y:Int=5
 constructor(){
 x=2
 y=2
 }
 constructor(x:Int,y:Int){
 this.x=x
 this.y=y
 }
}
```

```
fun main(args: Array<String>) {
 var a=A()
 var b=a
 b.y=8
 println("x=${a.x}, y=${a.y}")
}
```

    (a)   x=2, y=2
    (b)   x=2, y=8
    (c)   x=0, y=5
    (d)   x=0, y=8

24. What is the result after executing the code below?

Code

```
class A {
 var x:Int=0
 var y:Int=5
 constructor(){
 x=2
 y=2
 }
 constructor(x:Int,y:Int){
 this.x=x
 this.y=y
 }
}
```

```
var a=A(3,5)
var b=a
b.y=4
println("a(${a.x},${a.y})")
println("b(${b.x},${a.y})")
```

    (a)   a(3,5) and b(3,5)
    (b)   a(3,5) and b(2,4)
    (c)   a(3,5) and b(3,4)
    (d)   a(3,4) and b(3,4)

25. What is the result after executing the code below?

Code

```
open class C {                          class D:C {
  var x:Int = 5                           constructor()
  constructor(){x=2}                      override fun say(){
  open fun say(){                           super.say()
    println(x)                              println(x)
  }                                       }
}                                       }
```

```
fun main(args: Array<String>){
  var c1=C()
  c1.x=8
  var c2=D()
  c2.x=6
  c1.say()
  c2.say()
}
```

(a)	(b)	(c)	(d)
6	8	6	8
8	6	6	8
6	6	8	6

26. What is the result after executing the code below?

Code

```
class E {                               fun main(args: Array<String>) {
  companion object{                       var e1=E()
    var x:Int=10                          e1.print()
  }                                       var e2=E()
  constructor(){x+=5}                     E.x=8
  fun print(){                            e1.print()
    println(x)                            e2.print()
  }                                     }
}
```

(a)	(b)	(c)	(d)
15	8	15	8
8	15	15	8
8	8	8	15

27. After the process() function executes what value is printed to the screen?

```
class Outer {
    var x:Int=10
    class Data {
        fun process(){
            println(x)
        }
    }
}
```

    (a)   10

    (b)   Error because inner class cannot access x

    (c)   Error because nested class cannot access x

28. After the process() function executes what value is printed to the screen?

```
class Outer {
    private var x:Int=10
    inner class Data {
        fun process(){
            println(x)
        }
    }
}
```

    (a)   10

    (b)   Error because inner class cannot access x

    (c)   Error because cannot access private x

29. What is the result after executing the code below?

```
enum class Type {
    type1,type2,type3
}
var t:Type=Type.type2
println(t.ordinal)
```

    (a)   0 (b) 1 (c) 2

30. What is the result after executing the code below?

Code

```
interface X {
 fun func1()
}
interface Y {
 fun func2()
}
fun main(args: Array<String>){
 var x1:X
 x1=Z()
 x1.func3()}
```

```
class Z:X,Y {
 override fun func1() {
 println("a")
 }
 override fun func2() {
 println("b")
 }
 fun func3(){
 func1()
 func2()
 }
}
```

    (a) (b) (c)
    a   b a
    b   a a

31. Sales Management Software

    Sales management software according to the object-oriented model is illustrated as shown in Figure 26.

Figure 26.

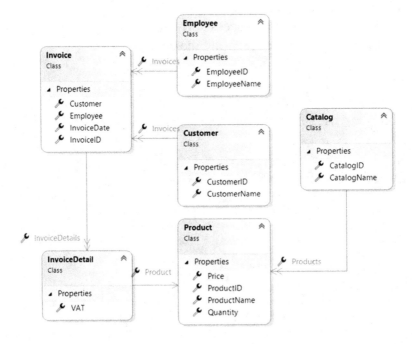

- ◦ Customer includes information: CustomerID, CustomerName
- ◦ Employee includes information: EmployeeID, EmployeeName
- ◦ Each sales order needs to store customer information, sales staff, invoice number and invoice date.
- ◦ Invoice detail is a list of Products including VAT.
- ◦ Each product is classified by category, the product's information includes: ProductID, ProductName, Quantity and Price.
- ◦ The Catalog includes the following information: CatalogID, CatalogName. A category contains multiple products, and a product belongs to only one category.
- ◦ Write class models that meet the requirements described above, provide methods to store invoice transactions, write functions that display and sort invoices by date, sort products by prices.

REFERENCES

Bailey, A., Greenhalgh, D., & Skeen, J. (2021). Kotlin Programming: The Big Nerd Ranch Guide (2nd ed.). Big Nerd Ranch, LLC.

Eckel, B., & Isakova, S. (2020). Atomic Kotlin. Mindview, LLC.

Griffiths, D., & Griffiths, D. (2019). Head First Kotlin. O'Reilly Media.

Jemerov & Isakova. (2017). *Kotlin in Action.* Manning.

Schild, H. (2019). Java the complete Reference (11th ed.). McGraw-Hill Education.

Chapter 11
File Processing

ABSTRACT

During software deployment, different kinds of file will be used depending on the specific case. The book will show the series of four file types: Text File, Serialize File, XML File, JSon File so that readers have more options in file processing. Why does program have to store data? As computer architecture is mentioned, a program wants to work, every resource must be loaded into memory, namely the RAM (Random Access Memory). The principle of RAM is the clipboard, when the software is turned off the data in the memory will no longer there. Assuming customers are entering 100 products, and the power is suddenly cut, if there is no mechanism to save data from RAM memory to the hard drive, customers will be losing all the data. Kotlin uses JVM libraries to interact with the file, so programmers can invoke these libraries. This chapter provides examples of handling saving and reading files with different cases, which help readers to cover most of the processing cases in practice. At the end of the chapter, there are exercises to improve readers skills with file processing.

FILE PROCESSING

During software deployment, different kinds of file will be used depending on the specific case. The book will show the series of four file types: Text File, Serialize File, XML File, JSon File so that readers have more options in file processing. Why does program have to store data? As computer architecture is mentioned, a program wants to work, every resource must

DOI: 10.4018/978-1-6684-6687-2.ch011

be loaded into memory, namely the RAM (Random Access Memory). The principle of RAM is the clipboard, when the software is turned off the data in the memory will no longer there. Assuming customers are entering 100 products, and the power is suddenly cut, if there is no mechanism to save data from RAM memory to the hard drive, customers will be losing all the data. Kotlin uses JVM libraries to interact with the file, so programmers can invoke these libraries. This chapter provides examples of handling saving and reading files with different cases, which help readers to cover most of the processing cases in practice. At the end of the chapter, there are exercises to improve readers skills with file processing.

Text File Processing

Text File is a way to store raw data, Readers can open the file to view the structure, content and edit.

Write Text File

To save text files, similar to Java, Kotlin will have to import the following libraries:

```
import java.io.FileOutputStream
import java.io.OutputStreamWriter
import java.io.BufferedWriter
```

The class FileOutputStream is a file output stream is an output stream for writing data to a File or to a FileDescriptor. Whether or not a file is available or may be created depends upon the underlying platform. FileOutputStream is meant for writing streams of raw bytes such as image data. For writing streams of characters, consider using FileWriter. The Table 1 shows constructor and Method summary for FileOutputStream.

Table 1. Constructor and method summary for FileOutputStream

Method	Description
FileOutputStream(String name)	Creates a file output stream to write to the file with the specified name.
void close()	Closes this file output stream and releases any system resources associated.
FileDescriptor getFD()	Returns the file descriptor associated.
void write(byte[] b)	Writes b bytes from the specified byte array.
void write(byte[] b, int off, int len)	Writes len bytes from the specified byte array starting at offset off.
void write(int b)	Writes the specified byte.

Example for declaring FileOutputStream object:

```
var fos = FileOutputStream(path)
```

We can set the path variable is "d:/data.txt"

The class OutputStreamWriter is a bridge from character streams to byte streams: Characters written to it are encoded into bytes using a specified charset. The charset that it uses may be specified by name or may be given explicitly, or the platform's default charset may be accepted. The Table 2 shows Constructor and Method summary for OutputStreamWriter.

Table 2. Constructor and method summary for OutputStreamWriter

Method	Description
OutputStreamWriter(OutputStream out, String charsetName)	Creates an OutputStreamWriter that uses the named charset.
void close()	Closes the stream, flushing it first.
void write(char[] cbuf, int off, int len)	Writes a portion of an array of characters.
void write(int c)	Writes a single character.
void write(String str)	Writes a string.

Example for declaring OutputStreamWriter object:

```
var osw = OutputStreamWriter(fos, "UTF-8")
```

The class BufferedWriter writes text to a character-output stream, buffering characters so as to provide for the efficient writing of single characters, arrays, and strings. The Table 3 shows Constructor and Method summary for BufferedWriter.

Table 3. Constructor and method summary for BufferedWriter

Method	Description
BufferedWriter(Writer out)	Creates a buffered character-output stream that uses a default-sized output buffer.
void close()	Closes the stream, flushing it first.
void newLine()	Writes a line separator.
void write(char[] cbuf, int off, int len)	Writes a portion of an array of characters.
void write(int c)	Writes a single character.
void write(String s, int off, int len)	Writes a portion of a String.

Example for declaring BufferedWriter object:

```
var bw = BufferedWriter(osw)
```

Note that when accessing the file, we must put it in a try…catch block or throw try catch. The Listing 1 is a complete illustration of the script to save the text file.

Listing 1. LearnTextFile/TestWriteTextFile.kt

```
1   import java.io.BufferedWriter
2   import java.io.FileOutputStream
3   import java.io.OutputStreamWriter
4   fun main(args: Array<String>) {
5   try {
6   var path="d:/data.txt"
7   var fos = FileOutputStream(path)
8   var osw = OutputStreamWriter(fos, "UTF-8")
9   var bw = BufferedWriter(osw)
10  bw.write("Kotlin")
11  bw.newLine()
12  bw.write("Programming")
13  bw.newLine()
14  bw.write("Language")
15  bw.close()
16  osw.close()
17  fos.close()
18  }
19  catch (ex:Exception)
20  {
21  ex.printStackTrace()
22  }
23  }
24
```

The above code is used to save 3 strings "Kotlin", "Programming", "Language" to the Text File in drive d:/data.txt. To enter a newline, we use the newLine() function.

Run the program and see the results in the Figure 1.

Figure 1. Stored text file

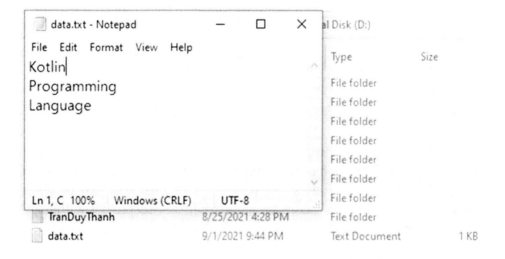

Read Text File

To read text files, similar to Java, Kotlin will have to import the following libraries:

```
import java.io.FileInputStream
import java.io.InputStreamReader
import java.io.BufferedReader
```

The class FileInputStream obtains input bytes from a file in a file system. What files are available depends on the host environment. FileInputStream is meant for reading streams of raw bytes such as image data. For reading streams of characters, consider using FileReader. The Table 4 shows Constructor and Method summary for FileInputStream.

Table 4. Constructor and method summary for FileInputStream

Method	Description
FileInputStream(String name)	Creates a FileInputStream by path name.
void close()	Closes this file input stream and releases any system resources associated.
FileDescriptor getFD()	Returns the FileDescriptor object that represents the connection to the actual file.
int read()	Reads a byte of data from this input stream.
int read(byte[] b)	Reads up to b bytes of data from this input stream into an array of bytes.
int read(byte[] b, int off, int len)	Reads up to len bytes of data from this input stream into an array of bytes.

Example for declaring FileInputStream object:

```
var path="d:/data.txt"
var fis = FileInputStream(path)
```

The class InputStreamReader is a bridge from byte streams to character streams: It reads bytes and decodes them into characters using a specified charset. The charset that it uses may be specified by name or may be given explicitly, or the platform's default charset may be accepted. The Table 5 shows Constructor and Method summary for InputStreamReader.

Table 5. Constructor and method summary for InputStreamReader

Method	Description
InputStreamReader(InputStream in, String charsetName)	Creates an InputStreamReader that uses the named charset.
void close()	Closes the stream and releases any system resources associated with it.
int read()	Reads a single character.
int read(char[] cbuf, int offset, int length)	Reads characters into a portion of an array.

Example for declaring InputStreamReader object:

```
var isr = InputStreamReader(fis, "UTF-8")
```

The class BufferedReader reads text from a character-input stream, buffering characters so as to provide for the efficient reading of characters, arrays, and lines. The Table 6 shows Constructor and Method summary for BufferedReader.

Table 6. Constructor and method summary for BufferedReader

Method	Description
BufferedReader(Reader in)	Creates a buffering character-input stream that uses a default-sized input buffer.
void close()	Closes the stream and releases any system resources associated with it.
int read()	Reads a single character.
int read(char[] cbuf, int off, int len)	Reads characters into a portion of an array.
String readLine()	Reads a line of text.

Example for declaring BufferedReader object:

```
var br = BufferedReader(isr)
```

Note that when accessing the file, we must put it in a try…catch block or throw try catch. The Listing 2 is a complete illustration of the script to read the text file.

Listing 2. LearnTextFile/TestReadTextFile.kt

```
1    import java.io.FileInputStream
2    import java.io.InputStreamReader
3    import java.io.BufferedReader
4    fun main(args: Array<String>) {
5    try {
6    var path="d:/data.txt"
7    var fis = FileInputStream(path)
8    var isr = InputStreamReader(fis, "UTF-8")
9    var br = BufferedReader(isr)
10   var line = br.readLine()
11   while (line != null) {
12   println(line)
13   line = br.readLine()
14   }
15   br.close()
16   isr.close()
17   fis.close()
18   }
19   catch (ex:Exception)
20   {
21   ex.printStackTrace()
22   }
23   }
24   }
```

Running the program, we have the results of reading data from d:/data.txt:

```
Kotlin
Programming
Language
```

The source code can be downloaded at the link:
https://github.com/thanhtd32/kotlin/tree/main/LearnTextFile

More Example With Text File

Now we make a project to save the file and read the file on the object, specifically we do it on the Product class (it has Code, Name, UnitPrice properties), the project structure will be as follows in the Figure 2.

Figure 2. More example with text file

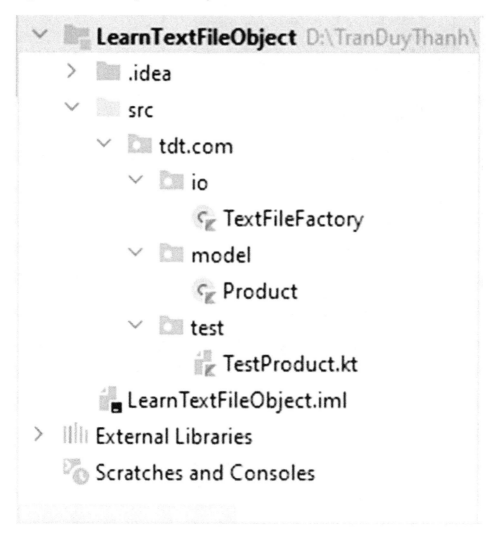

The package tdt.com.model will store the Product class with the following structure in the Listing 3.

Listing 3. LearnTextFileObject/tdt.com.model/Product

```
1
2    package tdt.com.model
3    class Product {
4    public var Code:Int=0
5    get() {return field}
6    set(value) {field=value}
7    public var Name:String=""
8    get() {return field}
9    set(value) {field=value}
10   public var UnitPrice:Double=0.0
11   get() {return field}
12   set(value) {field=value}
13   constructor()
14   constructor(code: Int, name: String,
15   unitPrice: Double) {
16   this.Code = code
17   this.Name = name
18   this.UnitPrice = unitPrice
19   }
20   override fun toString(): String {
21   return "$Code\t$Name\t$UnitPrice"
22   }
23   }
24
```

Now we will write the class to save the Product list as follows (TextFileFactory class), it is shown in the Listing 4.

Listing 4 (a). LearnTextFileObject/<u>tdt.com.io/TextFileFactory</u>

```
1   package tdt.com.io
2   import tdt.com.model.Product
3   import java.io.*
4   class TextFileFactory {
5   /**
6   * @author TranDuy Thanh
7   * @param data: Data is product list to be saved
8   * @param path: Storage path
9   * @return true if saved successfully, false if
10          saved fails
11          */
12          fun SaveFile(data:MutableList<Product>,
13          path:String):Boolean
14          {
15          try {
16          var fos = FileOutputStream(path)
17          var osw = OutputStreamWriter(fos, "UTF-8")
18          var bw = BufferedWriter(osw)
19          //convert product to string format:
20          //"$Code\t$Name\t$UnitPrice"
21          //and save to file line by line
22          for (product in data) {
23          bw.write(product.toString());
24          bw.newLine();
25          }
26          bw.close();
27          osw.close();
28          fos.close();
29          return true
30          }
31          catch (ex:Exception)
32          {
33          ex.printStackTrace()
34          }
35          return false
36          }
37          /**
38          * @author TranDuy Thanh
39          * @param path:storage path to read data
```

Listing 4 (b). LearnTextFileObject/tdt.com.io/TextFileFactory

```
40
41
42        * @return Product list MutableList
43        */
44        fun ReadFile(path:String):MutableList<Product>
45        {
46        var data:MutableList<Product>
47        = mutableListOf()
48        try {
49        var fis = FileInputStream(path)
50        var isr = InputStreamReader(fis, "UTF-8")
51        var br = BufferedReader(isr)
52        var line = br.readLine()
53        while (line != null) {
54        //string format:
55        "$Code\t$Name\t$UnitPrice"
56        //we split this string format
57         var arr = line.split("\t")
58        if (arr.size == 3) {
59        //remodel the Product object
60         var product: Product = Product()
61        product.Code = arr[0].toInt()
62        product.Name = arr[1]
63        product.UnitPrice =
64        arr[2].toDouble()
65        data.add(product)
66        }
67        line = br.readLine()
68        }
69        br.close()
70        isr.close()
71        fis.close()
72        }
73        catch (ex:Exception) {
74        ex.printStackTrace()
75        }
76        return data
77        }
78        }
79
80
```

Now create the main function in the file TestProduct.kt to test and save the Product List as a Text File. The saveProduct() function is used to demonstrate how to save a list of Products to a text file. The readProduct() function is used to demonstrate how to read a list of Products from a text file and re-model the object.

The main function provides options for the user to save the file, read the file, or exit the program. It is shown in the Listing 5.

Listing 5. LearnTextFileObject/tdt.com.test/TestProduct.kt

```
1
2     package tdt.com.test
3     import tdt.com.io.TextFileFactory
4     import tdt.com.model.Product
5     var path="d:/Productdata.txt"
6     fun saveProduct()
7     {
8     var data:MutableList<Product> = mutableListOf()
9     var p1=Product(1,"Coca",15.5)
10    data.add(p1)
11    var p2=Product(2,"Sting",25.0)
12    data.add(p2)
13    var p3=Product(3,"Redbull",17.0)
14    data.add(p3)
15    var tff= TextFileFactory()
16    var ret=tff.SaveFile(data,path)
17    if(ret)
18    {
19    println("Save text file successfully")
20    }
21    else
22    {
23    println("Save text file failed")
24    }
25    }
26    fun readProduct()
27    {
28    var tff= TextFileFactory()
29    var data:MutableList<Product> = tff.ReadFile(path)
30    for (product in data)
31    println(product)
32    }
33    fun main(args: Array<String>) {
34    while(true)
35    {
36    println("1.Save Product into File")
37    println("2.Open Product from File")
38    println("3.Exit")
39    println("Your choice:")
40    var s:String?= readLine()
41    if(s!=null)
42    {
43    if(s.equals("1"))
44    saveProduct()
45    else if(s.equals("2"))
46    readProduct()
47    else
48    break
49    }
50    }
51    }
52
```

When running the main function, we have the following result:

```
1.Save Product into File
2.Open Product from File
```

```
3.Exit
Your choice:
1
```

We choose 1 and then press Enter, the program will notify:
"Save text file successfully"

```
1.Save Product into File
2.Open Product from File
3.Exit
Your choice:
1
Save text file successfully
1.Save Product into File
2.Open Product from File
3.Exit
Your choice:
```

Now, we will see if the file Productdata.txt is successfully saved in the Figure 3.

Figure 3. ProductData.txt object data in text file

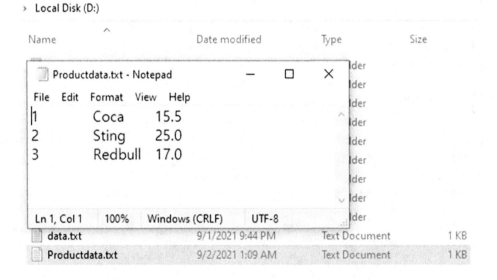

Apparently, the result is saved successfully, now we will choose 2 to read the product information:

```
1.Save Product into File
2.Open Product from File
3.Exit
Your choice:
2
1        Coca              15.5
2        Sting        25.0
3        Redbull       17.0
```

So, we have saved and read Text File successfully, Readers apply yourself to specific projects, save the structure of the Text File is by your decision, in the above examples, the book saves each object is a line, and attributes separated by a tab.

In the next lessons, the book will discuss the Serialize File Processing in Kotlin is very important in the process of data storage.

The source code can be downloaded at the link: https://github.com/thanhtd32/kotlin/tree/main/LearnTextFileO bject.

Serialize File Processing

The book has introduced Text File. In this lesson, the book will continue the tutorial series on file handling, which is Serialize File in Kotlin.

Like Text File, Kotlin also uses JVM libraries to process Serialize, so it is very similar to Java.

Serialize File allows us to "snap" the object onto the hard drive and restore the image from the hard drive to memory. To save the form of Serialize, the class stored on the hard drive must implement the Serializable interface.

Serializable Class

We see the structure of the Contact class as follows in the Listing 6. And we want to serialize the Contact object to the hard drive.

Listing 6. LearnSerializableFile/Contact

```
1   import java.io.Serializable
2   class Contact:Serializable {
3   public var Id:Int = 0
4   get() {return field}
5   set(value) {field=value}
6   public var Name:String=""
7   get() {return field}
8   set(value) {field=value}
9   public var Email:String=""
10  get() {return field}
11  set(value) {field=value}
12  constructor()
13  constructor(Id: Int,
14  Name: String,
15  Email: String) {
16  this.Id = Id
17  this.Name = Name
18  this.Email = Email
19  }
20  override fun toString(): String {
21  return "$Id\t$Name\t$Email"
22  }
23  }
24  }
```

To Serialize the Contact object to the hard drive, this class must implement the Serializable interface.

In the main function we create and use Contact class as in the Listing 7. But in this Listing we just create the contact object and print out the information.

Listing 7. LearnSerializableFile/TestSaveObject.kt

```
1   fun main(args: Array<String>) {
2   var c=Contact()
3   c.Id=100
4   c.Name="Dr. John"
5   c.Email="john@gmail.com"
6   println(c)
7   }
```

Output results when running the program:

```
100       Dr. John        john@gmail.com
```

Serialize Object Into the File

The question is how to serialize this Contact object to file by serializing its object to file? The library packages used to serialize the object into the file:

```
import java.io.FileOutputStream
import java.io.ObjectOutputStream
```

Class FileOutputStream was presented in the previous lesson, this lesson will describe how to use the ObjectOutputStream class.

The class ObjectOutputStream writes primitive data types and graphs of Java/Kotlin objects to an OutputStream. The objects can be read (reconstituted) using an ObjectInputStream. Persistent storage of objects can be accomplished by using a file for the stream. Only objects that support the java.io.Serializable interface can be written to streams. Table 7 shows Constructor and Method summary for ObjectOutputStream.

Table 7. Constructor and method summary for ObjectOutputStream

Method	Description
ObjectOutputStream (OutputStream out)	Creates an ObjectOutputStream that writes to the specified OutputStream.
void write(int val)	Writes a byte.
void writeByte(int val)	Writes an 8 bit byte.
void writeInt(int val)	Writes a 32 bit int.
void writeLong(long val)	Writes a 64 bit long.
void writeFloat(float val)	Writes a 32 bit float.
void writeDouble(double val)	Writes a 64 bit double.
void writeUTF(String str)	Primitive data write of this String in modified UTF-8 format.
void writeObject(Object obj)	Write the specified object to the ObjectOutputStream.
void close()	Closes the output stream.

Example for declaring ObjectOutputStream object:

```
var path="d:/contact.data"
var fos= FileOutputStream(path)
var oos= ObjectOutputStream(fos)
oos.writeObject(c)
```

```
oos.close()
fos.close()
```

The above code uses the FileOutputStream object and then passes it to the ObjectOutputStream object to use, to save the object we call the writeObject command. We need to call close() commands to close the file to finish saving the file. The Listing 8, we edit the code to illustrates serializing the Contact object to a file.

Listing 8. LearnSerializableFile/TestSaveObject.kt

```
1
2    import java.io.FileOutputStream
3    import java.io.ObjectOutputStream
4    fun main(args: Array<String>) {
5    var c=Contact()
6    c.Id=100
7    c.Name="Dr. John"
8    c.Email="john@gmail.com"
9    println(c)
10   var path="d:/contact.data"
11   try {
12   var fos= FileOutputStream(path)
13   var oos= ObjectOutputStream(fos)
14   oos.writeObject(c)
15   oos.close()
16   fos.close()
17   println("Save file successful!");
18   }
19   catch (ex:Exception)
20   {
21   ex.printStackTrace()
22   }
23   }
24
```

Running the above program code, we have the result message:

```
100       Dr. John        john@gmail.com
Save file successful!
```

Open drive D, we see the serialized file "contact.data" in the Figure 4.

Figure 4. The serialized contact.data file

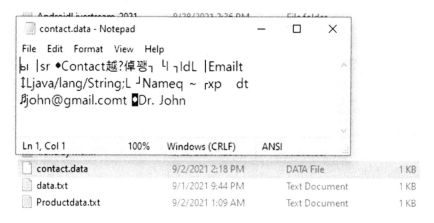

Deserialize Object from the File

The objects can be reconstituted using an ObjectInputStream. The class ObjectInputStream deserializes primitive data and objects previously written using an ObjectOutputStream.

ObjectOutputStream and ObjectInputStream can provide an application with persistent storage for graphs of objects when used with a FileOutputStream and FileInputStream respectively. ObjectInputStream is used to recover those objects previously serialized. The Table 8 shows Constructor and Method summary for ObjectInputStream.

Table 8. Constructor and method summary for ObjectInputStream

Method	Description
ObjectInputStream (InputStream in)	Creates an ObjectInputStream that reads from the specified InputStream.
int read()	Reads a byte of data.
byte readByte()	Reads an 8 bit byte.
int readInt()	Reads a 32 bit int.
long readLong()	Reads a 64 bit long.
float readFloat()	Reads a 32 bit float.
double readDouble()	Reads a 64 bit double.
String readUTF()	Reads a String in modified UTF-8 format.
Object readObject()	Read an object from the ObjectInputStream.
void close()	Closes the input stream.

Example for declaring ObjectInputStream object to deserializes the Contact object from the File, the codes are shown in the Listing 9.

Listing 9. LearnSerializableFile/TestOpenObject.kt

```
1   import java.io.FileInputStream
2   import java.io.ObjectInputStream
3   fun main(args: Array<String>) {
4   var path="d:/contact.data"
5   try
6   {
7   var fis= FileInputStream(path)
8   var ois= ObjectInputStream(fis)
9   var obj=ois.readObject()
10  var data= obj as Contact
11  ois.close()
12  fis.close()
13  println(data)
14  }
15  catch (ex:Exception)
16  {
17  ex.printStackTrace()
18  }
19  }
20
```

The above code uses FileInputStream and assigns it to ObjectInputStream, then uses the readObject() function to read the data.

Run the program, we get the result:

```
100      Dr. John        john@gmail.com
```

Here is the source code of the program, which can be downloaded at the following link: https://github.com/thanhtd32/kotlin/tree/main/LearnSerializableFile.

More Example with Serialize File

We upgrade the previous project by creating packages and classes to use for storing a list of Contact objects. It is shown in the Figure 5.

Figure 5. More example with serialize file

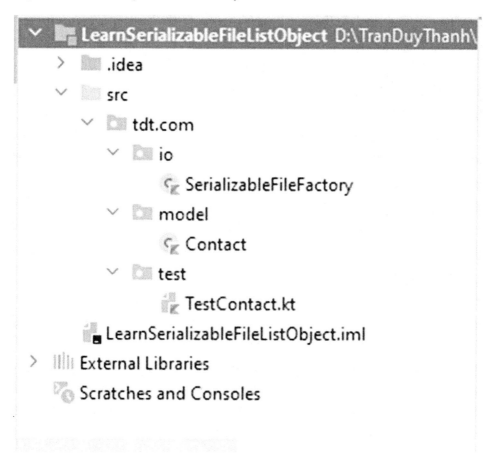

The Contact class contains Id, Name, and Email information.

The SerializableFileFactory class is used to serialize and deserialize a List of Contact objects.

TestContact.kt is used to test the functionality of the software.

And the program provides 5 functions as below:

```
1.Add new Contact
2.Print Contacts
3.Serialize Contacts
4.Deserialize Contacts
5.Exit
Your choice:1
```

The structure of the Contact class is described as follows in the Listing 10.

Listing 10. LearnSerializableFileListObject/tdt.com.model/Contact

```
1
2    package tdt.com.model
3    import java.io.Serializable
4    class Contact:Serializable {
5    public var Id:Int = 0
6    get() {return field}
7    set(value) {field=value}
8    public var Name:String?=null
9    get() {return field}
10   set(value) {field=value}
11   public var Email:String?=null
12   get() {return field}
13   set(value) {field=value}
14   constructor()
15   constructor(Id: Int,
16   Name: String?,
17   Email: String?) {
18   this.Id = Id
19   this.Name = Name
20   this.Email = Email
21   }
22   override fun toString(): String {
23   return "$Id\t$Name\t$Email"
24   }
25   }
26
```

Name and Email are declared with String? so that they can contain null values.

We create the SerializableFileFactory class provides two functions save File and open File in detail as below in the Listing 11.

Listing 11/ LearnSerializableFileListObject/<u>tdt.com.io/SerializableFileFactory</u>

```
1
2    package tdt.com.io
3    import java.io.FileInputStream
4    import java.io.FileOutputStream
5    import java.io.ObjectInputStream
6    import java.io.ObjectOutputStream
7    class SerializableFileFactory {
8      /**
9      * this function uses to save the object data
10     * into the file on the disk
11     * @param data the object to save
12     * @param path the path to save the data
13     * @return true/false
14     */
15      public fun saveFile(data:Any,path:String):Boolean
16    {
17    try {
18    var fos= FileOutputStream(path)
19    var oos= ObjectOutputStream(fos)
20    oos.writeObject(data)
21    oos.close()
22    fos.close()
23    return true
24    }
25    catch (ex:Exception)
26    {
27    ex.printStackTrace()
28    }
29    return false
30    }
31     /**
32     * this function use to deserialize the Object
33     * @param path the path of the file
34     * @return object or null
35     */
36      public fun openFile(path:String): Any?
37    {
38    try
39    {
40    var fis= FileInputStream(path)
41    var ois= ObjectInputStream(fis)
42    var data=ois.readObject()
43    ois.close()
44    fis.close()
45    return data
46    }
47    catch (ex:Exception)
48    {
49    ex.printStackTrace()
50    }
51    return null
52    }
53    }
54
```

Finally, we create the TestContact.kt as in the Listing 12 to test the List of Contact for serializing and deserializing.

Listing 12 (a). LearnSerializableFileListObject/tdt.com.test/TestContact.kt

```
1     package tdt.com.test
2     import tdt.com.io.SerializableFileFactory
3     import tdt.com.model.Contact
4     /**
5     * This function is used to add a new Contact
6     * data entered by the user
7     */
8     fun addNewContact():Contact
9     {
10    print("Id:")
11    var id= readLine()!!.toInt()
12    print("Name:")
13    var name= readLine()
14    print("Email:")
15    var email= readLine()
16    var c=Contact(id,name,email)
17    return c
18    }
19    /**
20    * This function is used to export the list of
21    * contacts to the screen
22    */
23    fun printContacts(contacts:MutableList<Contact>)
24    {
25    for (c in contacts)
26    {
27    println(c)
28    }
29    }
30    fun main(args: Array<String>) {
31    var contacts= mutableListOf<Contact>()
32    while(true)
33    {
34    println("1.Add new Contact")
35    println("2.Print Contacts")
36    println("3.Serialize Contacts")
37    println("4.Deserialize Contacts")
38    println("5.Exit")
39    print("Your choice:")
```

Listing 12 (b). LearnSerializableFileListObject/tdt.com.test/TestContact.kt

```
40
41
42    var s:String?= readLine()
43    if(s!=null)
44    {
45    if(s.equals("1"))
46    {
47    var c= addNewContact()
48    contacts.add(c)
49    }
50    else if(s.equals("2")) {
51    printContacts(contacts)
52    }
53    else if(s.equals("3"))
54    {
55    var sff=SerializableFileFactory()
56    var ret=sff.saveFile(contacts,
57    "d:/contacts.dat")
58    if(ret==true)
59    println("Save file successful!")
60    else
61    println("Save file Failed!")
62    }
63    else if(s.equals("4"))
64    {
65    var sff=SerializableFileFactory()
66    var data=
67    sff.openFile("d:/contacts.dat")
68    if(data!=null)
69    {
70    contacts=
71    data as MutableList<Contact>
72    printContacts(contacts)
73    }
74    }
75    else
76    break
77    }
78    }
79    }
80
```

Run the software to test the functions, we do the following test cases:

```
1.Add new Contact
2.Print Contacts
3.Serialize Contacts
4.Deserialize Contacts
5.Exit
Your choice:1
```

We enter 1 and then press the Enter key, repeat this operation until all 3 Contacts are entered:

```
1.Add new Contact
2.Print Contacts
3.Serialize Contacts
4.Deserialize Contacts
5.Exit
Your choice:1
Id:100
Name:John
Email:john@gmail.com
```

After entering all 3 contacts, we proceed to choose number 2 to display the Contacts list:

```
1.Add new Contact
2.Print Contacts
3.Serialize Contacts
4.Deserialize Contacts
5.Exit
Your choice:2
```

The list of 3 Contacts is output to the screen:

```
Your choice:2
100        John              john@gmail.com
200        Peter      peter@gmail.com
300        Lucy              lucy@gmail.com
1.Add new Contact
2.Print Contacts
3.Serialize Contacts
4.Deserialize Contacts
5.Exit
Your choice:3
```

Next, we enter 3 to serialize the contact list, result of successful file saving notification:

```
Your choice:3
Save file successful!
1.Add new Contact
2.Print Contacts
3.Serialize Contacts
4.Deserialize Contacts
5.Exit
Your choice:4
```

Next, we choose number 4 to deserialize the list of contacts again, the results are printed as below:

```
Your choice:4
100       John              john@gmail.com
200       Peter         peter@gmail.com
300       Lucy              lucy@gmail.com
1.Add new Contact
2.Print Contacts
3.Serialize Contacts
4.Deserialize Contacts
5.Exit
Your choice:5
```

So, the list of contacts has been deserialized back and output to the screen. We choose 5 to end the software. Readers can run the software and read the data again. We have serialized and deserialized successfully, readers apply yourself to the specific project. In the next lesson, the book will discuss XML File Handling in Kotlin which is very important in the process of data storage

The source code can be downloaded at the link: https://github.com/thanhtd32/kotlin/tree/main/LearnSerializableFileListObject.

XML File Processing

The book will guide how to save and read data with XML File. We still use the libraries in the JVM to handle Kotlin. The lesson focuses on modeling data from XML through objects and vice versa. As with previous file manipulation examples, we have the Product class with the following information in the Listing 13.

Listing 13. LearnXMLFile/tdt.com.model/Product

```
1    package tdt.com.model
2    class Product {
3    public var Code:Int=0
4    get() {return field}
5    set(value) {field=value}
6    public var Name:String=""
7    get() {return field}
8    set(value) {field=value}
9    public var UnitPrice:Double=0.0
10   get() {return field}
11   set(value) {field=value}
12   constructor()
13   constructor(code: Int, name: String,
14   unitPrice: Double) {
15   this.Code = code
16   this.Name = name
17   this.UnitPrice = unitPrice
18   }
19   override fun toString(): String {
20   return "$Code\t$Name\t$UnitPrice"
21   }
22   }
23   }
```

The Product class includes the Property Code, Name, and UnitPrice. Getters/setters as well as other structures are defined as above.

About the XML file structure, the book wants you to save the data XML with format as below in the Listing 14.

Listing 14. XML structure of Product object

```
1    <?xml version="1.0" encoding="UTF-8" standalone="no"?>
2    <Products>
3    <Product>
4    <Code>1</Code>
5    <Name>Coca cola</Name>
6    <Price>15.5</Price>
7    </Product>
8    <Product>
9    <Code>2</Code>
10   <Name>Sting</Name>
11   <Price>25.0</Price>
12   </Product>
13   <Product>
14   <Code>3</Code>
15   <Name>Redbull</Name>
16   <Price>17.0</Price>
17   </Product>
18   </Products>
```

The structure of the <Products> root tag, each element inside consists of a <Product> tag, the Product attributes are represented by the <Code>, <Name> and <Price> tags.

In order to save and read the XML File we have to use the following libraries:

```
import java.io.File
import javax.xml.parsers.DocumentBuilderFactory
import javax.xml.transform.TransformerFactory
import javax.xml.transform.dom.DOMSource
import javax.xml.transform.stream.StreamResult
import org.w3c.dom.Element
```

The book creates an XMLFileFactory class that has two methods for writing XML files and reading XML files. You want to know more about XML, you should do some extra research about XML. Please pay attention to this:

The SaveFile (data, path) function is a function that takes the Product List data into an XML file. The ReadFile (path) function modeled back from the XML datatype into object-oriented in Kotlin as a list of Product.

The source codes are shown in the Listing 15.

*Listing 15(a). LearnXMLFile/*tdt.com.io/XMLFileFactory

```
1     package tdt.com.io
2     import tdt.com.model.Product
3     import java.io.File
4     import javax.xml.parsers.DocumentBuilderFactory
5     import javax.xml.transform.TransformerFactory
6     import javax.xml.transform.dom.DOMSource
7     import javax.xml.transform.stream.StreamResult
8     import org.w3c.dom.Element
9     class XMLFileFactory {
10    /**
11    * @author Tran Duy Thanh
12    * @param data: Data is Product list to be saved
13    * @param path: Storage path
14    * @return true if saved successfully, false if save fails
15    */
16    fun SaveFile(data:MutableList<Product>, path:String):Boolean
17    {
18    try
19    {
20    var docFactory = DocumentBuilderFactory.newInstance()
21    var docBuilder = docFactory.newDocumentBuilder()
22    // create document object
23    var doc = docBuilder.newDocument()
24    //create root element <Products>
25    var rootElement = doc.createElement("Products")
26    //add rootElement to document
27    doc.appendChild(rootElement)
28    for(product in data)
29    {
30    //create Product element <Product>
31    var productElement = doc.createElement("Product")
32    //create Code element <Code>
33    var codeElement=doc.createElement("Code")
34    codeElement.textContent=product.Code.toString()
35    //add <Code> tag into <Product> tag
36    productElement.appendChild(codeElement)
37    //create Name element <Name>
38    var nameElement=doc.createElement("Name")
39    nameElement.textContent=product.Name
40    //add <Name> tag into <Product> tag
41    productElement.appendChild(nameElement)
42    //create Price element <Price>
43    var priceElement=doc.createElement("Price")
44    priceElement.textContent=
45    product.UnitPrice.toString()
46    //add <Price> tag into <Product> tag
47    productElement.appendChild(priceElement)
48    ////add <Product> tag into <Products> tag
49    rootElement.appendChild(productElement)
```

Listing 15(b). LearnXMLFile/tdt.com.io/XMLFileFactory

```
50
51
52    }
53    // write the content into xml file
54    var transformerFactory =
55    TransformerFactory.newInstance()
56    var transformer = transformerFactory.newTransformer()
57    var source = DOMSource(doc)
58    var result = StreamResult(File(path).absolutePath)
59    // Output to console for testing          .
60    transformer.transform(source, result)
61    return true
62    }
63    catch (ex:Exception)
64    {
65    ex.printStackTrace()
66    }
67    return false
68    }
69    /**
70     * @author TranDuy Thanh
71     * @param path:storage path to read data
72     * @return Product list MutableList
73     */
74    fun ReadFile(path:String):MutableList<Product>
75    {
76    var data:MutableList<Product> = mutableListOf()
77    try {
78    //Get the DOM Builder Factory
79    var factory = DocumentBuilderFactory.newInstance()
80    //Get the DOM Builder
81    var builder = factory.newDocumentBuilder()
82    //Load and Parse the XML document
83    //document contains the complete XML as a Tree.
84    var xmlfile = File(path)
85    var document = builder.parse(xmlfile)
86    //Iterating the nodes and extracting the data.
87    var nodeList = document.documentElement.childNodes
88    for (i in 0..nodeList.length - 1) {
89
```

*Listing 15(c). LearnXMLFile/*tdt.com.io/XMLFileFactory

```
90
91      //We have encountered an <Product> tag.
92       var node = nodeList.item(i)
93      if (node is Element) {
94      var product = Product()
95      var childNodes = node.getChildNodes()
96      for (j in 0..childNodes.getLength() - 1) {
97      var cNode = childNodes.item(j)
98      //Identifying the child tag of Product
99      if (cNode is Element) {
100     var content = cNode.getLastChild()
101     .getTextContent().trim()
102     when (cNode.getNodeName()) {
103     "Code" ->
104     product.Code= content.toInt()
105     "Name" ->
106     product.Name= content
107     "Price" ->
108     product.UnitPrice=
109     content.toDouble()
110     }
111     }
112     }
113     data.add(product)
114     }
115     }
116     }
117     catch (ex:Exception)
118     {
119     ex.printStackTrace()
120     }
121     return data
122     }
123     }
124
```

We create a main function to test writing the XML FILE, the codes are in the Listing 16.

Listing 16. LearnXMLFile/tdt.com.test/TestProductWriteXML.kt

```
package tdt.com.test
import tdt.com.io.XMLFileFactory
import tdt.com.model.Product
fun main(args: Array<String>) {
var data:MutableList<Product> = mutableListOf()
var product1=Product(1,"Coca cola",15.5)
data.add(product1)
var product2=Product(2,"Sting",25.0)
data.add(product2)
var product3=Product(3,"Redbull",17.0)
data.add(product3)
var xmlff=XMLFileFactory()
var ret=xmlff.SaveFile(data,"d:/Productdata.xml")
if(ret)
{
println("Save text file successfully")
}
else
{
println("Save text file failed")
}
}
```

The code above creates 3 Products and puts them in a MutableList, and then passes them to the SaveFile function of the XMLFileFactory class. Run the program, we have the following result:

```
Save text file successfully
```

We check the results by going to the D:/Productdata.xml drive, using the browser to open it, we see the xml structure as below in the Figure 6.

Figure 6. Productdata.xml file

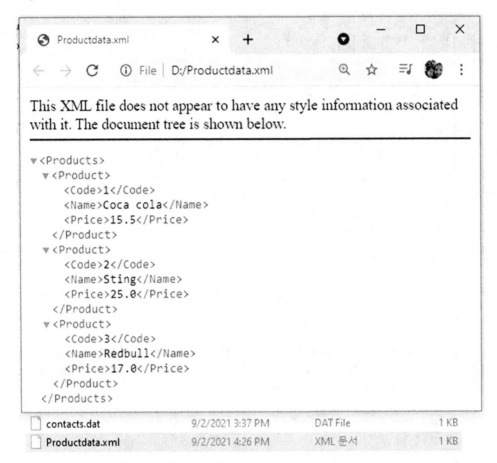

Apparently, the list Product object has saved successfully in XML format, now we will call the function ReadFile to restore the list Product object from XML, the codes are shown in the Listing 17.

Listing 17. LearnXMLFile/tdt.com.test/TestProductReadXML.kt

```
1
2    package tdt.com.test
3    import tdt.com.io.XMLFileFactory
4    import tdt.com.model.Product
5    fun main(args: Array<String>) {
6    var path="d:/Productdata.xml"
7    var xmlff=XMLFileFactory()
8    var data:MutableList<Product>
9    data=xmlff.ReadFile(path)
10   for (product in data)
11   println(product)
12   }
13
```

When running the main function, we have the following result:

```
1        Coca cola        15.5
2        Sting        25.0
3        Redbull        17.0
```

We have saved and read XML File successfully, you apply yourself to specific projects, structure XML File is how you decide. In the next lessons, the book will discuss JSON File Handling in Kotlin which is very important in the process of data storage. The source code can be downloaded at the link: https://github.com/thanhtd32/kotlin/tree/main/LearnXMLFile.

JSon File Processing

Readers have known three types of file interaction: Text File, Serialize File, XML file. Now the book is going to write about a very popular file format that is the Json format.

JSON Format

JSON (JavaScript Object Notation) is defined data according to the JavaScript language, ECMA-262 standard 1999, the structure is a simple text format with nested data fields. JSON is used to exchange data between components of a system that is compatible with most languages C, C++, C#, Java, Kotlin, JavaScript, Perl, Python, etc.

JSON is built on two main structures:

- A set of name/value pairs, in many different languages this value pair can be object, record, struct, dictionary, hash table, keyed list, etc.
- A collection of lists of values, which can be array, vector, list or sequence.

a JSonObject contains unordered string/value pairs, enclosed in a "{ }" pair, the values inside are formatted "string:value" and separated by a ",". Value here can be string, number, true- false, null, etc. Figure 7 shows the JSonObject structure.

Figure 7. JSonObject structure

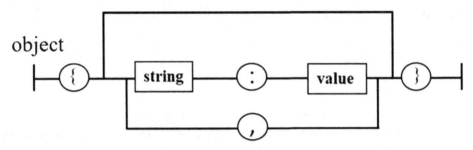

Below is an illustration of the structure of a JSonObject:

```
{
    firstName:"Susan",
        lastName:"Happy",
        age:18,
        email:"susan@gmail.com"
}
```

The above JSonObject has the properties: firstName, lastName, age and email, with their respective values.

An array object that contains many ordered children. The subword parts are enclosed in "[]" pairs and separated by a ",". Each child element can be a single value like: number, string, true-false, null or another object, maybe even an array.

Figure 8. JSonArray structure

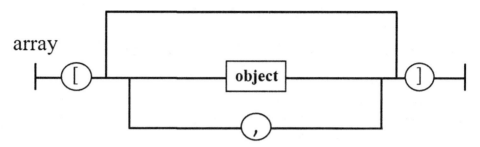

Here is a sample JSonArray example:

```
[
    {
      "Code": "P1",
      "Name": "DELL Inspiron 14NR",
      "Quantity": 100,
      "UnitPrice": 2000
    },
    {
      " Code": "P2",
       " Name": "HP Inspiron 113",
        "Quantity": 130,
        "UnitPrice": 1400
    }
]
```

Kotlin also has classes available for Json interactions, or there are many well-known external libraries such as GSon, Klaxon etc., which make it easy to convert Object Model to Json, and Json to Object Model vice versa.

GSon for JSon

In this lesson, the book will show how to use GSon in Kotlin to convert between Object Model and Json. We download GSon library and reference it to Project in your IntelliJ IDEA, the link can be downloaded at the link: https://repo1.maven.org/maven2/com/google/code/gson/gson/2.8 .8/.

Readers can download another GSon version at the link: https://repo1. maven.org/maven2/com/google/code/gson/gson/.

Download the gson-2.8.8.jar (about 237kb file) from the link above to the computer. The book briefly explains how GSon works:

1.Convert the Kotlin Model to Json String, do the following:

```
var gson = Gson()
var obj = KotlinModel()//some class in Kotlin
//convert KotlinModel object to JSON:
var jsonInString = gson.toJson(obj)
```

2.Save the Kotlin Model to Json File, do the following:

```
var gson = Gson()
var obj = KotlinModel()//some class in Kotlin
//save KotlinModel into a json file
var file=FileWriter("D:\\file.json")
gson.toJson(obj, file)
file.close()
```

3.Convert JSon String to Kotlin Model, we do the following:

```
var gson = Gson()
var jsonInString = "{'name': 'cocacola'}"
var obj= gson.fromJson(jsonInString, KotlinModel::class.java)
```

4.Convert JSon from file to Kotlin Model, we do the following:

```
var gson = Gson()
//JSON to Kotlin model, read it from a file.
var obj = gson.fromJson(FileReader("D:\\file.json"),
KotlinModel::class.java)
```

5.The Json data is a JsonArray

If the Json data is a JsonAray, then for the Kotlin Model we should do the following to conver the JsonArray to a list of KotlinModel:

```
var gson = Gson()
var json = "[{\"name\":\"cocacola\"},
            {\"name\":\"pepsi\"}]"
var data:MutableList = gson.fromJson(json,
       object: TypeToken()
       {}.type)
```

1.4.3 Reference GSon Library

The book will show the instructions so that readers can easily understand and manipulate the GSon library. We create a project named LearnJSonFile, and from this project, we create a directory named libs to copy gson-2.8.8.jar library into libs. The figure 11.9 shows how to select the Directory.

Figure 9. Select new/directory

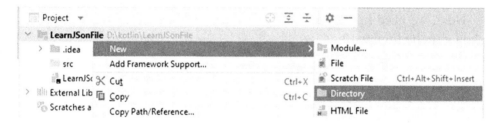

Right-click on Project / select New / select Directory, the New Directory is shown in the Figure 10.

Figure 10. Select new/directory

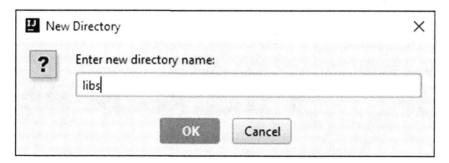

We define the name of the directory is "libs" and click **OK**, the libs directory will be created in the project. And then we copy the gson-2.8.8.jar file to this folder as shown in the Figure 11.

Figure 11. Add gson library to project

Next, we need to put gson-2.8.8.jar into the library used in Project, it is shown in the Figure 12.

Figure 12. Add as library

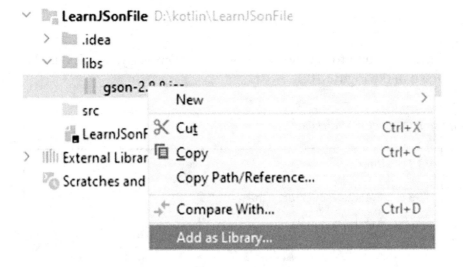

Right-click on gson-2.8.8.jar and select add as Library as shown above, the configuration screen will appear as in the Figure 13.

Figure 13. Create library

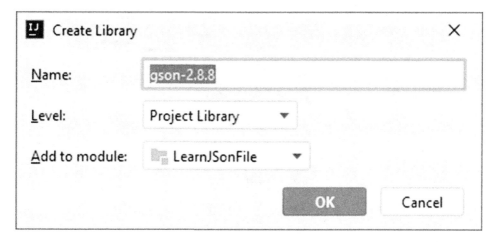

Name item is default and we click **OK**, and readers see a change in the way that readers see the set of GSon classes in the Figure 14.

Figure 14. Set of GSon classes

Create Model Class

Throughout the following content we focus on creating a Course class and writing the code to save the Course object as well as the Course list to JSon format and vice versa. Now, we create the Course class as below in the Listing 18.

Listing 18. LearnJSonFile/tdt.com.model/Course

```
1
2     package tdt.com.model
3     import java.io.Serializable
4     class Course: Serializable{
5     public var Id:String?=null
6     get() {return field}
7     set(value) {field=value}
8     public var Name:String?=null
9     get() {return field}
10    set(value) {field=value}
11    public var Credit:Int=0
12    get() {return field}
13    set(value) {field=value}
14    constructor()
15    constructor(Id: String?,
16    Name: String?,
17    Credit: Int) {
18    this.Id = Id
19    this.Name = Name
20    this.Credit = Credit
21    }
22    override fun toString(): String {
23    return "$Id\t$Name\t$Credit"
24    }
25    }
26
```

Convert Model Class to String JSon

We write codes to convert the Course object into the JSon String format, we create TestCourseToJSonString.kt and write code as the listing 19.

Listing 19. LearnJSonFile/tdt.com.test/TestCourseToJSonString.kt

```
package tdt.com.test
import com.google.gson.Gson
import tdt.com.model.Course
fun main(args: Array<String>) {
  //Create a GSon object
  var gson = Gson()
  //create a course object
  var course = Course()
  course.Id="C12"
  course.Name="Kotlin Language"
  course.Credit=3
  //convert course object to json string
  var jsonInString = gson.toJson(course)
  //print the course information by json string
  println(jsonInString)
  //print the course information by object model
  println(course)
}
```

Running the above program, we get the following results:

```
{"Id":"C12","Name":"Kotlin Language", "Credit":3}
C12          Kotlin Programming Language          3
```

We see the string Json format of the course object displayed as above.

Convert String Json to Model Class

We continue create the TestJSonStringToCourse.kt to convert String Json format to Course object model by GSon.

```
{"Id":"C12","Name":"Kotlin Language", "Credit":3}
```

The Listing 20 shows how to convert the string Json format to the Course object.

Listing 20. LearnJSonFile/tdt.com.test/TestJSonStringToCourse.kt

```
1
2
3     package tdt.com.test
4     import com.google.gson.Gson
5     import tdt.com.model.Course
6     fun main(args: Array<String>) {
7     //Create a GSon object
8      var gson = Gson()
9     //create a string json:
10     var json = "{\"Id\":\"C12\",\"Name\":\"Kotlin Language\", \"Credit\":3}"
11    //print the course information by json string
12    println(json)
13    //print the course information by object model
14     var course = gson.fromJson(json, Course::class.java)
15    println(course)
16    }
17
```

Running the above program, we get the following results:

```
{"Id":"C12","Name":"Kotlin Language", "Credit":3}
C12        Kotlin Language        3
```

We see the Json structure and the Course object model displayed as above.

Convert Model Class to Json File

We continue create TestCourseToJSonFile.kt file to convert Course object to Json File by GSon, it shown in the Listing 21.

Listing 21. LearnJSonFile/tdt.com.test/TestCourseToJSonFile.kt

```
1
2     package tdt.com.test
3     import com.google.gson.Gson
4     import tdt.com.model.Course
5     import java.io.FileWriter
6     fun main(args: Array<String>) {
7     //Create a GSon object
8     var gson = Gson()
9     //create a course object
10    var course = Course()
11    course.Id="C12"
12    course.Name="Kotlin Language"
13    course.Credit=3
14    //create a FileWriter object
15    //this is location to save the data
16    var file= FileWriter("D:\\course.json")
17    //call toJson to convert course to json
18    //and save this data to file
19    gson.toJson(course, file)
20    //We have to call close() method
21    file.close()
22    }
23
```

We run the code above and then go to the drive D to see the json file is created, it is shown in the Figure 15.

Figure 15. Course.json file

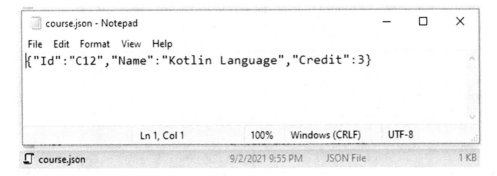

Convert Json File to Model Class

Next, we proceed to convert the data in course.json file into Course object model, we create a TestCourseFromJSonFile.kt and write code as the Listing 22.

Listing 22. LearnJSonFile/tdt.com.test/TestCourseFromJSonFile.kt

```
1   package tdt.com.test
2   import com.google.gson.Gson
3   import tdt.com.model.Course
4   import java.io.FileReader
5   fun main(args: Array<String>) {
6      //Create a GSon object
7      var gson = Gson()
8      //create a FileReader object
9      //this is location to read the data
10     var fr=FileReader("D:\\course.json")
11     //call fromJson method
12     //Course::class.java is syntax to convert
13     var course = gson.fromJson(fr, Course::class.java)
14     println(course)
15  }
16
```

Running the program, we get the following output:

```
C12        Kotlin Language        3
```

We have known how to convert an object model to Json format and vice versa. Readers can apply the technique to another projects. Source code can be downloaded at the link: https://github.com/thanhtd32/kotlin/tree/main/LearnJSonFile.

List Object Model With Json Processing

In addition, we often encounter data in the form of lists of objects, how to convert between object list model and JSon format? Such as the list of the Courses object. We create a new project with name LearnJSonFileListObject and create the packages and classes as the Figure 16.

Figure 16. Packages structure of the project

The Course class is the same structure.

We create an additional class JSonFileFactory and provide 2 functions SaveFile and OpenFile, the code is as follows in the Listing 23.

*Listing 23. LearnJSonFileListObject/*tdt.com.io/JSonFileFactory

```
package tdt.com.io
import com.google.gson.Gson
import java.io.FileWriter
import java.io.FileReader
import com.google.gson.reflect.TypeToken
import tdt.com.model.Course
class JSonFileFactory {
    /**
     * @author TranDuy Thanh
     * @param data: Data is Course list to be saved
     * @param path: Storage path
     * @return true if saved successfully,
     * false if save fails
     */
    fun SaveFile(data:MutableList<Course>,
    path:String):Boolean
    {
    try {
    val gs= Gson()
    val file=FileWriter(path)
    gs.toJson(data,file)
    file.close()
    return true
    }
    catch (ex:Exception)
    {
    ex.printStackTrace()
    }
    return false
    }
    /**
     * @author TranDuy Thanh
     * @param path:storage path to read data
     * @return Course list MutableList
     */
    fun ReadFile(path:String):MutableList<Course>
    {
    var data:MutableList<Course> = mutableListOf()
    try
    {
    val gson = Gson()
    var file=FileReader(path)
    data = gson.fromJson(file,
    object:
    TypeToken<MutableList<Course>>()
    {
    }.type
    )
    file.close()
    }
    catch (ex:Exception)
    {
    ex.printStackTrace()
    }
    return data
    }
}
```

Gson helps us to simplify the storage and reading of data. This is one of the most popular libraries used in projects, and the JSon data format is becoming more popular, possibly more than XML File.

We create the TestCourseListToJSon.kt file with main function to convert the list of courses to Json as the Listing 24.

Listing 24. LearnJSonFileListObject/tdt.com.test/TestCourseListToJSon.kt

```
package tdt.com.test
import tdt.com.io.JSonFileFactory
import tdt.com.model.Course
fun main(args: Array<String>) {
var data:MutableList<Course> = mutableListOf()
//create c1 course object
var c1=Course()
c1.Id="C12"
c1.Name="Kotlin Language"
c1.Credit=3
//add c1 to list
 data.add(c1)
//create c2 course object
 var c2=Course()
c2.Id="C21"
c2.Name="CSharp Language"
c2.Credit=2
//add c2 to list
 data.add(c2)
//create c3 course object
 var c3=Course()
c3.Id="C45"
c3.Name="Edge Computing"
c3.Credit=3
//add c3 to list
 data.add(c3)
//create JSonFileFactory object
 var jsff=JSonFileFactory()
//call SaveFile
 var ret=jsff.SaveFile(data,"d:/courses.json")
if(ret)
{
println("Save json file successfully")
}
else
{
println("Save json file failed")
}
}
```

Run the program, we get the following results from d:/courses.json, it is shown in the Figure 17.

Figure 17. Courses.json

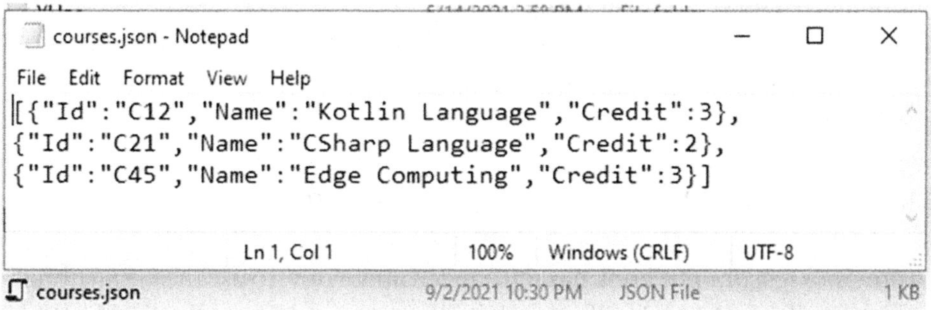

Apparently, the result is saved successfully, now we will create TestCourseListFromJSon.kt and write main method to call the function reading information as in the Listing 25.

Listing 25. LearnJSonFileListObject/tdt.com.test/TestCourseListFromJSon.kt

```
1
2     package tdt.com.test
3     import tdt.com.io.JSonFileFactory
4     import tdt.com.model.Course
5     fun main(args: Array<String>) {
6     //create courses list object
7     var courses:MutableList<Course>
8     //create JSonFileFactory object
9     var jsff= JSonFileFactory()
10    //call ReadFile method
11    courses=jsff.ReadFile("d:/courses.json")
12    //print all
13    for (course in courses)
14    println(course)
15    }
16
```

When running the main function, we have the following result:

```
C12        Kotlin Language      3
C21        CSharp Language      2
C45        Edge Computing           3
```

We have saved and read JSon File successfully, Readers can apply yourself to specific projects, JSon File structure in this case it will automatically build based on Class structure and relationship between Class that readers created.

In the next lesson, the book will show how to retrieve Json data has a complex structure, you pay attention to it.

The source code can be downloaded at the link: https://github.com/thanhtd32/kotlin/tree/main/LearnJSonFileListObject.

More Complex Object Model and JSon Processing

In previous lesson, The book has introduced about how to use the GSon library to save the Kotlin Model to JSon and read converting JSon to Kotlin Model. In this lesson, the book continues to add a more complex JSon example in Kotlin, which is to create two classes that have a Master-Detail relationship, which is one of the most common cases in the deployment process of actual projects. Specifically, the book will add a Student Class that has a relationship with the Course Class: A Student has many courses, it is shown in the Figure 18.

Figure 18. Class diagram of student and course

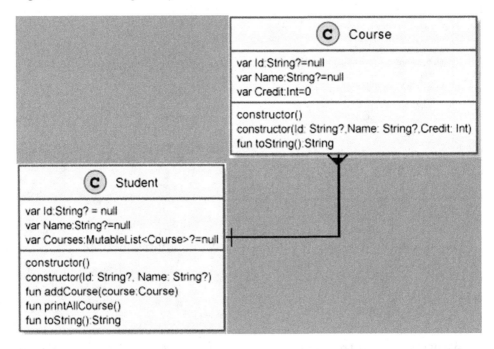

Let's look at how GSon creates the JSon file as well as how to restore the Kotlin Model. The book will go directly to the programming techniques.

We create a project with name LearnJSonFileComplex, the project structure is shown in the Figure 19.

Figure 19. Project structure

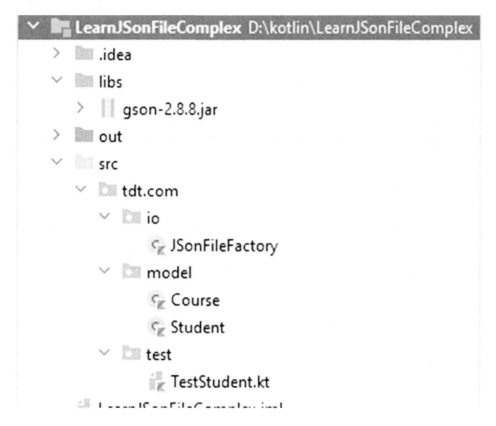

The Course Class is structured as follows in the Listing 26.

Listing 26. LearnJSonFileComplex/tdt.com.model/Course

```
package tdt.com.model
class Course{
public var Id:String?=null
get() {return field}
set(value) {field=value}
public var Name:String?=null
get() {return field}
set(value) {field=value}
public var Credit:Int=0
get() {return field}
set(value) {field=value}
constructor()
constructor(Id: String?,
Name: String?,
Credit: Int) {
this.Id = Id
this.Name = Name
this.Credit = Credit
}
override fun toString(): String {
return "$Id\t$Name\t$Credit"
}
}
```

And the Structure of class Student as in the Listing 27.

Listing 27. LearnJSonFileComplex/tdt.com.model/Student

```
1
2    package tdt.com.model
3    class Student {
4    public var Id:String? = null
5    get() {return field}
6    set(value) {field=value}
7    public var Name:String?=null
8    get() {return field}
9    set(value) {field=value}
10   public var Courses:MutableList<Course>?=null
11   get() {return field}
12   set(value) {field=value}
13   constructor()
14   {
15   Courses= mutableListOf()
16   }
17   constructor(Id: String?, Name: String?) {
18   this.Id = Id
19   this.Name = Name
20   Courses= mutableListOf()
21   }
22   //Add new course for student
23    fun addCourse(course:Course)
24   {
25   if(Courses!=null)
26   Courses!!.add(course)
27   }
28   //print all student's courses
29    fun printAllCourse()
30   {
31   if(Courses==null)return
32   for (course in Courses!!)
33   {
34   println(course)
35   }
36   }
37   override fun toString(): String {
38   return "$Id\t$Name"
39   }
40   }
41
```

And then we create the JSonFileFactory class, it has the following structure as in the Listing 28.

Listing 28. LearnJSonFileComplex/tdt.com.io/JSonFileFactory

```
1
2     package tdt.com.io
3     import com.google.gson.Gson
4     import java.io.FileWriter
5     import java.io.FileReader
6     import com.google.gson.reflect.TypeToken
7     import tdt.com.model.Course
8     import tdt.com.model.Student
9     class JSonFileFactory {
10    /**
11     * @author Tran Duy Thanh
12     * @param data: Data is Student list to be saved
13     * @param path: Storage path
14     * @return true if saved successfully,
15     * false if save fails
16    */
17    fun SaveFile(data:MutableList<Student>,
18    path:String):Boolean
19    {
20    try {
21    val gs= Gson()
22    val file=FileWriter(path)
23    gs.toJson(data,file)
24    file.close()
25    return true
26    }
27    catch (ex:Exception)
28    {
29    ex.printStackTrace()
30    }
31    return false
32    }
33    /**
34     * @author Tran Duy Thanh
35     * @param path:storage path to read data
36     * @return Any list MutableList
37    */
38    fun ReadFile(path:String):MutableList<Student>
39    {
40    var data:MutableList<Student>
41    data= mutableListOf()
42    try
43    {
44    val gson = Gson()
45    var file=FileReader(path)
46    data = gson.fromJson(file,
47    object:
48    TypeToken<MutableList<Student>>()
49    {
50    }.type
51    )
52    file.close()
53    }
54    catch (ex:Exception)
55    {
56    ex.printStackTrace()
57    }
58    return data
59    }
60    }
61
```

Finally, we create the main function to test with 5 options (TestStudent.kt):

```
1.Create Sample Data
2.Print Sample Data
3.Write Sample JsonData
4.Read Samle JsonData
5.Exit
Your choice:2
```

Here are the code details as in the Listing 29.

Listing 29(a). LearnJSonFileComplex/tdt.com.test/TestStudent.kt

```
1    package tdt.com.test
2    import tdt.com.io.JSonFileFactory
3    import tdt.com.model.Course
4    import tdt.com.model.Student
5    var path="D:/students.json"
6    var students:MutableList<Student> = mutableListOf()
7    fun main(args: Array<String>) {
8    while(true)
9    {
10   println("1.Create Sample Data")
11   println("2.Print Sample Data")
12   println("3.Write Sample JsonData")
13   println("4.Read Samle JsonData")
14   println("5.Exit")
15   print("Your choice:")
16   var s:String?= readLine()
17   if(s!=null)
18   {
19   if(s.equals("1"))
20   {
21   createSampledata()
22   }
23   else if(s.equals("2")) {
24   printSampleData()
25   }
26   else if(s.equals("3"))
27   {
28   writeSampleJsonData()
29   }
30   else if(s.equals("4"))
31   {
32   readSampleJsonData()
33   }
34   else
35   break
36   }
37   }
38   }
39   //create sample data list
40   fun createSampledata()
41   {
42   students.clear()
43   //create Student 1
44    var st1=Student("ID1","John")
45   students.add(st1)
46   //create Student 2
47    var st2=Student("ID2","Peter")
48   students.add(st2)
49    //create Student 3
50    var st3=Student("ID3","Lucy")
51   students.add(st3)
52   //create c1 course object
53   var c1= Course("C12","Kotlin Language",3)
54   //create c2 course object
55   var c2= Course("C21","CSharp Language",2)
56   //create c3 course object
57   var c3= Course("C45","Edge Computing",3)
58   //add new courses for student
59   st1.addCourse(c1)
```

Listing 29(b). LearnJSonFileComplex/tdt.com.test/TestStudent.kt

60	
61	
62	
63	st1.addCourse(c3)
64	st2.addCourse(c1)
65	st2.addCourse(c2)
66	st2.addCourse(c3)
67	st3.addCourse(c2)
68	}
69	*//print all sample data*
70	fun printSampleData()
71	{
72	for (student in *students*)
73	{
74	*println*(student)
75	*println*("----------------------------")
76	for(course in student.Courses!!)
77	{
78	*println*("\t$course")
79	}
80	*println*("----------------------------")
81	}
82	}
83	*//write sample data to json format*
84	fun writeSampleJsonData()
85	{
86	var jsff=JSonFileFactory()
87	var ret= jsff.SaveFile(*students*, *path*)
88	if(ret)
89	{
90	*println*("Save Json file successfully")
91	}
92	else
93	{
94	*println*("Save Json file failed")
95	}
96	}
97	*//read sample json data*
98	fun readSampleJsonData()
99	{
100	var jsff=JSonFileFactory()
101	*students*=jsff.ReadFile(*path*)
102	*println*("Open JSon File successfully")
103	}
104	
105	

When running the main function, we have the following result:

```
1.Create Sample Data
2.Print Sample Data
3.Write Sample JsonData
4.Read Samle JsonData
5.Exit
Your choice:1
```

We choose 1 to create Sample data.
And then choose 2 to print sample data:

```
1.Create Sample Data
2.Print Sample Data
3.Write Sample JsonData
4.Read Samle JsonData
5.Exit
Your choice:2
```

The student list and their courses:

```
ID1        John
----------------------------
       C12          Kotlin Language       3
       C45          Edge Computing                  3
----------------------------
ID2        Peter
----------------------------
       C12          Kotlin Language       3
       C21          CSharp Language       2
       C45          Edge Computing                  3
----------------------------
ID3        Lucy
----------------------------
       C21          CSharp Language       2
----------------------------
```

And then we choose 3 to write the student list into Json file, we check "D:/ students.json" to see the data format as in the Figure 20.

Figure 20. Students.json

```
students.json - Notepad                              —   □   ×

File  Edit  Format  View  Help
[{"Id":"ID1","Name":"John","Courses":[{"Id":"C12","Name":"Kotlin
Language","Credit":3},{"Id":"C45","Name":"Edge
Computing","Credit":3}]},{"Id":"ID2","Name":"Peter","Courses":
[{"Id":"C12","Name":"Kotlin Language","Credit":3},
{"Id":"C21","Name":"CSharp Language","Credit":2},
{"Id":"C45","Name":"Edge Computing","Credit":3}]},
{"Id":"ID3","Name":"Lucy","Courses":[{"Id":"C21","Name":"CSharp
Language","Credit":2}]}]

                        Ln 1, Col 1        100%   Windows (CRLF)   UTF-8
```

students.json   9/3/2021 12:01 AM   JSON File   1 KB

Apparently, the results have been saved successfully, do Readers see if there are any differences in Json structure? That is, each Student has a Courses array-> that is automatically generated by the GSon from the relationship of the 2 classes: Student+ Course.

Now, comeback to the program and we choose 4 to read sample data.

```
1.Create Sample Data
2.Print Sample Data
3.Write Sample JsonData
4.Read Samle JsonData
5.Exit
Your choice:4
Open JSon File successfully
```

And then choose 2 to see the data again.

```
Your choice:2
ID1        John
----------------------------
        C12        Kotlin Language     3
        C45        Edge Computing          3
----------------------------
ID2        Peter
----------------------------
        C12        Kotlin Language     3
        C21        CSharp Language     2
        C45        Edge Computing          3
----------------------------
ID3        Lucy
----------------------------
        C21        CSharp Language     2
----------------------------
```

Readers see that JSon is easier more than Text File, Serialize File, and XML File, right to program. The JSon structure is used a lot nowadays, and more and more developers like it. We have completed the complex case of JSon File that is the relationship between the classes, readers apply yourself to specific projects.

The source code can be downloaded at the link: https://github.com/thanhtd32/kotlin/tree/main/LearnJSonFileComplex.

Readers can read more explanations of the conditional structure in the authors' books (Jemerov et al., 2017; Griffiths & Griffiths, 2019; Eckel

& Isakova, 2020; Bailey et al., 2021). Additionally, Java Object Oriented Programming book is referenced in Schild (2019).

Exercises

1. Why do we have to store data?
2. What library classes do we use to interact with Text File?
3. What library classes do we use to interact with Serialize File?
4. What library classes do we use to interact with XML File?
5. What library classes do we use to interact with JSon File?
6. What is the difference in data structure of JSonObject and JSonArray?
7. bw is an object variable of BufferedWriter, what command do we use to write a string "hello"?
    (a) bw.write("hello")
    (b) bw.writeString("hello")
    (c) bw.writeData("hello")
    (d) bw.writeObject("hello")
8. br is an object variable of BufferedReader, what command do we use to read all string in the text file?
    (a) br.readAllLine()
    (b) br.readLines()
    (c) br.readAlls()
    (d) br.readToEnd()
9. Write a program to write and read a list of Students with the following structure, using Text File

```
class Student
{
    var Id:String?=null
    var Name:String?=null
}
```

10. oos is an object variable of ObjectOutputStream, what command do we use to Serializable the object obj into the File?
    (a) oos.writeObject(obj)
    (b) oos.write (obj)
    (c) oos.saveObject(obj)
    (d) oos.save(obj)
11. ois is an object variable of ObjectInputStream, what command do we use to Deserializable the object from the File?

(a) ois.readObject()

(b) ois.read ()

(c) ois.openObject()

(d) ois.open()

12. Write a program to write and read a list of Employees with the following structure, using Serializable File

```
class Employee
{
    var Id:Int=0
    var Name:String?=null
    var Birthday:Date? = null
}
```

13. Write a program to write and read a list of Assets with the following structure, using XML File

```
<assets>
        <asset>
                <id>id1</id>
                <name>asset 1</name>
        </asset>
        <asset>
                <id>id2</id>
                <name>asset 2</name>
        </asset>
</assets>
```

14. Write a program to write and read a list of Employee with the following the class Diagram, using JSon File

Figure 21.

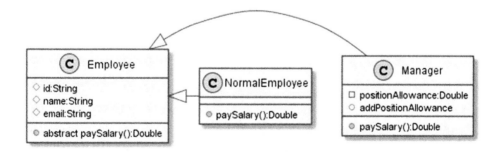

Employee is an abstract class, including id, name, email and paySalary() abstract method.

NormalEmployee class inherits Employee, overriding paySalary() method, default is 3000$, Manager class inherits Employee, including positionAllowance, and overriding paySalary method (Manager's salary is equal to NormalEmployee's salary plus positionAllowance).

The program provides the following functions: add new Employee, edit Employee, Display Employee list, delete Employee, Save Employee to hard drive with Json format, load Json data from hard drive into memory.

REFERENCES

Bailey, A., Greenhalgh, D., & Skeen, J. (2021). *Kotlin Programming: The Big Nerd Ranch Guide* (2nd ed.). Big Nerd Ranch, LLC.

Eckel, B., & Isakova, S. (2020). Atomic Kotlin. *Mindview, LLC.*

Griffiths, D., & Griffiths, D. (2019). Head First Kotlin. O'Reilly Media.

Jemerov & Isakova. (2017). *Kotlin in Action.* Manning.

Schild, H. (2019). Java the complete Reference (11th ed.). McGraw-Hill Education.

Chapter 12
Graphic User Interface

ABSTRACT

For customers, providing interactive user interfaces is very important because customers can only manipulate on the intuitive screen. There are many types of interfaces provided by different programming languages and dependent on the case that programmer used. In addition, with the development of programming languages, it is possible to use interfaces between different programming languages. This chapter presents graphic user interface, guides learners on how to write classes that inherit interfaces as well as how to drag and drop controls on the interface to get the desired interface. In this chapter, readers will discover layout, basic controls label, button, etc. and list, table, tree, etc. For each type of control, detailed instructions are provided, which makes it easy for readers to grasp the theory and implement the practical parts. The chapter also presents how to create executables for Kotlin. At the end of the chapter, there are exercises to help readers practice user interface handling skills.

DOI: 10.4018/978-1-6684-6687-2.ch012

INTRODUCTION GUI FORM

In this lesson, the book will introduce how to design and display interfaces using Kotiln. We create a Project named LearnGUIPart1, then we create a GUI Form, select the GUI form as in the Figure 1.

Figure 1. Select GUI form

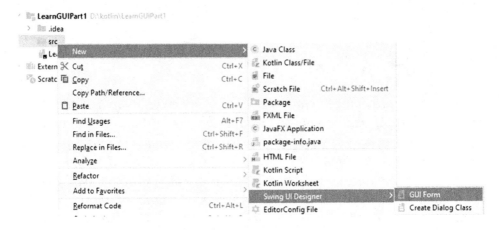

Right-click on src → select New→then select the Swing UI Designer→ select GUI Form, the New GUI Form screen will appear as below in the Figure 2.

Figure 2. New GUI form

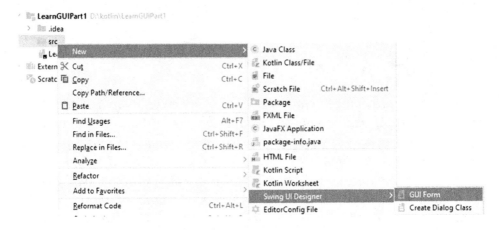

Form Name: Name of the user interface. We define name HelloWorldUI.

Base Layout Manager: Choose the default layout for the interface, of course we can change later. Layout is where the organizer arranges Controls on the interface. At this screen, IntelliJ IDEA offers the following layouts as in the Figure 3.

Figure 3. New GUI form

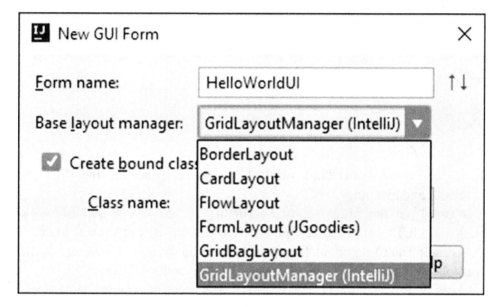

For the first time, just leave it as default as IDEA chooses. And the book will explain the layout manager in the next lessons.

Create Bound Class: We check it, and the logic class is automatically created for the Form name. Then click OK to create, the tool will look like as the Figure 4.

Figure 4. GUI Form designer

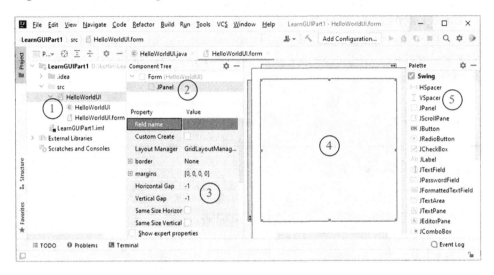

At the Figure 4, the book marked 5 areas, each section has different functions and meanings:

Area 1: Is the organizational structure of the Class, and libraries. HelloWorldUI.form use to design, HelloWorldUI class use to code logic.

Area 2: The Component Tree, which tells you the layout structure of the controls on the interface, lets you drag and drop controls here.

Area 3: Properties window, which allows you to configure parameters for the control as: Colors, letters, sizes, names ...

Area 4: The interface design, allows us to drag the control here.

Area 5: The Pallette window, which displays the list of controls (JLabel, JTextField, JButton, JRadioButon, JCheckBox, JList, JTable, JTree…), it allows you to drag the controls in and drop off area 4.

Now, we drag and drop few Controls in the HelloWorldUI.form like Figure 5.

Figure 5. Drag and drop control

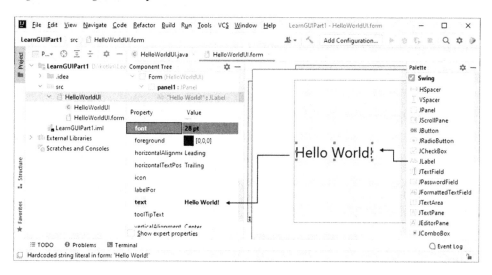

Drag the JLabel to drop in the Palette to the Designer area, then in the Property area we set font and text, or another property.

By default, the program will have a JPanel layout named panel1 for us to drag and drop and design controls on this panel.

Now, Readers observe the HelloWorldUI class that will automatically declare the variable of this control (panel1, it comes from HelloWorldUI. form), it is shown like in the Figure 6.

Figure 6. HelloWorldUI logic class

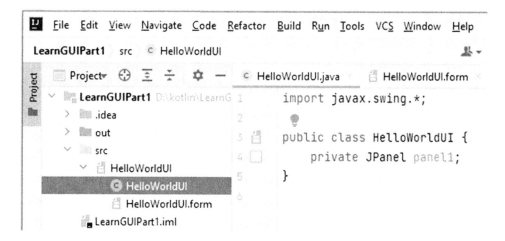

We change the visibility modifier to protected for panel1 as in the Listing 1.

Listing 1. LearnGUIPart1/HelloWorldUI.java

```
1
2    import javax.swing.*;
3    public class HelloWorldUI {
4      protected JPanel panel1;
5    }
6
```

We create a kotlin class extends from HelloWorldUI with name HelloWorldKotlinUI as in the Listing 2.

Listing 2. LearnGUIPart1/HelloWorldKotlinUI

```
1
2    import javax.swing.JFrame
3    class HelloWorldKotlinUI: HelloWorldUI {
4    //create frame object for window
5     lateinit var frame: JFrame
6    constructor()
7    constructor(title:String)
8    {
9    frame = JFrame(title)
10   //set the panel1 for frame
11   //the UI from HellWorldUI.form
12   //set the panel1 for frame
13   //the UI from HellWorldUI.form
14   frame.contentPane = panel1
15   }
16   //this method uses to show the UI
17   fun showUI() {
18   //set 'X' corner button to close the window
19   frame.defaultCloseOperation =JFrame.EXIT_ON_CLOSE
20   //set size for window: width=500, height=300
21   frame.setSize(500, 300)
22   //set centering desktop for the window
23   frame.setLocationRelativeTo(null)
24   //show the window
25   frame.isVisible = true
26   }
27   }
28
```

And then we create a new file Kotlin (TestHelloWorldUI.kt) like Figure 7.

310

Figure 7. TestHelloWorldUI

We add the following commands to show the Window as in the Listing 3.

Listing 3. LearnGUIPart1/TestHelloWorldUI

```
1    fun main(args: Array<String>) {
2    var hwui=HelloWorldUI("Learn GUI")
3    hwui.showUI()
4    }
```

We run the program and see the GUI shows as the Figure 8.

Figure 8. HelloWorld window

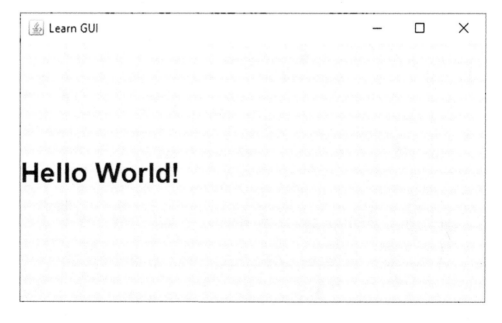

As such, the book has completed the tutorial on how to create graphic user interface in Kotlin. Next lesson, the book will explain how to use the Window and layout manager. Please pay proper attention to the tutorial.

The source code can be downloaded at the link: https://github.com/thanhtd32/kotlin/tree/main/LearnGUIPart1;

WINDOW AND LAYOUT MANAGER

The book has shown how to create the graphic user interface in Kotlin. Now, the book will explain the JFrame, JPanel, Layout manager and common controls such as JLabel, JTextField, JButton.

JFrame

Readers have known how to create a project with Graphic User Interface. Now, the book will explain how the Window is created.

To create a Window, we use the JFrame class, and the Graphic is shown as in the Figure 9.

Figure 9. JFrame window

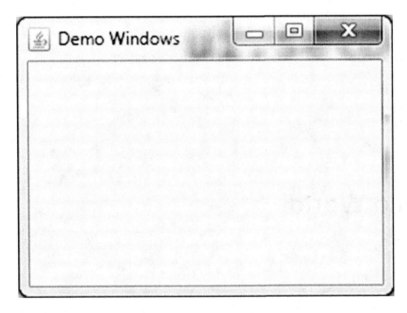

Libraries for graphic design is swing, and awt for events listener:

```
import java.awt.*;
import java.awt.event.*;
import javax.swing.*;
```

The Table 1 shows Constructors and methods of JFrame.

Table 1. Constructors and methods of JFrame

Method	Description
JFrame()	Create the window object by JFrame
title	The title of the window
defaultCloseOperation= JFrame.EXIT_ON_CLOSE	Set the operation that will happen by default when closes the window.
setSize(500, 300)	set the initial size with setSize. Width = 500, height=300
setLocationRelativeTo(null)	Set center the window on the screen.
isVisible = true	Show the window

To design a good user graphic interface, we need to know how to use JPanel's Layout Manager. These categories include:

- Flowlayout
- Boxlayout
- Borderlayout
- CardLayout
- FormLayout

FlowLayout Manager

FlowLayout allows adding controls on the same line, when it runs out of space, it will automatically go down the line, we can also adjust the direction of the control's appearance. By default, when a JPanel is instantiated, the container class itself will have a Layout type of FlowLayout. The Figure 10 shows the Flowlayout.

Figure 10. FlowLayout manager

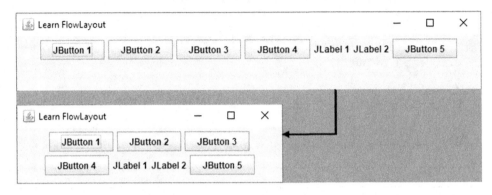

The code examples in Kotlin language are shown in the Listing 4.

Listing 4. FlowLayoutManager

```
1    //create a JPanel object containing the interface:
2    var pn = JPanel()
3    //Set the layout for this container:
4    pn.layout = FlowLayout()
5    //create JButton, JLabel control
6    var btn1 = JButton("JButton 1")
7    var btn2 = JButton("JButton 2")
8    var btn3 = JButton("JButton 3")
9    var btn4 = JButton("JButton 4")
10   var lbl5 = JLabel("JLabel 1")
11   var lbl6 = JLabel("JLabel 2")
12   var btn5 = JButton("JButton 5")
13   //add the control to panel
14   pn.add(btn1)
15   pn.add(btn2)
16   pn.add(btn3)
17   pn.add(btn4)
18   pn.add(lbl5)
19   pn.add(lbl6)
20   pn.add(btn5)
21
```

BoxLayout Manager

BoxLayout allows adding controls by row or column, at each add position it only accepts 1 control, so if you want to appear multiple controls at one location, you should add that position as a JPanel and then add the controls. else to this JPanel.

BoxLayout.X_AXIS allows adding controls from left to right.

BoxLayout.Y_AXIS allows adding controls from top to bottom.

BoxLayout will not automatically line up when it runs out of space, controls will be obscured if there is a lack of space to contain it. The Figure 11 shows the BoxLayout Manager.

Figure 11. BoxLayout manager

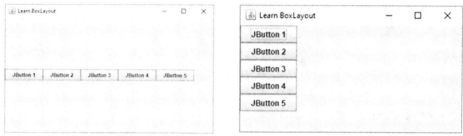

BoxLayout.X AXIS   BoxLayout.Y AXIS

The code examples the Kotlin as below in the Listing 5.

Listing 5. BoxLayoutManager

```
1    //Create a JPanel object
2    var pn = JPanel()
3    //set layout to BoxLayout
4    pn.layout = BoxLayout(pn, BoxLayout.X_AXIS)
5    //create JButton control
6    var btn1 = JButton("JButton 1")
7    var btn2 = JButton("JButton 2")
8    var btn3 = JButton("JButton 3")
9    var btn4 = JButton("JButton 4")
10   val btn5 = JButton("JButton 5")
11   //add the buttons to panel:
12   pn.add(btn1)
13   pn.add(btn2)
14   pn.add(btn3)
15   pn.add(btn4)
16   pn.add(btn5)
17
```

BorderLayout Manager

BorderLayout helps us display controls in 5 regions: North, South, West, East, Center. If there were not 4 regions: North, West, South, East. Then the

Center area will fill the window, usually when putting controls JTable, JTree, ListView, JScrollpane ... we usually put in the Center area so that it can scale itself according to the window size to make the interface more beautiful. The Figure 12 shows the BoxLayout manager.

Figure 12. BoxLayout manager

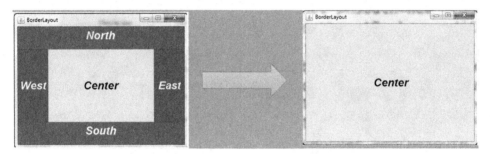

The code examples in the Kotlin language as below is in the Listing 6.

Listing 6. BorderLayoutManager

```
//create JPanel object
var pn = JPanel()
//set border layout
pn.layout = BorderLayout()
//create north panel
var pnNorth = JPanel()
pnNorth.background = Color.RED
pn.add(pnNorth, BorderLayout.NORTH)
//create south panel
var pnSouth = JPanel()
pnSouth.background = Color.RED
pn.add(pnSouth, BorderLayout.SOUTH)
//create west panel
var pnWest = JPanel()
pnWest.background = Color.BLUE
pn.add(pnWest, BorderLayout.WEST)
//create east panel
var pnEast = JPanel()
pnEast.background = Color.BLUE
pn.add(pnEast, BorderLayout.EAST)
//create center panel
var pnCenter = JPanel()
pnCenter.background = Color.YELLOW
pn.add(pnCenter, BorderLayout.CENTER)
```

CardLayout Manager

CardLayout allows to share the display position of the controls, which means that for the same display position, we can let other controls display at different times, by default the first added control will be displayed.

The Figure 13 shows the CardLayout manager: When the user clicks "Show Card1", the graphic user interface of Card1 will appear, and when the user clicks "Show Card2", the graphic user interface of Card2 will appear, and they appear at the same location.

Figure 13. CardLayout manager

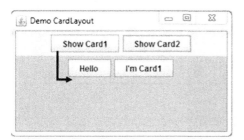 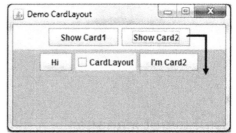

The code examples in Kotlin language as below is shown in the Listing 7.

Listing 7. CardLayoutManager

```
1
2    var pn = JPanel()
3    pn.layout = CardLayout()
4    var pnCard1 = JPanel()
5    pnCard1.background = Color.LIGHT_GRAY
6    var pnCard2 = JPanel()
7    pnCard2.background = Color.PINK
8    pn.add(pnCard1, "mycard1")
9    pn.add(pnCard2, "mycard2")
10   btnShowCard1.addActionListener(ActionListener {
11    val cl = pn.layout as CardLayout
12   cl.show(pn, "mycard1")
13   })
14
```

Figure 14. GridLayout manager

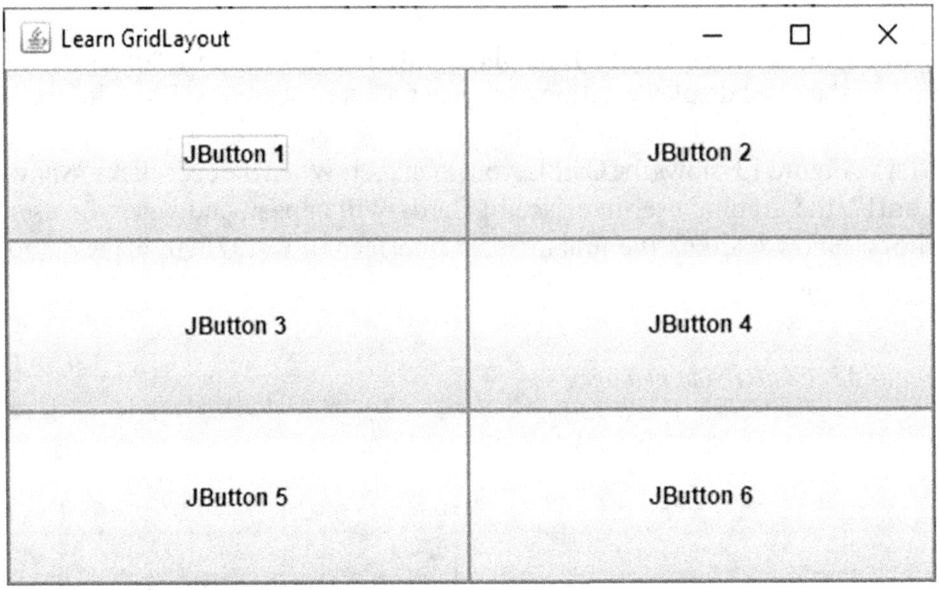

GridLayout Manager

GridLayout allows to arrange controls by row and column. We often use the GridLayout (row, column) constructor to set the number of rows and columns when designing the graphic user interface. The Figure 14 shows how to create a layout with 3 rows and 2 columns.

The code examples in the Kotlin language as below is shown in the Listing 8.

Listing 8. GridLayoutManager

```
1
2
3    //create a JPanel object containing the interface:
4    var pn = JPanel()
5    //Set the layout for this container:
6    //3 rows, 2 columns
7    pn.layout = GridLayout(3, 2)
8    //create JButton, JLabel control
9    var btn1 = JButton("JButton 1")
10   var btn2 = JButton("JButton 2")
11   var btn3 = JButton("JButton 3")
12   var btn4 = JButton("JButton 4")
13   var btn5 = JButton("JButton 5")
14   var btn6 = JButton("JButton 6")
15   //add the control to panel
16   pn.add(btn1)
17   pn.add(btn2)
18   pn.add(btn3)
19   pn.add(btn4)
20   pn.add(btn5)
21   pn.add(btn6)
22
```

Thus, the book introduced several layout managers when designing interfaces, depending on different situations, we can combine many types of layouts.

COMMON CONTROLS

In the previous lesson, the book has shown you how to create a user graphic interface in Kotlin. Now, the book continues guide how to use the common controls, such as JLable, JTextField, JButton and set the event for JButton, JRadioButton, JCheckBox...

JLabel

JLabel is used to display text, image, and not editable the text.

The Table 2 shows constructors and methods of JLabel

Table 2. Constructors and methods of JLabel

Method	Description
JLabel()	Creates a JLabel instance with no image and with an empty string for the title.
JLabel(String text)	Creates a JLabel instance with the specified text.
JLabel(Icon image)	Creates a JLabel instance with the specified image.
text	Set/Get the text string for the label displays.
icon	Set/Get the icon that the label displays.
foreground	Set/Get the text color
background	Set/Get the background color

JTextField

JTextField is used to display the text, and allow text editing.
The Table 3 shows constructors and methods of JTextField.

Table 3. Constructors and methods of JTextField

Method	Description
JTextField()	Constructs a new TextField.
JTextField(String text)	Constructs a new TextField initialized with the specified text.
JTextField(int columns)	Constructs a new empty TextField with the specified number of columns.
text	Set/Get the text for textfield to display.

JButton

JButton is very important to attach event to do something that you want.
The Table 4 shows Constructors and methods of JButton.

Table 4. Constructors and methods of JButton

Method	Description
JButton()	Creates a button with no set text or icon.
JButton(String text)	Creates a button with text.
icon	Set/Get the Icon for button
text	Set/Get the text for textfield to display.
mnemonic	Set/Get the shortcut key for button

Add event for the button is shown in the Listing 9.

Listing 9. Add event for the button

```
1
2   btn.addActionListener(ActionListener {
3   //do something here,coding here
4   })
5
```

The book will continue to add an example of the user graphic interface design using the Gridlayout manager and how to assign events to the Controls. We create the project "QuadraticEquationUI", the user graphic user interface as below is shown in the Figure 15.

Figure 15. Quadratic equation

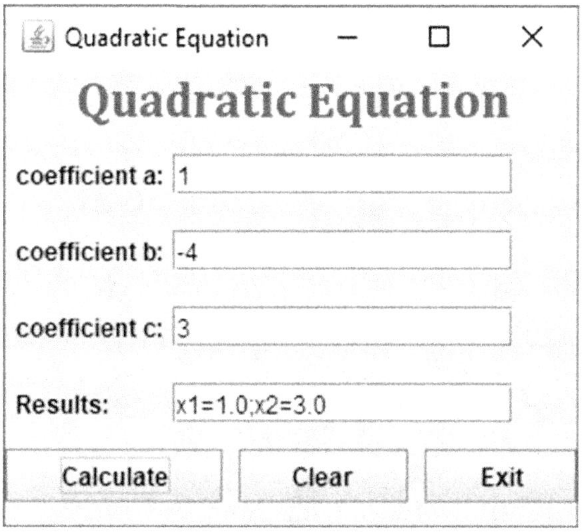

We create Swing GUI with name "MainUI" and set the layout manager is the GridLayout Manager, defined name is pnMain (MainUI.form is the design layout, MainUI class is java code logic), the Figure 16 shows how to layout for the Quadratic equation.

Figure 16. Layout for quadratic equation

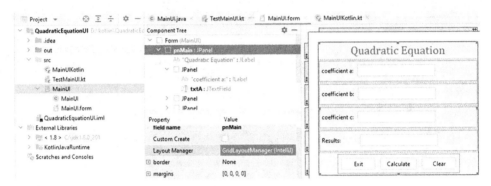

Then about the JPanel of the Coefficient a, Coefficient b, Coefficient c, the result, the buttons, you choose Layout Manager as FlowLayout for all JPanels.

Name for the Controls are shown in the Figure 17 (select the field name in the Property window to define name for the Controls in the MainUI.form).

Figure 17. Names for controls in the quadratic equation

pnMain

	Quadratic Equation	
coefficient a:		txtA
coefficient b:		txtB
coefficient c:		txtC
Results:		txtResult
Calculate	Clear	Exit
btnCalculate	btnClear	btnExit

Now we observe that the MainUI class appears these control variable names as follows in the Listing 10.

Listing 10. QuadraticEquationUI/MainUI

```
1
2     import javax.swing.*;
3     public class MainUI {
4     private JPanel pnMain;
5     private JTextField txtA;
6     private JTextField txtB;
7     private JTextField txtC;
8     private JTextField txtResult;
9     private JButton btnCalculate;
10    private JButton btnClear;
11    private JButton btnExit;
12    }
13
14
```

We change private visibility modifier in MainUI class to protected as below is shown in the Listing 11.

Listing 11. QuadraticEquationUI/MainUI

```
1
2     import javax.swing.*;
3     public class MainUI {
4     protected JPanel pnMain;
5     protected JTextField txtA;
6     protected JTextField txtB;
7     protected JTextField txtC;
8     protected JTextField txtResult;
9     protected JButton btnCalculate;
10    protected JButton btnClear;
11    protected JButton btnExit;
12    }
13
14
```

Then we create a MainUIKotlin class extends from MainUI java class as below is shown in the Listing 12.

Listing 12. QuadraticEquationUI/MainUIKotlin

```
1
2    import javax.swing.JFrame
3    class MainUIKotlin: MainUI{
4    var frame: JFrame
5    constructor() {
6    frame = JFrame("Quadratic Equation")
7    frame.contentPane = pnMain
8    }
9    //this method uses to show the UI
10   fun showUI() {
11   //set 'X' corner button to close the window
12   frame.defaultCloseOperation =JFrame.EXIT_ON_CLOSE
13   //set size for window: width=300, height=260
14   frame.setSize(300, 260)
15   //set centering desktop for the window
16   frame.setLocationRelativeTo(null)
17   //show the window
18   frame.isVisible = true
19   }
20   }
21
```

We continue to create TestMainUI.kt kotlin to create the window as follows is shown in the Listing 13.

Listing 13. QuadraticEquationUI/TestMainUI.kt

```
1    fun main(args: Array<String>) {
2    var mainUI=MainUIKotlin()
3    mainUI.showUI()
4    }
5
```

Run the code, we get the graphic user interface as below is shown in the Figure 18 (but without event for the Buttons).

Figure 18. Quadratic equation

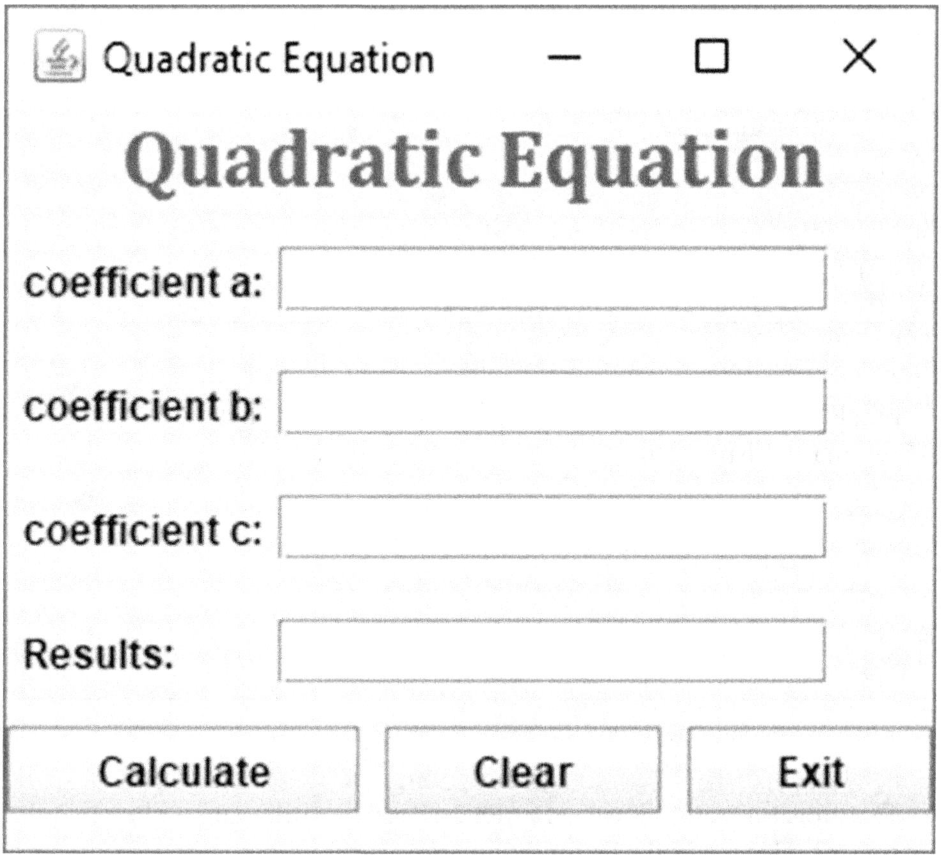

We need to create events for Buttons for Exit, Clear and Calculate button. In the MainUIKotlin class, we modify the code.

The Listing 14 shows how to add event for button exit

```
constructor() {
frame = JFrame("Quadratic Equation")
frame.contentPane = pnMain
btnExit.addActionListener { System.exit(0) }
}
```

Similarly, we add the event for the clear Button, it is shown in the Listing 15.

Listing 15. QuadraticEquationUI/MainUIKotlin

```
constructor() {
  frame = JFrame("Quadratic Equation")
  frame.contentPane = pnMain
  btnExit.addActionListener { System.exit(0) }
  btnClear.addActionListener {
    txtA.text = ""
    txtB.text = ""
    txtC.text = ""
    txtResult.text = ""
    txtA.requestFocus()
  }
}
```

Finally, we repeat the operation to set event for Calculate button, it is shown in the Listing 16.

Listing 16. QuadraticEquationUI/MainUIKotlin

```
btnCalculate.addActionListener{
  processQuaraticEquation()
}
```

The processQuarateEquation function does the following is shown in the Listing 17. This method will solve and argue cases with quadratic equations.

Listing 17. QuadraticEquationUI/MainUIKotlin/processQuarateEquation

```
1   private fun processQuaraticEquation() {
2   var a = txtA.text.toDouble()
3   var b = txtB.text.toDouble()
4   var c = txtC.text.toDouble()
5   if (a == 0.0) {
6   var msg = "a must be different from 0"
7   JOptionPane.showMessageDialog(null, msg)
8   }
9   if (a != 0.0) {
10  var delta = Math.pow(b, 2.0) - 4 * a * c
11  if (delta < 0)
12  txtResult.text = "No solution!"
13  else if (delta == 0.0)
14  {
15  var result= "x1=x2=" + -b / 2 * a
16  txtResult.text =result
17  }
18  else {
19  var x1 = (-b - Math.sqrt(delta)) / (2 * a)
20  var x2 = (-b + Math.sqrt(delta)) / (2 * a)
21  txtResult.text = "x1=$x1;x2=$x2"
22  }
23  }
24  }
25  }
```

Here is the full of coding for MainUIKotlin class, and the whole codes are shown in the Listing 18.

Listing 18. QuadraticEquationUI/MainUIKotlin

```
1
2    import javax.swing.JFrame
3    import javax.swing.JOptionPane
4    class MainUIKotlin: MainUI{
5    var frame: JFrame
6    constructor() {
7    frame = JFrame("Quadratic Equation")
8    frame.contentPane = pnMain
9    btnExit.addActionListener { System.exit(0) }
10    btnClear.addActionListener {
11    txtA.text = ""
12    txtB.text = ""
13    txtC.text = ""
14    txtResult.text = ""
15    txtA.requestFocus()
16    }
17    btnCalculate.addActionListener{
18    processQuaraticEquation()
19    }
20    }
21    private fun processQuaraticEquation() {
22    var a = txtA.text.toDouble()
23    var b = txtB.text.toDouble()
24    var c = txtC.text.toDouble()
25    if (a == 0.0) {
26    var msg = "a must be different from 0"
27    JOptionPane.showMessageDialog(null, msg)
28    }
29    if (a != 0.0) {
30    var delta = Math.pow(b, 2.0) - 4 * a * c
31    if (delta < 0)
32    txtResult.text = "No solution!"
33    else if (delta == 0.0)
34    {
35    var result= "x1=x2=" + -b / 2 * a
36    txtResult.text =result
37    }
38    else {
39    var x1 = (-b - Math.sqrt(delta)) / (2 * a)
40    var x2 = (-b + Math.sqrt(delta)) / (2 * a)
41    txtResult.text = "x1=$x1;x2=$x2"
42    }
43    }
44    }
45    //this method uses to show the UI
46    fun showUI() {
47    //set 'X' corner button to close the window
48    frame.defaultCloseOperation =JFrame.EXIT_ON_CLOSE
49    //set size for window: width=300, height=260
50    frame.setSize(300, 260)
51    //set centering desktop for the window
52    frame.setLocationRelativeTo(null)
53    //show the window
54    frame.isVisible = true
55    }
56    }
57
```

Run the program, we will have the graphic user interface as above requirements, we test some test cases in the Figure 19.

Figure 19. Test cases for quadratic equation

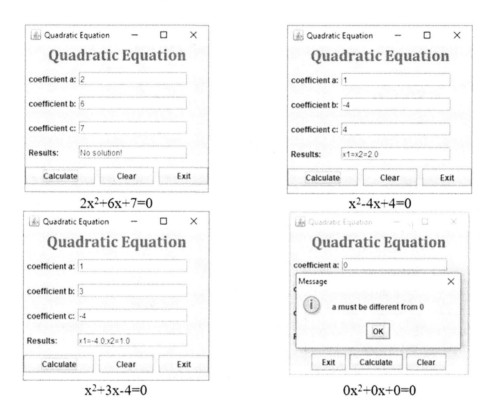

$$2x^2+6x+7=0 \qquad x^2-4x+4=0$$

$$x^2+3x-4=0 \qquad 0x^2+0x+0=0$$

The book has completed the tutorial on how to create an interface in Kotlin, how to assign events, layout the interface, use GridLayout. Next lesson, the book will introduce the JCheckBox and JRadioButton. The source code can be downloaded the the link: https://github.com/thanhtd32/kotlin/tree/main/QuadraticEquationUI.

JCheckBox

JCheckBox can be selected or deselected, and which displays its state to the user. By convention, any number of check boxes in a group can be selected. The Figure 20 shows the example for using JCheckBox.

Figure 20. JCheckBox: Language favorites

The Table 5 shows Constructors and methods of JCheckBox.

Table 5. Constructors and methods of JCheckBox

Method	Description
JCheckBox()	Creates an initially unselected check box button with no text, no icon.
JCheckBox(String text)	Creates an initially unselected check box with text.
isSelected	Set/Get the state of the checkbox.
text	Set/Get the text this component will display.
foreground	Set/Get the text color
background	Set/Get the background color

We design a software with CheckBoxUI name to confirm our favorite programming language as follows is shown in the Figure 21.

Figure 21. Design for language favorites GUI

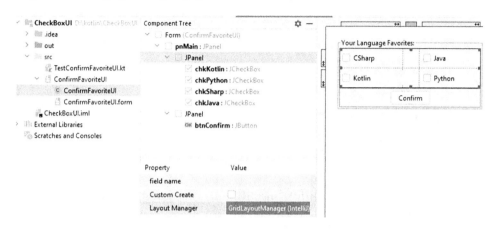

Create the ConfirmFavoriteUI form then drag and drop the controls as above.

pnMain is Border layout manager.

JPanel for 4 JCheckBox is Grid layout manager and we set the name for the JCheckBox is shown in the Table 6.

Table 6. Define the name for JCheckBox

Control	Name	Description
JCheckBox	chkKotlin	Show the text Kotlin language
JCheckBox	chkPython	Show the text Python language
JCheckBox	chkSharp	Show the text C# language
JCheckBox	chkJava	Show the text Java language
JButton	btnConfirm	Button to confirm language favorites

The code of ConfirmFavoriteUI class is automatic generating as below is shown in the Listing 19.

Listing 19. CheckBoxUI/ConfirmFavoriteUI

```
1
2    import javax.swing.*;
3    public class ConfirmFavoriteUI {
4    private JPanel pnMain;
5    private JCheckBox chkKotlin;
6    private JCheckBox chkPython;
7    private JCheckBox chkSharp;
8    private JCheckBox chkJava;
9    private JButton btnConfirm;
10   }
11
```

We change private visibility modifier to protected, it is shown in the Listing 20.

Listing 20. CheckBoxUI/ConfirmFavoriteUI

```
1
2    import javax.swing.*;
3    public class ConfirmFavoriteUI {
4    protected JPanel pnMain;
5    protected JCheckBox chkKotlin;
6    protected JCheckBox chkPython;
7    protected JCheckBox chkSharp;
8    protected JCheckBox chkJava;
9    protected JButton btnConfirm;
10   }
11
```

And then we create ConfirmFavoriteUIKotlin class extends from ConfirmFavoriteUI java class, whole code of the class as follows are shown in the Listing 21.

Listing 21. CheckBoxUI/ConfirmFavoriteUIKotlin

```
1
2
3      import java.awt.event.ActionListener
4      import javax.swing.JFrame
5      import javax.swing.JOptionPane
6      class ConfirmFavoriteUIKotlin:ConfirmFavoriteUI {
7      var frame: JFrame
8      constructor() {
9      frame = JFrame("Learn Checkbox")
10     frame.contentPane = pnMain
11     btnConfirm.addActionListener(
12     ActionListener {
13      processConfirmation()
14      })
15     }
16     private fun processConfirmation() {
17     val builder = StringBuilder()
18     if (chkJava.isSelected) {
19     builder.append(chkJava.text)
20     builder.append("\n")
21     }
22     if (chkKotlin.isSelected) {
23     builder.append(chkKotlin.text)
24     builder.append("\n")
25     }
26     if (chkPython.isSelected) {
27     builder.append(chkPython.text)
28     builder.append("\n")
29     }
30     if (chkSharp.isSelected) {
31     builder.append(chkSharp.text)
32     builder.append("\n")
33     }
34     JOptionPane.showMessageDialog(null, builder)
35     }
36     //this method uses to show the UI
37     fun showUI() {
38     //set 'X' corner button to close the window
39     frame.defaultCloseOperation =JFrame.EXIT_ON_CLOSE
40     //set size for window: width=300, height=150
41     frame.setSize(300, 150)
42     //set centering desktop for the window
43     frame.setLocationRelativeTo(null)
44     //show the window
45     frame.isVisible = true
46     }
47     }
48
```

Create TestConfirmFavoriteUI.kt and write the code to run the application, it is shown in the Listing 22.

Listing 22. CheckBoxUI/TestConfirmFavoriteUI.kt

```
1   fun main(args: Array<String>) {
2   var cfui=ConfirmFavoriteUIKotlin()
3   cfui.showUI()
4   }
5
```

All done, we run the program and test some test cases, they are shown in the Figure 22.

Figure 22. Test cases for language favorites
The source code can be downloaded at the link: https://github.com/thanhtd32/kotlin/tree/main/ CheckBoxUI.

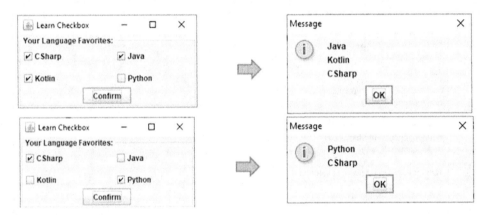

JRadioButton

JRadioButton can be selected or deselected, and which displays its state to the user. Used with a ButtonGroup object to create a group of buttons in which only one button at a time can be selected.

The Table 7 shows Constructors and methods of JRadioButton.

334

Table 7. Constructors and methods of JRadioButton

Method	Description
JRadioButton ()	Creates an initially unselected JRadioButton with no text, no icon.
JRadioButton(String text)	Creates an initially unselected JRadioButton with text.
isSelected	Set/Get the state of the checkbox.
text	Set/Get the text this component will display.
foreground	Set/Get the text color
background	Set/Get the background color

We design a project with RadioButtonUI name to change the Image Icon as follows (Rose and Orchid) is shown in the Figure 23.

Figure 23. JRadioButton: Change image

We design the graphic user interface for project is shown in the Figure 24.

Figure 24. Design layout for change image

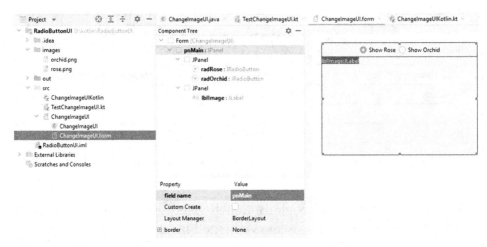

We set the layout manager for pnMain is Border Layout.

The JPanel contains the JRadioButtons, we set the layout manager is FlowLayout.

The JPanel contains the JLabel, we set the layout manager Border layout and the lblImage is placed in the center.

Create the images directory and save 2 images rose.png and orchid.png into this directory. And we define the name for controls is shown in the Table 8.

Table 8. Define the name for the controls

Control	Name	Description
JRadioButton	radRose	RadioButton to show Rose
JRadioButton	radOrchid	RadioButton to show Orchid
JLabel	lblImage	Label to show images following the radiobutton

We design the graphic user interface as above by dragging and dropping the controls into the Panel.

The code of ChangeImageUI class is automatic generating as below is shown in the Listing 23.

Listing 23. RadioButtonUI/ChangeImageUI

```
1
2
3    import javax.swing.*;
4    public class ChangeImageUI {
5    private JPanel pnMain;
6    private JRadioButton radRose;
7    private JRadioButton radOrchid;
8    private JLabel lblImage;
9
10   }
11
```

We change private visibility modifier to protected and add more icon variable (icon is ImageIcon), it is shown in the Listing 24.

Listing 24. RadioButtonUI/ChangeImageUI

```
1
2
3    import javax.swing.*;
4    public class ChangeImageUI {
5    protected JPanel pnMain;
6    protected JRadioButton radRose;
7    protected JRadioButton radOrchid;
8    protected JLabel lblImage;
9    protected ImageIcon icon;
10   }
11
```

ImageIcon will be used to show the Image corresponding to the selected JRadioButtons.

We create ChangeImageUIKotlin class extends ChangeImageU java class, using JFrame is the same previous lesson, and we also assign events to 2 JRadioButtons, it is shown in the Listing 25.

Listing 25. RadioButtonUI/ChangeImageUIKotlin

```
1    radRose.addActionListener(
2    ActionListener {
3    if (radRose.isSelected()) {
4    icon = ImageIcon("images/rose.png")
5    lblImage.setIcon(icon)
6    }
7    })
8
```

To create an ImageIcon object and set the image for this Icon, we use the command: icon = ImageIcon("images/rose.png").

To assign this Icon to JLabel we call the method: lblImage.setIcon(icon).

The final source code of the ChangeImageUIKotlin class, it is shown in the Listing 26.

Listing 26. RadioButtonUI/ChangeImageUIKotlin

```
1
2    import java.awt.event.ActionListener
3    import javax.swing.ButtonGroup
4    import javax.swing.ImageIcon
5    import javax.swing.JFrame
6    class ChangeImageUIKotlin:ChangeImageUI{
7    var frame: JFrame
8    constructor() {
9    frame = JFrame("Change Image- JRadioButton")
10   frame.contentPane = pnMain
11   val bg = ButtonGroup()
12   bg.add(radRose)
13   bg.add(radOrchid)
14   //set default image for
15    icon = ImageIcon("images/rose.png")
16   lblImage.setIcon(icon)
17   //check if the Rose JRadioButton is checked
18    radRose.addActionListener(
19   ActionListener {
20    if (radRose.isSelected()) {
21   icon = ImageIcon("images/rose.png")
22   lblImage.setIcon(icon)
23    }
24    })
25   //check if the Orchid JRadioButton is checked
26    radOrchid.addActionListener(
27   ActionListener {
28    if (radOrchid.isSelected()) {
29   icon = ImageIcon("images/orchid.png")
30   lblImage.setIcon(icon)
31    }
32    })
33    }
34   //this method uses to show the UI
35   fun showUI() {
36   //set 'X' corner button to close the window
37   frame.defaultCloseOperation = JFrame.EXIT_ON_CLOSE
38   //set size for window: width=500, height=300
39   frame.setSize(500, 300)
40   //set centering desktop for the window
41   frame.setLocationRelativeTo(null)
42   //show the window
43   frame.isVisible = true
44    }
45    }
46
```

We create TestChangeImageUI.kt kotlin file and write main function to run the project, it is shown in the Listing 27.

Listing 27. RadioButtonUI/TestChangeImageUI.kt

```
1   fun main(args: Array<String>) {
2   var ciu= ChangeImageUIKotlin()
3   ciu.showUI()
4   }
```

Run the program and select the JRadioButton to change the image, it is shown in the Figure 25.

Figure 25. Test cases for change image
The source code can be downloaded at the link: https://github.com/thanhtd32/kotlin/tree/main/RadioButtonUI.

ADVANCED CONTROLS

In this part, the book continues guide how to use the advanced controls, such as JComboBox, JList, JTable, JTree.

JComboBox

JComboBox combines a button or editable field and a drop-down list. The user can select a value from the drop-down list, which appears at the user's request. If you make the combo box editable, then the combo box includes an editable field into which the user can type a value. Example for JComboBox is shown in the Figure 26.

Figure 26. Employee GUI

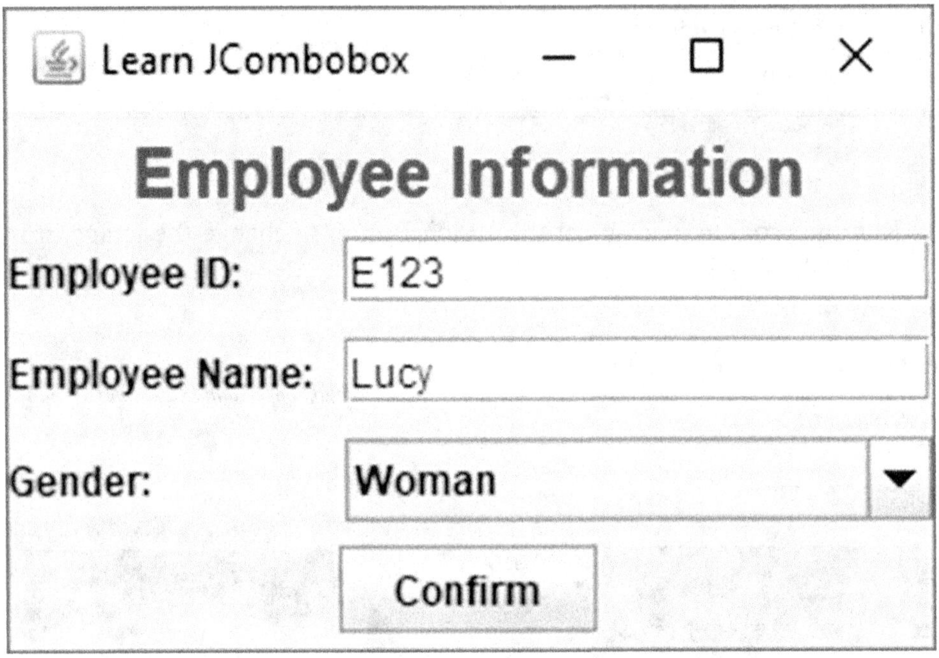

The Table 9 shows Constructors and methods of JComboBox.

Table 9. Constructors and methods of JComboBox

Method	Description
JComboBox()	Creates a JComboBox with a default data model.
void addItem(E item)	Adds an item to the item list.
selectedItem	Set/Get the selected item.
selectedIndex	Set/Get the selected index
void removeItem(Object anObject)	Removes an item from the item list.
void removeItemAt(int anIndex)	Removes the item at anIndex This method works only if the JComboBox uses a mutable data model.
void removeAllItems()	Removes all items from the item list.
void addItemListener (ItemListener aListener)	Adds an ItemListener.

We design the graphic user interface with JComboBoxUI name to confirm Employee Information as follows is shown in the Figure 27.

Figure 27. Design for employee GUI

We create the EmployeeUI form then drag and drop the controls as above. pnMain is Border layout manager.

JPanel for Employee Id, Name and Gender is Grid layout manager. And this JPanel is placed center of the pnMain. The name for controls is shown in the Table 10.

Table 10. Define the name for controls

Control	Name	Description
JTextField	txtEmployeeID	Store and show the Employee ID
JTextField	txtEmployeeName	Store and show the Employee Name
JComboBox	cboEmployeeGender	Store and show the Employee Gender
JButton	btnConfirm	Button to confirm Employee information

We create the Employee kotin class as below is shown in the Listing 28.

Listing 28. JComboBoxUI/Employee

```
1   class Employee {
2   public var EmployeeID:String=""
3   get() {return field}
4   set(value) {field=value}
5   public var EmployeeName:String=""
6   get() {return field}
7   set(value) {field=value}
8   public var EmployeeGender=""
9   get() {return field}
10  set(value) {field=value}
11  constructor()
12  constructor(EmployeeID: String,
13  EmployeeName: String,
14  EmployeeGender: String) {
15  this.EmployeeID = EmployeeID
16  this.EmployeeName = EmployeeName
17  this.EmployeeGender = EmployeeGender
18  }
19  override fun toString(): String {
20  return "Employee ID:$EmployeeID\n" +
21  "Employee Name:$EmployeeName\n" +
22  "Employee Gender:$EmployeeGender"
23  }
24  }
25  }
```

We open the EmployeeUI java class, the code is generated as below is shown in the Listing 29.

Listing 29. JComboBoxUI/EmployeeUI

```
1
2   import javax.swing.*;
3   public class EmployeeUI {
4   private JPanel pnMain;
5   private JButton btnAdd;
6   private JTextField txtEmployeeID;
7   private JTextField txtEmployeeName;
8   private JComboBox cboEmployeeGender;
9   private JButton btnConfirm;
10  }
11
```

We change private visibility modifier to protected as below in shown in the Listing 30.

Listing 30. JComboBoxUI/EmployeeUI

```
1
2
3     import javax.swing.*;
4     public class EmployeeUI {
5     protected JPanel pnMain;
6     protected JButton btnAdd;
7     protected JTextField txtEmployeeID;
8     protected JTextField txtEmployeeName;
9     protected JComboBox cboEmployeeGender;
10    protected JButton btnConfirm;
11    }
12
```

And then we create EmployeeUIKotlin class extends EmployeeUI java class and write the function for Confirmation Employee in this class as follows is shown in the Listing 31.

Listing 31. JComboBoxUI/EmployeeUIKotlin/processConfirmation

```
1
2     private fun processConfirmation() {
3     //create Employee object(Kotlin class)
4     var em = Employee()
5     em.EmployeeID = txtEmployeeID.getText()
6     em.EmployeeName = txtEmployeeName.getText()
7     //check if user chooses the item in the JCombobox
8     if (cboEmployeeGender.selectedIndex!= -1) {
9     var gender =
10    cboEmployeeGender.selectedItem as String
11    em.EmployeeGender = gender
12    }
13    JOptionPane.showMessageDialog(null, em)
14    }
```

cboEmployeeGender.selectedIndex!=-1 use to check if user choose the item in the JCombobox.

All done code of the EmployeeUIKotlin class is shown in the Listing 32.

Listing 32. JComboBoxUI/EmployeeUIKotlin

```
1
2
3     import java.awt.event.ActionListener
4     import javax.swing.JFrame
5     import javax.swing.JOptionPane
6     class EmployeeUIKotlin:EmployeeUI {
7     var frame: JFrame
8     constructor() {
9     frame = JFrame("Learn JCombobox")
10    frame.contentPane = pnMain
11    //add item for JCombobox
12    cboEmployeeGender.addItem("Woman")
13    cboEmployeeGender.addItem("Man")
14    btnConfirm.addActionListener(
15    ActionListener {
16    processConfirmation()
17    })
18    }
19    private fun processConfirmation() {
20    //create Employee object(Kotlin class)
21    var em = Employee()
22    em.EmployeeID = txtEmployeeID.getText()
23    em.EmployeeName = txtEmployeeName.getText()
24    //check if user chooses the item
25    if (cboEmployeeGender.selectedIndex!= -1) {
26    var gender =
27    cboEmployeeGender.selectedItem as String
28    em.EmployeeGender = gender
29    }
30    JOptionPane.showMessageDialog(null, em)
31    }
32    //this method uses to show the UI
33    fun showUI() {
34    //set 'X' corner button to close the window
35    frame.defaultCloseOperation = JFrame.EXIT_ON_CLOSE
36    //set size for window: width=300, height=200
37    frame.setSize(300, 200)
38    //set centering desktop for the window
39    frame.setLocationRelativeTo(null)
40    //show the window
41    frame.isVisible = true
42    }
43    }
44
45
```

We create TestEmployeeUI.kt kotlin with main method to run application, it is shown in the Listing 33.

Listing 33. JComboBoxUI/TestEmployeeUI.kt

```
1     fun main(args: Array<String>) {
2     var eui= EmployeeUIKotlin()
3     eui.showUI()
4     }
```

We run the program and test some cases. It is shown in the Figure 28.

Figure 28. Test cases for Employee GUI
The source code can be downloaded at the link: *https://github.com/thanhtd32/kotlin/tree/main/ JComboBoxUI.*

JList

JList displays a list of objects and allows the user to select one or more items. A separate model, ListModel, maintains the contents of the list. It can display an array or Vector of objects by using the JList constructor or call addItem method.

The Figure 29 shows the example for using the JList.

Figure 29. JList for employee GUI

The Table 11 shows Constructors and methods of JList.

Table 11. Constructors and methods of JList

Method	Description
JList()	Constructs a JList with an empty, read-only, model.
JList(E[] listData)	Constructs a JList that displays the elements in the specified array.
selectedIndex	Set/Get a selected index from the list.
selectedValue	Set/Get a seleceted value from the list.
void setListData(E[] listData)	Constructs a read-only ListModel from an array of items.
void setListData(Vector<? extends E> listData)	Constructs a read-only ListModel from a Vector and calls setModel with this model.
void setModel (ListModel<E> model)	Sets the model that represents the contents or "value" of the list.
void clearSelection()	Clears the selection
void addListSelectionListener (ListSelectionListener listener)	Adds a listener to the list, to be notified each time a change to the selection occurs.

We design the graphic user interface with JListUI project name for Employee Information as follows is shown in the Figure 30.

Figure 30. Design employee GUI

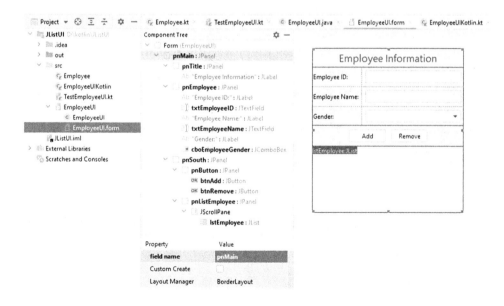

Create the EmployeeUI form then drag and drop the controls as above.

JPanel(pnMain) is Border Layout manager.

JPanel(pnTitle) is Flow Layout manager and set it to North of the pnMain.

JPanel(pnEmployee) for Employee Id, Name and Gender is Grid layout manager. And this JPanel is placed center of the pnMain.

JPanel(pnSouth) contains JButton add, remove and JList is Border Layout manager, and this JPanel is set South in the pnMain.

JPanel(pnButton) is Flow Layout manager, and this JPanel is set North of the pnSouth.

JPanel(pnListEmployee) is Border Layout manager, and this JPanel is set Center of the pnSouth. We have to use JScrollPane with JList, and set JScrollPane into the Center of the pnListEmployee.

The Table 12 shows the name defining for the controls.

Table 12. Define name for the controls

Control	Name	Description
JTextField	txtEmployeeID	Store and show the Employee ID
JTextField	txtEmployeeName	Store and show the Employee Name
JComboBox	cboEmployeeGender	Store and show the Employee Gender
JButton	btnAdd	Button to add new Employee to JList
JButton	btnRemove	Button to remove selected Employee
JList	lstEmployee	JList to show list Employee

The program allows users to enter Employee's information, press the "Add" button, and Empoyee information will be added in the JList.

Each time user clicks on each Employee in the JList, the details of the Employee will be displayed again into the JTextField and JComboBox.

Pressing the "Remove" Button, it will remove Employee from the JList.

We create Employee kotin class as below is shown in the Listing 34.

Listing 34. JListUI/Employee

```
1
2    class Employee {
3    public var EmployeeID:String=""
4    get() {return field}
5    set(value) {field=value}
6    public var EmployeeName:String=""
7    get() {return field}
8    set(value) {field=value}
9    public var EmployeeGender=""
10   get() {return field}
11   set(value) {field=value}
12   constructor()
13   constructor(EmployeeID: String,
14   EmployeeName: String,
15   EmployeeGender: String) {
16   this.EmployeeID = EmployeeID
17   this.EmployeeName = EmployeeName
18   this.EmployeeGender = EmployeeGender
19   }
20   override fun toString(): String {
21   return "$EmployeeName"
22   }
23   }
24
```

We open the EmployeeUI java class, the code is generated as below is shown in the Listing 35.

Listing 35. JListUI/EmployeeUI

```
1
2
3    import javax.swing.*;
4    public class EmployeeUI {
5    private JTextField txtEmployeeID;
6    private JTextField txtEmployeeName;
7    private JComboBox cboEmployeeGender;
8    private JButton btnAdd;
9    private JButton btnRemove;
10   private JList lstEmployee;
11   private JPanel pnMain;
12   private JPanel pnSouth;
13   private JPanel pnEmployee;
14   private JPanel pnButton;
15   private JPanel pnListEmployee;
16   private JPanel pnTitle;
17   }
18
```

We change private visibility modifier to protected, it is shown in the Listing 36.

Listing 36. JListUI/EmployeeUI

```
1
2    import javax.swing.*;
3    public class EmployeeUI {
4    protected JTextField txtEmployeeID;
5    protected JTextField txtEmployeeName;
6    protected JComboBox cboEmployeeGender;
7    protected JButton btnAdd;
8    protected JButton btnRemove;
9    protected JList lstEmployee;
10   protected JPanel pnMain;
11   protected JPanel pnSouth;
12   protected JPanel pnEmployee;
13   protected JPanel pnButton;
14   protected JPanel pnListEmployee;
15   protected JPanel pnTitle;
16   }
17
18
```

We create EmployeeUIKotlin class extends EmployeeUI java class. To set model for JList we write code like the Listing 37.

Listing 37. JListUI/EmployeeUIKotlin

```
1    var model: DefaultListModel<Employee>
2    //assign model for JList
3    model = DefaultListModel()
4    lstEmployee.setModel(model)
5
```

We create the addEmployeeToList() function to add an Employee to the JList when the user clicks the Add button, it is shown in the Listing 38.

Listing 38. JListUI/EmployeeUIKotlin/addEmployeeToList

```
1    private fun addEmployeeToList() {
2    var em = Employee()
3    em.EmployeeID = txtEmployeeID.text
4    em.EmployeeName = txtEmployeeName.text
5    if (cboEmployeeGender.selectedIndex != -1) {
6    var gender=cboEmployeeGender.selectedItem
7    em.EmployeeGender = gender.toString()
8    }
9    model.addElement(em)
10   }
11
```

We create the removeEmployee() function to remove selected Employee from the JList when the user clicks the Add Remove, it is shown in the Listing 39.

Listing 39. JListUI/EmployeeUIKotlin/removeEmployee

```
1  private fun removeEmployee() {
2  var obj = lstEmployee.selectedValue
3  if (obj != null) {
4  model.removeElement(obj)
5  }
6  }
7
```

Finally, We create the showDetailEmployee() function to show details of the selected Employee from the JList when the user clicks on the JList, it is shown in the Listing 40.

Listing 40. JListUI/EmployeeUIKotlin/showDetailEmployee

```
1  private fun showDetailEmployee() {
2  var obj = lstEmployee.selectedValue
3  if (obj != null) {
4  var em = obj as Employee
5  txtEmployeeID.text = em.EmployeeID
6  txtEmployeeName.text = em.EmployeeName
7  var gender = em.EmployeeGender
8  cboEmployeeGender.selectedItem = gender
9  }
10 }
11
```

Here is the detailed program of the EmployeeUIKotlin class, how to create JFrame and the events we apply similar to the previous examples. The full of code is shown in the Listing 41.

Listing 41(a). JListUI/EmployeeUIKotlin

```
1    import javax.swing.DefaultListModel
2    import javax.swing.JFrame
3    class EmployeeUIKotlin:EmployeeUI {
4    var frame: JFrame
5    var model: DefaultListModel<Employee>
6    constructor() {
7    frame = JFrame("Learn JList")
8    frame.contentPane = pnMain
9    //add item for JCombobox
10   cboEmployeeGender.addItem("Woman")
11   cboEmployeeGender.addItem("Man")
12   //assign model for JList
13   model = DefaultListModel()
14   lstEmployee.setModel(model)
15   btnAdd.addActionListener {
16   addEmployeeToList()
17   }
18   btnRemove.addActionListener {
19   removeEmployee()
20   }
21   lstEmployee.addListSelectionListener {
22   showDetailEmployee()
23   }
24   }
25   //show detail employee when user click on JList
26   private fun showDetailEmployee() {
27   var obj = lstEmployee.selectedValue
28   if (obj != null) {
29   var em = obj as Employee
```

Listing 41(b). JListUI/EmployeeUIKotlin

30	txtEmployeeID.*text* = em.EmployeeID
31	txtEmployeeName.*text* = em.EmployeeName
32	var gender = em.EmployeeGender
33	cboEmployeeGender.*selectedItem* = gender
34	}
35	}
36	//*remove the selected employee*
37	private fun removeEmployee() {
38	var obj = lstEmployee.*selectedValue*
39	if (obj != null) {
40	model.removeElement(obj)
41	}
42	}
43	//*add a new employee into the JList*
44	private fun addEmployeeToList() {
45	var em = Employee()
46	em.EmployeeID = txtEmployeeID.*text*
47	em.EmployeeName = txtEmployeeName.*text*
48	if (cboEmployeeGender.*selectedIndex* != -1) {
49	var gender=cboEmployeeGender.*selectedItem*
50	em.EmployeeGender = gender.toString()
51	}
52	model.addElement(em)
53	}
54	//*this method uses to show the UI*
55	fun showUI() {
56	//*set 'X' corner button to close the window*
57	frame.*defaultCloseOperation* = JFrame.*EXIT_ON_CLOSE*
58	
59	//*set size for window: width=300, height=200*
60	frame.setSize(300, 380)
61	//*set centering desktop for the window*
62	frame.setLocationRelativeTo(null)
63	//*show the window*
64	frame.*isVisible* = true
65	}
66	}
67	}

Finally, we create TestEmployeeUI.kt kotlin file with main method to run the program, let's see the Listing 42.

Listing 42. JListUI/TestEmployeeUI.kt

1	fun main(args: Array<String>) {
2	var eui= EmployeeUIKotlin()
3	eui.showUI()
4	}

We run program and test some cases:

- Add a new Employee into the JList
- View detail of the Employee information when user click on the JList
- Remove selected Employee from the JList

The Figure 31 shows the Employee JList GUI, we take some test cases.

Figure 31. Test case for employee JList GUI
The source code can be downloaded at the link: https://github.com/thanhtd32/kotlin/tree/main/JListUI.

JTable

In the previous lessons, Readers already have known the graphic user interface design as well as the event handling in Kotlin. The book continues to show an advanced control that is JTable so that you can display list data as well to reinforce the knowledge you have learned.

JTable is used to display and edit regular two-dimensional tables of cells. It is shown in the Figure 32.

Figure 32. JTable

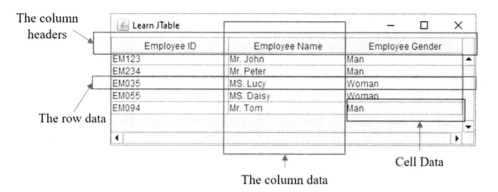

Figure 32 illustrates a JTable with 3 columns: Employee ID, Employee Name and Employee Gender. The data of each Employee is displayed on each line.

Table 13 shows Constructors and methods of JTable.

Table 13. Constructors and methods of JTable

Method	Description
JTable()	Constructs a default JTable that is initialized with a default data model, a default column model, and a default selection model.
JTable(TableModel dm)	Constructs a JTable that is initialized with dm as the data model, a default column model, and a default selection model.
selectedRow	Get the index of the first selected row, -1 if no row is selected.
selectedColumn	Get the index of the first selected column, -1 if no column is selected.
Object getValueAt (int row, int column)	Returns the cell value at row and column.
void addMouseListener (MouseListener l)	Adds the specified mouse listener to receive mouse events from this component. If listener l is null, no exception is thrown and no action is performed.
void addKeyListener (KeyListener l)	Adds the specified key listener to receive key events from this component. If l is null, no exception is thrown and no action is performed.

The Listing 43 illustrates how to use DefaultTableModel in JTable (demonstration for the Figure 32).

Listing 43. Demostration for JTable

1	//Declare the DefaultTableModel object
2	var tableModel: DefaultTableModel
3	//Declare the JTable object
4	var table: JTable
5	//Create the DefaultTableModel object
6	tableModel = DefaultTableModel()
7	//add 3 columns for DefaultTableModel
8	tableModel.addColumn("Employee ID")
9	tableModel.addColumn("Employee Name")
10	tableModel.addColumn("Employee Gender")
11	//Assign tableModel for table
12	table = JTable(tableModel)
13	//add new rows for JTable
14	var arr1 = arrayOf("EM123", "Mr. John", "Man")
15	tableModel.addRow(arr1)
16	var arr2 = arrayOf("EM035", "MS. Lucy", "Woman")
17	tableModel.addRow(arr2)
18	var arr3 = arrayOf("EM055", "MS. Daisy", "Woman")
19	tableModel.addRow(arr3)
20	var arr4 = arrayOf("EM094", "Mr. Tom", "Man")
21	tableModel.addRow(arr4)

DefaultTableModel is an implementation of TableModel that uses a Vector of Vectors to store the cell value objects.

The Table 14 shows Constructors and methods of DefaultTableModel.

Table 14. Constructors and methods of DefaultTableModel

Method	Description
DefaultTableModel()	Constructs a DefaultTableModel which is a table of zero columns and zero rows.
void addColumn(Object columnName)	Adds a column to the model.
void addRow(Object[] rowData)	Adds a row to the end of the model.
void addRow(Vector rowData)	Adds a row to the end of the model.
columnCount	Set/Get the number of columns
rowCount	Set/Get the number of rows in this data table.
Object getValueAt(int row, int column)	Returns an attribute value for the cell at row and column.
void insertRow(int r, Object[] rowData)	Inserts a row at r index in the model.
void insertRow(int r, Vector rowData)	Inserts a row at r index in the model.
void removeRow(int r)	Removes the row at r index
void setValueAt(Object aValue, int row, int column)	Sets the object value for the cell at column and row.

We design the graphic user interface with JTableUI project name for Employee Information as follows is shown in the Figure 33.

Figure 33. JTable: Employee

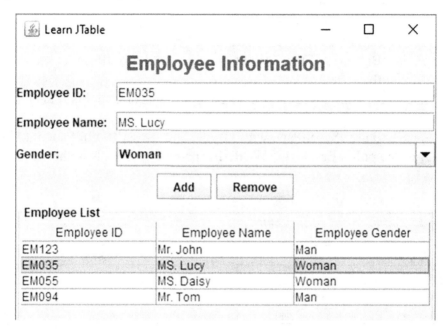

We create EmployeeUI and design the controls is shown in the Figure 34.

Figure 34. Desgin JTable for employee

Create the EmployeeUI form then drag and drop the controls as above.

JPanel(pnMain) is Border Layout manager.

JPanel(pnTitle) is Flow Layout manager and set it to North of the pnMain.

JPanel(pnEmployee) for Employee Id, Name and Gender is Grid layout manager. And this JPanel is placed center of the pnMain.

JPanel(pnSouth) contains JButton add, remove and JList is Border Layout manager, and this JPanel is set South in the pnMain.

JPanel(pnButton) is Flow Layout manager, and this JPanel is set North of the pnSouth.

JPanel(pnListEmployee) is Border Layout manager, and this JPanel is set Center of the pnSouth.

We have to use JScrollPane with JTable, and we set JScrollPane into the Center of the pnListEmployee. We define name for controls is shown in the Table 15.

Table 15. Define the name for controls

Control	Name	Description
JTextField	txtEmployeeID	Store and show the Employee ID
JTextField	txtEmployeeName	Store and show the Employee Name
JComboBox	cboEmployeeGender	Store and show the Employee Gender
JButton	btnAdd	Button to add new Employee to JList
JButton	btnRemove	Button to remove selected Employee
JTable	tblEmployee	JTable to show list Employee

The program allows users to enter Employee's information, press the "Add" button, and Empoyee information will be added in the JTable.

Each time you click on each Employee in the JTable, the details of the Employee will be displayed again into the JTextField and JComboBox.

Pressing the "Remove" Button, it will remove Employee from the JTable.

We create Employee kotin class as below is shown in the Listing 44.

Listing 44. JTableUI/Employee

```
1
2    class Employee {
3    public var EmployeeID:String=""
4    get() {return field}
5    set(value) {field=value}
6    public var EmployeeName:String=""
7    get() {return field}
8    set(value) {field=value}
9    public var EmployeeGender=""
10   get() {return field}
11   set(value) {field=value}
12   constructor()
13   constructor(EmployeeID: String,
14   EmployeeName: String,
15   EmployeeGender: String) {
16   this.EmployeeID = EmployeeID
17   this.EmployeeName = EmployeeName
18   this.EmployeeGender = EmployeeGender
19   }
20   override fun toString(): String {
21   return "$EmployeeName"
22   }
23   }
24
```

We open the EmployeeUI java class, the code is generated as below is shown in the Listing 45.

Listing 45. JTableUI/EmployeeUI

```
1
2    import javax.swing.*;
3    public class EmployeeUI {
4    private JPanel pnTitle;
5    private JPanel pnEmployee;
6    private JTextField txtEmployeeID;
7    private JTextField txtEmployeeName;
8    private JComboBox cboEmployeeGender;
9    private JPanel pnSouth;
10   private JPanel pnButton;
11   private JButton btnAdd;
12   private JButton btnRemove;
13   private JPanel pnListEmployee;
14   private JPanel pnMain;
15   private JTable tblEmployee;
16
17   }
18
```

We change private visibility modifier to protected, it is shown in the Listing 46.

Listing 46. JTableUI/EmployeeUI

```
1
2     import javax.swing.*;
3     public class EmployeeUI {
4     protected JPanel pnTitle;
5     protected JPanel pnEmployee;
6     protected JTextField txtEmployeeID;
7     protected JTextField txtEmployeeName;
8     protected JComboBox cboEmployeeGender;
9     protected JPanel pnSouth;
10    protected JPanel pnButton;
11    protected JButton btnAdd;
12    protected JButton btnRemove;
13    protected JPanel pnListEmployee;
14    protected JPanel pnMain;
15    protected JTable tblEmployee;
16    }
17
18
```

And then we create EmployeeUIKotlin class extends EmployeeUI java class and modify this class to set the DefaulTableModel for JTable, it is shown in the Listing 47.

Listing 47. JTableUI/EmployeeUIKotlin

```
1     var tableModel: DefaultTableModel
2     //Create the DefaultTableModel object
3     tableModel = DefaultTableModel()
4     //add 3 columns for DefaultTableModel
5     tableModel.addColumn("Employee ID")
6     tableModel.addColumn("Employee Name")
7     tableModel.addColumn("Employee Gender")
8     //setmodel for JTable
9     tblEmployee.setModel(tableModel)
10
```

We assign the event for JButton Add to insert new Employee in the JTable, let's see the Listing 48 how to add event and insert a new row into the JTable.

Listing 48. JTableUI/EmployeeUIKotlin

```
1    btnAdd.addActionListener{
2      processAddNewEmployee()
3    }
4    //add new employee
5    private fun processAddNewEmployee() {
6    var id: String = txtEmployeeID.getText()
7    var name: String = txtEmployeeName.getText()
8    var gender = ""
9    if (cboEmployeeGender.selectedIndex == 0)
10   gender = "Woman"
11   else
12   gender ="Man"
13   var row = arrayOf(id, name, gender)
14   //insert new row
15    tableModel.addRow(row)
16   }
17
```

We assign the addMouseListener event to the JTable to view the Employee details when the user clicks on each Employee in the JTable. We write the code for this event as follows is shown in the Listing 49.

Listing 49. JTableUI/EmployeeUIKotlin

```
1    tblEmployee.addMouseListener(
2    object: MouseAdapter() {
3    override fun mousePressed(e: MouseEvent) {
4    super.mousePressed(e)
5    showDetailEmployee()
6    }
7    })
8    //Show detail employee information
9    private fun showDetailEmployee() {
10   if (tblEmployee.selectedRow == -1)
11   return
12   var row: Int = tblEmployee.selectedRow
13    var id = tblEmployee.getValueAt(row, 0)
14   var name = tblEmployee.getValueAt(row, 1)
15   var gender = tblEmployee.getValueAt(row, 2)
16   txtEmployeeID.setText(id.toString())
17   txtEmployeeName.setText(name.toString())
18   cboEmployeeGender.
19   setSelectedItem(gender.toString())
20   }
21
```

Finally, we process the Employee delete button, the code as follows is shown in the Listing 50.

Listing 50. JTableUI/EmployeeUIKotlin

```
1    btnRemove.addActionListener{
2     processRemoveEmployee()
3    }
4    //remove employee from the JTable
5    private fun processRemoveEmployee() {
6    if (tblEmployee.selectedRow == -1)
7    return
8    var row: Int = tblEmployee.selectedRow
9     tableModel.removeRow(row)
10   }
11
```

The Listing 51 shows the full code of the EmployeeUIKotlin class.

Listing 51(a). JTableUI/EmployeeUIKotlin

```
1    import java.awt.event.MouseAdapter
2    import java.awt.event.MouseEvent
3    import javax.swing.JFrame
4    import javax.swing.table.DefaultTableModel
5    class EmployeeUIKotlin: EmployeeUI {
6    var tableModel: DefaultTableModel
7    var frame: JFrame
8    constructor() {
9    frame = JFrame("Learn JTable")
10   frame.contentPane = pnMain
11   //add item for JCombobox
12    cboEmployeeGender.addItem("Woman")
13   cboEmployeeGender.addItem("Man")
14   //Create the DefaultTableModel object
15    tableModel = DefaultTableModel()
16   //add 3 columns for DefaultTableModel
17    tableModel.addColumn("Employee ID")
18   tableModel.addColumn("Employee Name")
19   tableModel.addColumn("Employee Gender")
20   //setmodel for JTable
21    tblEmployee.setModel(tableModel)
22   btnAdd.addActionListener{
23    processAddNewEmployee()
24   }
25    tblEmployee.addMouseListener(
26   object: MouseAdapter() {
27   override fun mousePressed(e: MouseEvent) {
28   super.mousePressed(e)
29   showDetailEmployee()
30   }
31   })
32   btnRemove.addActionListener{
33    processRemoveEmployee()
34   }
35   }
36   //remove employee from the JTable
37    private fun processRemoveEmployee() {
38   if (tblEmployee.selectedRow == -1)
39   return
```

Listing 51(b). JTableUI/EmployeeUIKotlin

```
40
41          var row: Int = tblEmployee.selectedRow
42          tableModel.removeRow(row)
43        }
44        //Show detail employee information
45        private fun showDetailEmployee() {
46        if (tblEmployee.selectedRow == -1)
47        return
48        var row: Int = tblEmployee.selectedRow
49        var id = tblEmployee.getValueAt(row, 0)
50        var name = tblEmployee.getValueAt(row, 1)
51        var gender = tblEmployee.getValueAt(row, 2)
52        txtEmployeeID.setText(id.toString())
53        txtEmployeeName.setText(name.toString())
54        cboEmployeeGender.
55        setSelectedItem(gender.toString())
56        }
57        //add new employee
58        private fun processAddNewEmployee() {
59        var id: String = txtEmployeeID.getText()
60        var name: String = txtEmployeeName.getText()
61        var gender = ""
62        if (cboEmployeeGender.selectedIndex == 0)
63        gender = "Woman"
64        else
65        gender ="Man"
66        var row = arrayOf(id, name, gender)
67        //insert new row
68        tableModel.addRow(row)
69        }
70        //this method uses to show the UI
71        fun showUI() {
72        //set 'X' corner button to close the window
73        frame.defaultCloseOperation = JFrame.EXIT_ON_
74        CLOSE
75        //set size for window: width=450, height=430
76        frame.setSize(450, 430)
77        //set centering desktop for the window
78        frame.setLocationRelativeTo(null)
79        //show the window
80        frame.isVisible = true
81        }
82        }
83
```

Finally, The Listing 52, we create TestEmployeeUI.kt and write the main function to run the program.

Listing 52. JTableUI/TestEmployeeUI.kt

```
1    fun main(args: Array<String>) {
2    var eui= EmployeeUIKotlin ()
3    eui.showUI()
4    }
```

We run program and test some cases is shown in the Figure 35.

- Insert new employee
- View employee's detail information
- Remove employee from the JTable

Figure 35. Test cases for JTable employee
The source code can be download at the link: https://github.com/thanhtd32/kotlin/tree/main/JTableUI.

JTree

This is the last lesson for Graphic User Interface. The book will introduce how to create a JTree, get the DefaultMutableTreeNode into JTree Especially use Object-oriented programming to put data on this tree, as well as know how to handle events when users click on each node on the tree. JTree displays a set of hierarchical data as an outline is shown in the Figure 36.

Figure 36. JTree

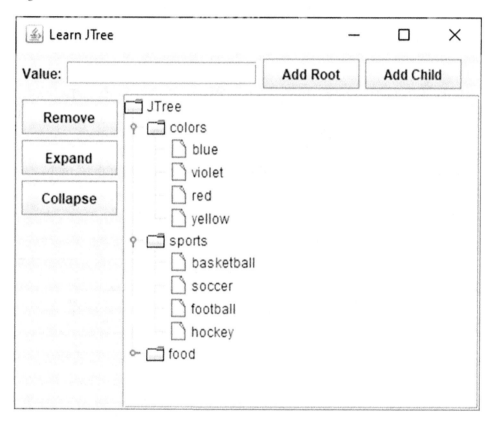

Table 16 shows Constructors and methods of JTree.

Table 16. Constructors and methods of JTree

Method	Description
JTree()	Returns a JTree with a sample model.
JTree(TreeModel newModel)	Returns an instance of JTree which displays the root node. And the tree is created using the specified data model.
void collapsePath(TreePath path)	Ensures that the node identified by the specified path is collapsed and viewable.
void collapseRow(int row)	Ensures that the node in the specified row is collapsed.
void expandPath(TreePath path)	Ensures that the node identified by the specified path is expanded and viewable.
void expandRow(int row)	Ensures that the node in the specified row is expanded and viewable.
lastSelectedPathComponent	Returns the last path component of the selected path.

We use DefaultMutableTreeNode for JTree. A DefaultMutableTreeNode is a general-purpose node in a tree data structure. A tree node may have at most one parent and 0 or more children. A tree may consist of many subtrees, each node acting as the root for its own subtree.

Table 17 shows Constructors and methods of DefaultMutableTreeNode.

Table 17. Constructors and methods of DefaultMutableTreeNode

Method	Description
DefaultMutableTreeNode()	Creates a tree node that has no parent and no children, but which allows children.
DefaultMutableTreeNode(Object userObject)	Creates a tree node with no parent, no children, but which allows children, and initializes it with the specified user object.
void add(MutableTreeNode newChild)	Removes newChild from its parent and makes it a child of this node by adding it to the end of this node's child array.
level	Returns the number of levels above this node. The distance from the root to this node.
userObject	Set/Get user object.
parent	Returns this node's parent or null if this node has no parent.
void remove(int childIndex)	Removes the child at the specified index from this node's children and sets that node's parent to null.

The Listing 53 illustrates how to use DefaultMutableTreeNode into JTree.

Listing 53. Demo add DefaultMutableTreeNode into JTree

```
1    //Create a root node
2    var root = DefaultMutableTreeNode("JTree")
3    //Create a Tree
4    var tree = JTree(root)
5    //create Colors node
6    var colorsNode = DefaultMutableTreeNode("colors")
7    root.add(colorsNode)
8    //create blue node
9    var blueNode = DefaultMutableTreeNode("blue")
10   colorsNode.add(blueNode)
11   //create violetNode node
12   var violetNode = DefaultMutableTreeNode("violet")
13   colorsNode.add(violetNode)
14   //create Sports node
15   var sportsNode = DefaultMutableTreeNode("sports")
16   root.add(sportsNode)
17   //create soccer node
18   var soccerNode = DefaultMutableTreeNode("soccer")
19   sportsNode.add(soccerNode)
20   //create Food node
21   var foodNode = DefaultMutableTreeNode("food")
22   root.add(foodNode)
23
```

The Listing 54 illustrates how to assign events when user selects Nodes on JTree.

Listing 54. Add mouse listener for JTree

```
1    tree.addMouseListener(object: MouseListener {
2    override fun mouseReleased(e: MouseEvent?) { }
3    override fun mousePressed(e: MouseEvent?) { }
4    override fun mouseExited(e: MouseEvent?) { }
5    override fun mouseEntered(e: MouseEvent?) { }
6    override fun mouseClicked(e: MouseEvent?) {
7    //get the selected node
8    var obj = tree.lastSelectedPathComponent
9    var selectedNode = obj as DefaultMutableTreeNode
10   //process selectedNode
11   }
12   })
13
```

In addition, when a JTree has configurations available, we can delete the Root Node and re-initialize the Root Node for it as follows is shown in the Listing 55.

Listing 55. Reset root for JTree

```
1    //Remove all nodes in the tree
2    var model = tvDemo.model
3     as DefaultTreeModel
4    var root = model.root
5     as DefaultMutableTreeNode
6    root.removeAllChildren()
7    model.reload()
8    model.setRoot(null)
9    //create the root in the tree
10   root = DefaultMutableTreeNode("JTree")
11   model.setRoot(root)
12
```

We design the graphic user interface with JTreeUI project as follows is shown in the Figure 37.

Figure 37. Design for JTree

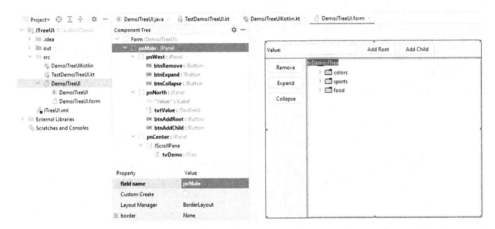

And we add the DemoJTreeUI form then drag and drop the controls as above.

JPanel(pnMain) is Border Layout manager.

JPanel(pnWest) is Flow Layout manager and set it to West of the pnMain.

JPanel(pnNorth) for JTextField and Buttons is Flow layout manager. And this JPanel is placed North of the pnMain.

JPanel(pnCenter) contains JTree is Border Layout manager, and this JPanel is set Center in the pnMain.

We have to use JScrollPane with JTree, and we set JScrollPane into the Center of the pnCenter.

368

Table 18.

Control	Name	Description
JTextField	txtValue	Store and show the value
JButton	btnAddRoot	Add the root into the JTree
JButton	btnAddChild	Add a child node in a parent node
JButton	btnRemove	Remomve a selected node
JButton	btnExpand	Expand node
JButton	btnCollapse	Collapse node
JTree	tvDemo	JTree shows values as hierarchical structure

We open the DemoJTreeUI java class, the code is generated as below is shown in the Listing 56.

Listing 56. JTreeUI/DemoJTreeUI

```
1   import javax.swing.*;
2   public class DemoJTreeUI {
3   private JPanel pnMain;
4   private JTree tvDemo;
5   private JTextField txtValue;
6   private JButton btnAddRoot;
7   private JButton btnAddChild;
8   private JButton btnRemove;
9   private JButton btnExpand;
10  private JButton btnCollapse;
11  private JPanel pnWest;
12  private JPanel pnNorth;
13  private JPanel pnCenter;
14  }
15
```

We change private visibility modifier to protected is shown in the Listing 57.

Listing 57. JTreeUI/DemoJTreeUI

```
1
2    import javax.swing.*;
3    public class DemoJTreeUI {
4    protected JPanel pnMain;
5    protected JTree tvDemo;
6    protected JTextField txtValue;
7    protected JButton btnAddRoot;
8    protected JButton btnAddChild;
9    protected JButton btnRemove;
10   protected JButton btnExpand;
11   protected JButton btnCollapse;
12   protected JPanel pnWest;
13   protected JPanel pnNorth;
14   protected JPanel pnCenter;
15   }
16
```

And then we create DemoJTreeUIKotlin class extends DemoJTreeUI java class and modify this class. We clear JTree's default data is shown in the Listing 58.

Listing 58. JTreeUI/DemoJTreeUIKotlin

```
1
2    //Remove all nodes in the tree
3    var model = tvDemo.model as DefaultTreeModel
4    var root = model.root as DefaultMutableTreeNode
5    root.removeAllChildren()
6    model.reload()
7    model.setRoot(null)
```

Next we assign the event to the btnAddRoot button to handle creating Root for JTree is shown in the Listing 59.

Listing 59. JTreeUI/DemoJTreeUIKotlin

```
1    btnAddRoot.addActionListener {
2      addRoot()
3    }
4    //add a root
5    private fun addRoot() {
6    var model = tvDemo.model as DefaultTreeModel
7    var root: DefaultMutableTreeNode
8    var value = txtValue.text
9      root = DefaultMutableTreeNode(value)
10   model.setRoot(root)
11   }
```

To add a Child Node into the selected Node, we add event for btnAddChild and call the addChild() method as follows is shown in the Listing 60.

Listing 60. JTreeUI/DemoJTreeUIKotlin

```
1   //add a new node
2   private fun addChild() {
3     //get the selected node
4     var obj = tvDemo.lastSelectedPathComponent
5     if(obj == null)
6     return
7     var selectedNode = obj as DefaultMutableTreeNode
8     //create a new Node:
9     var value = txtValue.text
10    var childNode = DefaultMutableTreeNode(value)
11    selectedNode.add(childNode)
12    //update the UI
13    tvDemo.updateUI()
14  }
15
```

To remove the selected Node, we add event for btnRemove and program it as follows is shown in the Listing 61.

Listing 61. JTreeUI/DemoJTreeUIKotlin

```
1   btnRemove.addActionListener { removeNode() }
2   //remove selected node
3   private fun removeNode() {
4   var obj = tvDemo.lastSelectedPathComponent
5     if(obj == null)
6     return
7     var model = tvDemo.model as DefaultTreeModel
8     var node = obj as DefaultMutableTreeNode
9     if (node.parent != null) {
10    model.removeNodeFromParent(node)
11    } else {
12    //remove the Root
13     var root = model.root as DefaultMutableTreeNode
14    root.removeAllChildren()
15    model.reload()
16    model.setRoot(null)
17    }
18  }
19
```

In case of deleting Node from JTree, we need to check that Node is Root Node or not. If it is the root node, we delete all nodes in the tree. If it is not the root node, we will remove selected node from the Parent node.

With the expanding all the nodes in the JTree, we add event for btnExpand as program below is shown in the Listing 62.

Listing 62. JTreeUI/DemoJTreeUIKotlin

```
btnExpand.addActionListener { expandAll() }
//expand all nodes
fun expandAll() {
    var row = 0
    while (row < tvDemo.rowCount) {
        tvDemo.expandRow(row)
        row++
    }
}
```

And the last one, with the collapsing all the nodes in the JTree, we add event for btnCollapse as program below is shown in the Listing 63.

Listing 63. JTreeUI/DemoJTreeUIKotlin

```
btnCollapse.addActionListener { collapseAll() }
//collapse all nodes
private fun collapseAll() {
    var row = 0
    while (row < tvDemo.rowCount) {
        tvDemo.collapseRow(row)
        row++
    }
}
```

Finally, we have the whole program for this JTreeUI application, DemoJTreeUIKotlin class as below is shown in the Listing 64.

Listing 64(a). JTreeUI/DemoJTreeUIKotlin

```
1    import javax.swing.JFrame
2    import javax.swing.tree.DefaultMutableTreeNode
3    import javax.swing.tree.DefaultTreeModel
4    class DemoJTreeUIKotlin:DemoJTreeUI {
5    var frame: JFrame
6    constructor() {
7    frame = JFrame("Learn JTree")
8    frame.contentPane = pnMain
9    //Remove all nodes in the tree
10   var model = tvDemo.model as DefaultTreeModel
11   var root = model.root as DefaultMutableTreeNode
12   root.removeAllChildren()
13   model.reload()
14   model.setRoot(null)
15   btnAddRoot.addActionListener {
16   addRoot()
17   }
18   btnAddChild.addActionListener { addChild() }
19   btnRemove.addActionListener { removeNode() }
20   btnExpand.addActionListener { expandAll() }
21   btnCollapse.addActionListener { collapseAll() }
22   }
23   //collapse all nodes
24   private fun collapseAll() {
25   var row = 0
26   while (row < tvDemo.rowCount) {
27   tvDemo.collapseRow(row)
28   row++
29   }
30   }
31   //expand all nodes
32   fun expandAll() {
33   var row = 0
34   while (row < tvDemo.rowCount) {
35   tvDemo.expandRow(row)
36   row++
37   }
38   }
39   //remove selected node
40   private fun removeNode() {
41   var obj = tvDemo.lastSelectedPathComponent
42   if(obj == null)
43   return
44   var model = tvDemo.model as DefaultTreeModel
45   var node = obj as DefaultMutableTreeNode
46   if (node.parent != null) {
47   model.removeNodeFromParent(node)
48   } else {
49   //remove the Root
50   var root = model.root as
51   DefaultMutableTreeNode
52   root.removeAllChildren()
53   model.reload()
54   model.setRoot(null)
55   }
56   }
57   //add a new node
58   private fun addChild() {
59   //get the selected node
```

Listing 64(b). JTreeUI/DemoJTreeUIKotlin

```
60
61
62
63      var obj = tvDemo.lastSelectedPathComponent
64      if(obj == null)
65      return
66      var selectedNode = obj as
67      DefaultMutableTreeNode
68      //create a new Node:
69      var value = txtValue.text
70      var childNode = DefaultMutableTreeNode(value)
71      selectedNode.add(childNode)
72      //update the UI
73      tvDemo.updateUI()
74      }
75      //add a root
76      private fun addRoot() {
77      var model = tvDemo.model as DefaultTreeModel
78      var root: DefaultMutableTreeNode
79      var value = txtValue.text
80      root = DefaultMutableTreeNode(value)
81      model.setRoot(root)
82      }
83      //this method uses to show the UI
84      fun showUI() {
85      //set 'X' corner button to close the window
86      frame.defaultCloseOperation = JFrame.EXIT_ON_
87      CLOSE
88      //set size for window: width=450, height=430
89      frame.setSize(450, 430)
90      //set centering desktop for the window
91      frame.setLocationRelativeTo(null)
92      //show the window
93      frame.isVisible = true
94      }
95      }
96
97
98
```

And we create TestDemoJTreeUI.kt kotlin class to run the application is shown in the Listing 65.

Listing 65. JTreeUI/TestDemoJTreeUI.kt

1	fun main(args: Array<String>) {
2	var dmtui= DemoJTreeUIKotlin()
3	dmtui.showUI()
4	}

The source code can be downloaded here: https://github.com/thanhtd32/kotlin/tree/main/JTreeUI.

EXECUTABLE FOR KOTLIN

Thus, the book has completed the knowledge related to Kotlin, including data types, variable declarations, conditional statement, loops, functions, strings, arrays, lists, object-oriented, lamda expressions, file handling, graphic user interface… in this lesson, the book will show how to package the software into an executable file.

IntelliJ IDEA provides us with the Tool to package software into executable file, which is so simple that we do not need to even think of it. Let's begin:

Step 1: Open a project, such as JTreeUI in the previous lesson.

Readers make sure that the project has file TestDemoJTreeUI.kt with main method is shown in the Listing 66.

Listing 66. JTreeUI/TestDemoJTreeUI.kt

1	fun main(args: Array<String>) {
2	var dmtui=DemoJTreeUIKotlin()
3	dmtui.showUI()
4	}
5	

Step 2: Go to File / select Project Structure is shown in the Figure 38.

Figure 38. Select project structer

Step 3: Select artifacts / click on the + marker / select JAR / select From Modules with dependencies is shown in the Figure 39.

Figure 39. Select from modules with dependencies

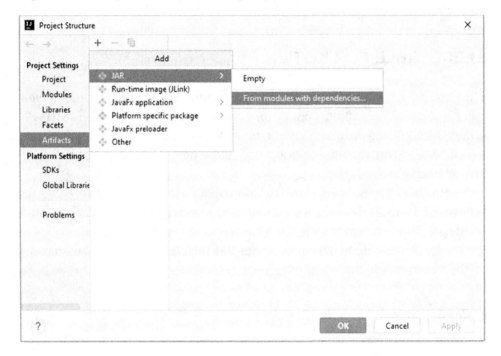

After choose "From modules with dependencies…", the screen "Create JAR from Modules" will show and asks for the Main Class appears, see Figure 40.

Figure 40. Choose main class

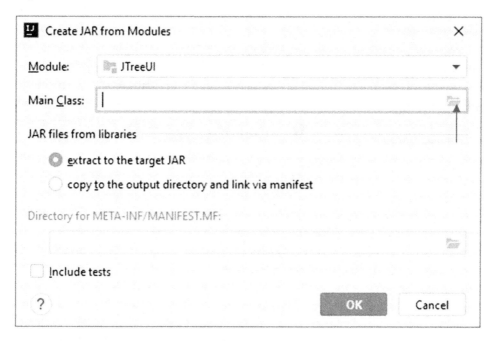

We click on the Main Class button and Choose the main class, it is shown in the Figure 41.

Figure 41. Choose main class

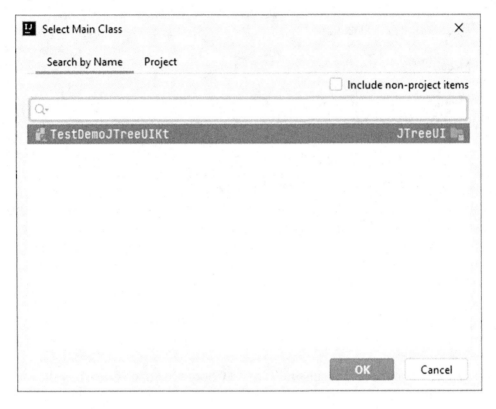

Readers can choose TestDemoJTreeUIkt, then click OK, the main class is shown in the Figure 42.

Figure 42. Choose TestDemoJTreeUIKt main class

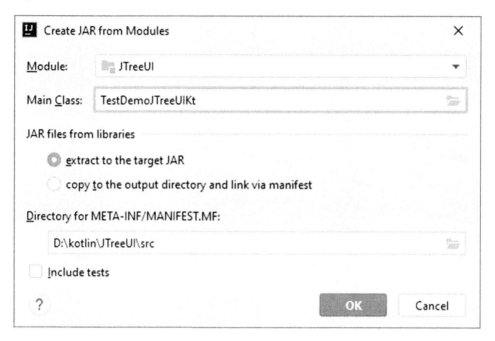

We click OK, the configuration parameters will display out as below is shown in the Figure 43.

Figure 43. Artifacts configuration

Item 1 is the jar name created; item 2 is where the jar is stored. Select OK to return to the main screen. We select Build menu and then choose Build Artifacts…is shown in the Figure 44.

Figure 44. Build artifacts

We choose the action Build in the Build Artifact and wait for executing the jar file output, it is shown in the Figure 45.

Figure 45. Action build artifacts

We choose the action Build in the Build Artifact and wait for executing the jar file output. When the compilation is done, we see the artifacts directory as below is shown in the Figure 46.

Figure 46. Out put artifacts folder

We go to the artifacts directory and JTreeUI_jar sub directory, readers will see JTreeUI.jar is shown in the Figure 47.

Figure 47. Executable jar file

double click on the JTreeUI.jar to run the software, it is shown in the Figure 48.

Figure 48. Run jar file

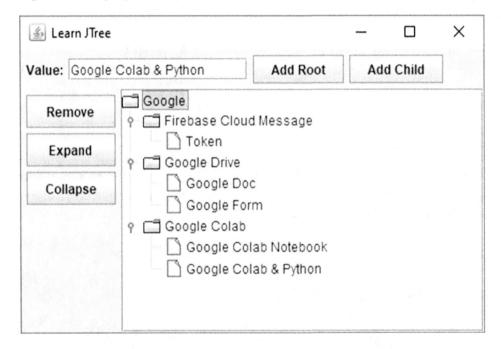

We have completed the steps to create the jar file in Intellij IDEA. Readers try to learn the programming language well, please train yourself to have more knowledge of the technology. To learn programming well, readers have to work hard, learn day by day and practice a lot.

Readers can read more explanations of the conditional structure in the authors' books (Jemerov et al., 2017; Griffiths & Griffiths, 2019; Eckel & Isakova, 2020; Bailey et al., 2021). Additional Java Object Oriented Programming book is referenced (Schild, 2019).

EXERCISES

1. How do we create a Window in Kotlin?
2. What is the working principle of FlowLayout Manager?
3. What is the working principle of BoxLayout Manager?
4. What is the working principle of BorderLayout Manager?
5. What is the working principle of CardLayout Manager?
6. What is the working principle of GridLayout Manager?
7. How to assign events to controls on the graphic user interface?
8. btn is a JButton variable, what command do we use to assign an Icon to it?
    (a) btn.setIcon(new ImageIcon("path"))
    (b) btn.setImage(new ImageIcon("path"))
    (c) btn.setIcon(new Icon("path"))
    (d) btn.setImage(new Icon("path"))
9. Design and solve the first-degree equations like the interface in Figure 49.

Figure 49.

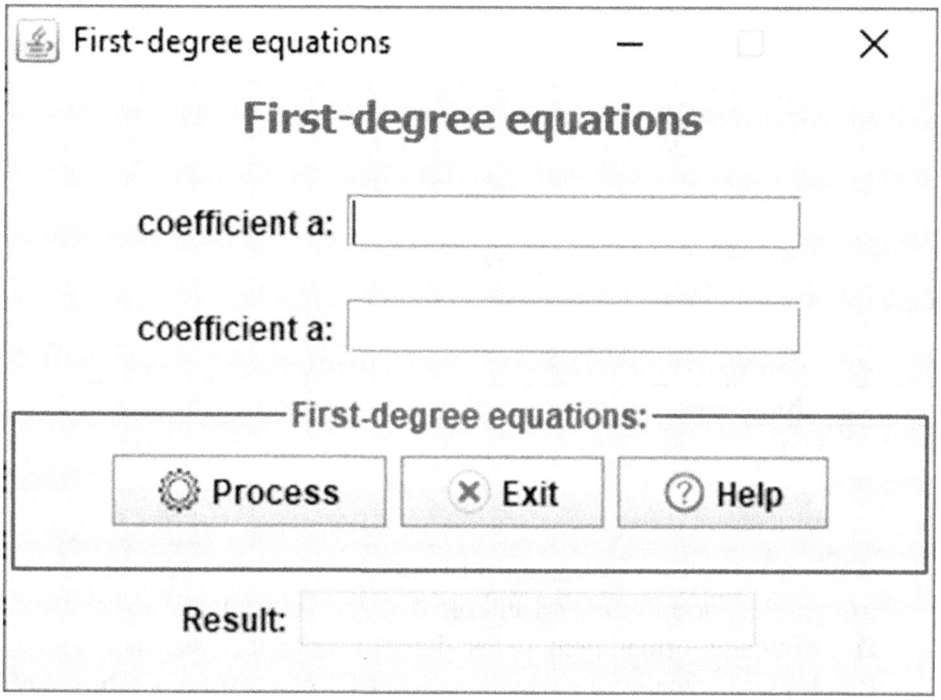

Process JButton: Program will solve the first-degree equations

Exit JButton: Program will be killed

Help JButton: Use JOptionPane to show the instruction.

10. Write a program to test common knowledge. Combine object-oriented programming with file saving function to mark questions that candidates are unfinished. Simulate 10 questions for the software, Click Submit will display the number of correct sentences, the number of incorrect sentences.

Figure 50.

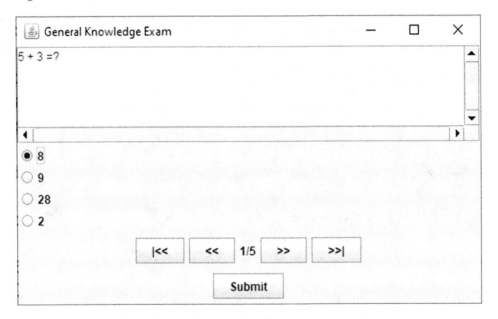

Table 19.

First question	|<<	Next question	>>
Previous question	<<	Last question	>>|

11. Write an employee management program like the interface below, using object-oriented model and file interaction techniques to handle it. Department information includes: department code, department name. Employee information includes: Employee ID, employee name, birthday. Each employee belongs to only one department.

Figure 51.

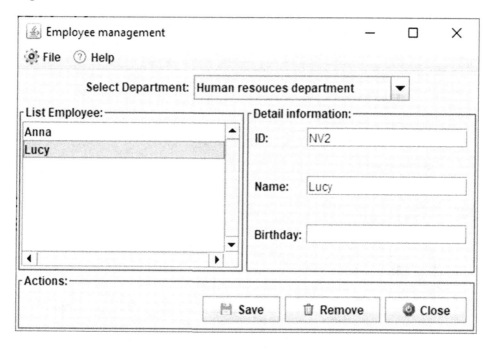

○   Simulate any 3 departments and shows them into the JCombobox.
○   Select a department to display the list of employees of that department in JList.
○   Select any employee in JList to display employee details.
○   Pressing the "Save" button will save employees by department.
○   Pressing the "Remove" button will remove the employee from the department.
○   Press the "Close" button to exit the software.
○   Menus to save files, open files: use Json to interact with files.
○   Help and About: Readers choose how to display.

Figure 52.

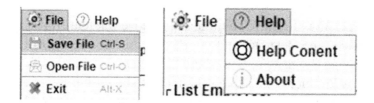

12. Write a Student management program like the interface below. A Student includes: ID, name, gender and grade.

Figure 53.

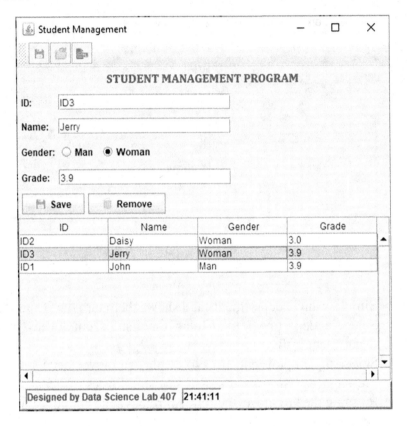

- ○ **JToolbar:** Save(Save to Serializable file format), Open(Open Serializable file format), Html (export Student list into HTML file format).
- ○ Pressing the "Save" button will take the Student to the JTable.
- ○ Clicking on each Student will display detailed information on the interface.
- ○ Pressing "Remove" button will remove Student from JTable.
- ○ Show the Designer and digital timer at the bottom of the Screen. Using SwingWorker to show the timer.
13. Write a Product management system as shown below. A catalog has many products, a catalog's information includes: category code, category

name. Information on a product includes: Product code, product name, quantity, unit price, and total amount.

Figure 54.

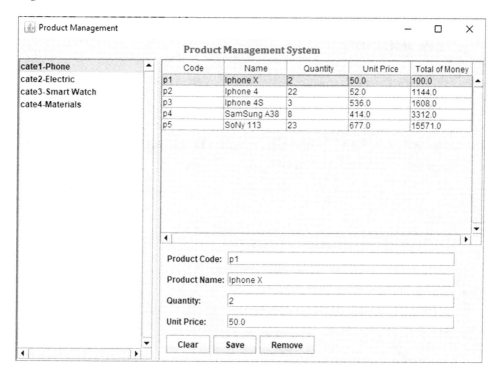

- ○ The list of categories is displayed into the JList, each time the Category is selected, the product list of the category will be displayed in the JTable.
- ○ Clicking on JTable will display product details down to the section below.
- ○ Click "Clear": Clear data in the JTextField.
- ○ Click "Save": Save the product to the selected category.
- ○ Click "Remove": Remove the product from the catalog.
- ○ Right-click on JList: Display Popup menu with 3 items: Add new Catalog, View detail CataLog, Delete Catalog.
  - • **Add New Catalog:** Open a Window to create a new Catalog.
  - • **View Detail Catalog:** Open detail information of selected Catalog.
  - • **Delete Catalog:** Remove selected Catalog.

Figure 55.

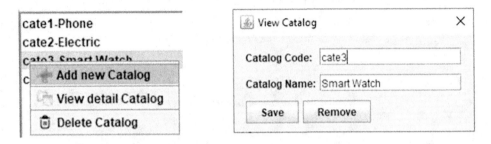

The program uses JSon to store data.
14. Improve exercise 13, replace JList with JTree as shown below. Provides the same functions as exercise 13.

Figure 56.

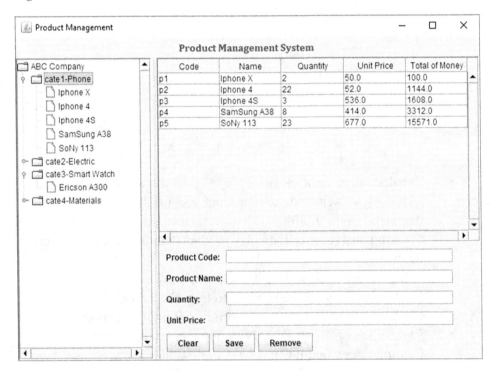

Categories and Products are hierarchical in JTree.

15. Use JSplitPane to write software that displays images as shown below. Use JSplitPane to divide the screen into 3 areas. Using object-oriented, Initialize a list of images into a JList, each time clicking on any image will display the image and description for that image.

Figure 57.

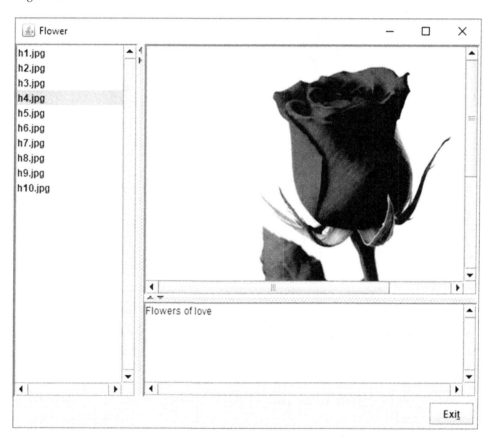

   ○   Press the Exit button to exit the software.

16. Export exercise 15 to an executable jar file.

17. Multiple File Type Processing software.
    Write product management software with the following interface:
    The software provides functions for users to manipulate the product list, product information including Product ID, Product Name, UnitPrice.

   ○   **Add Button:** Add a new Product to the table.

Figure 58.

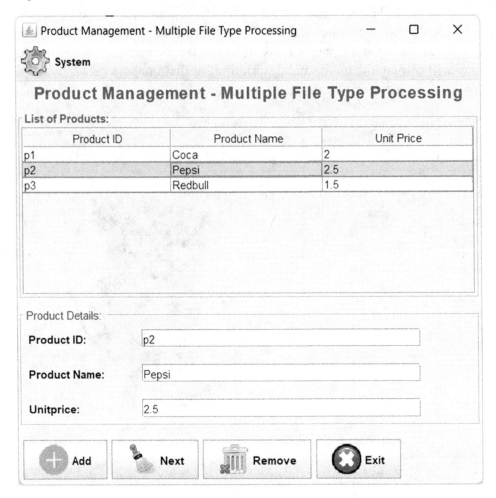

- ○ **Next Button:** Clear data in input fields, and focus on input field for Product ID.
- ○ **Remove Button:** Removes the currently selected Product from the table.
- ○ **Table:** Displays a list of Products when there is a change, each time you click on a line, display product details in the details section.
- ○ **Menus:** Provide many options to save files and read files in different formats (Text file, Serialize file, XML file and Json File).

Figure 59 shows the functions for saving data in different file formats:

Figure 59.

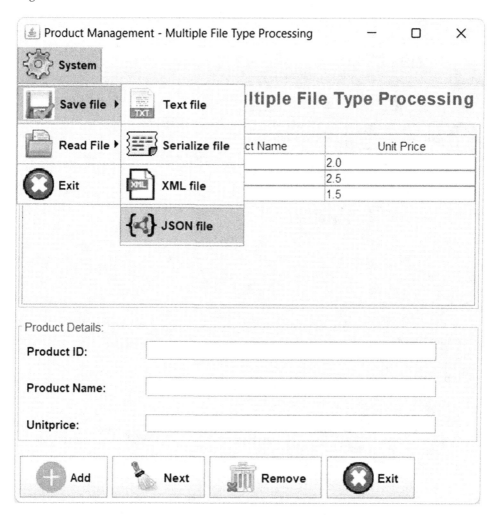

Figure 60 illustrates the functions that read data from different file formats:

Figure 60.

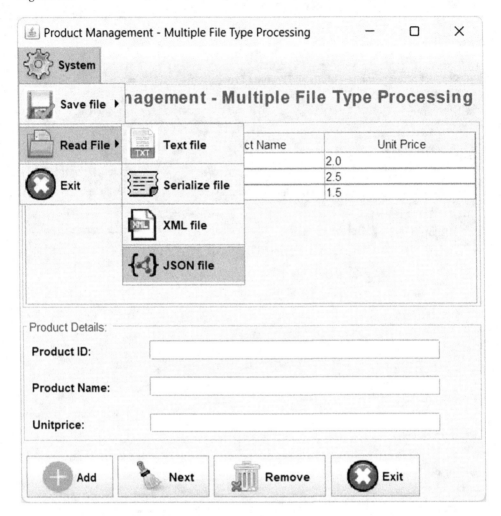

REFERENCES

Bailey, Greenhalgh, & Skeen. (2021). Kotlin Programming: The Big Nerd Ranch Guide (2nd ed.). Big Nerd Ranch, LLC.

Eckel & Isakova. (2020). Atomic Kotlin. Mindview LLC.

Griffiths, D., & Griffiths, D. (2019). Head First Kotlin. O'Reilly Media.

Jemerov & Isakova. (2017). *Kotlin in Action.* Manning.

Schild, H. (2019). Java the complete Reference (11th ed.). McGraw-Hill Education.

Chapter 13
Vert.X for Kotlin Restful API

ABSTRACT

Kotlin as well as other programming languages can be applied to writing service APIs. This chapter presents a new framework called Vert.X. It is considered as one of the powerful frameworks. It can support the implementation of many services including Restful API. Kotlin is used as the main programming language of Android mobile. When deploying Mobile, Restful API is used to interact with data on the server, so how to create Restful APIs is very important. Using Vert.X will help programmers save a lot of time, and Vert.X is considered to be very optimal when deploying services. This chapter will demonstrate the knowledge of how to build and deploy Restful APIs using Vert.X and demonstrate how to write code in Kotlin to call these APIs and how Postman platform interacts the API. This chapter includes brief of Restful API, overview Vert.X, creating Restful API by Kotlin in Vert.X, calling API in Postman, and authentication for Restful API. At the end of the chapter, there are exercises to help readers improve their programming skills using Vert.X to create Restful API.

DOI: 10.4018/978-1-6684-6687-2.ch013

BRIEF OF RESTFUL API

In this section, we briefly introduce Restful API, its benefits, structure and working mechanism.

What Is Restful API?

Web developers often refer to the REST principle and RESTful data structure because it is a very important part of the development of web applications.

RESTful API is a standard used in the design of APIs for web applications to facilitate resource management. It focuses on system resources (text files, images, audio, video, or dynamic data, etc.), including resource states that are formatted and transmitted over HTTP or HTTPs.

Web Services as well as Restful API have several benefits such as:

- Provides broad interoperability with different software applications running on different platforms (Mobile, Web, Desktop...).
- Use open standards and protocols.
- Improve reusability.
- Promote investment in existing software systems.
- Create interactive and flexible relationships between components in the system, easy for the development of distributed applications.
- Promote system integration, reduce system complexity, lower operating costs, develop systems quickly, and effectively interact with other enterprises' systems.

Figure 1. Restful API benefits

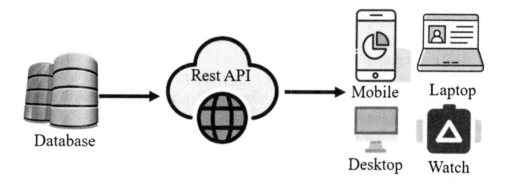

Database → Rest API → Mobile Laptop Desktop Watch

Figure 1 illustrates the benefits of Restful API, we only need to build the API once, from which the different platforms can access it without having to rewrite it. Thus, it reduces labor and financial costs to implement the project, making the project more efficient.

Structures of Restful

Rest API when designed will have many methods, mainly including GET, POST, PUT and DELETE.

Figure 2. Restful API structure

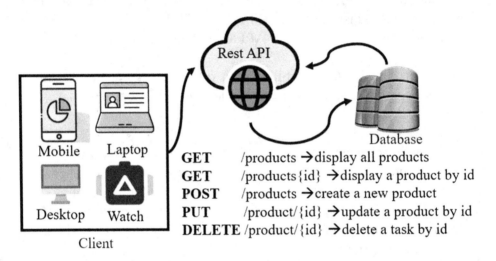

GET	/products	→display all products
GET	/products{id}	→display a product by id
POST	/products	→create a new product
PUT	/product/{id}	→update a product by id
DELETE	/product/{id}	→delete a task by id

An API (Application Programming Interface) is a set of rules and mechanisms by which an application or component interacts with another application or component. The API can return the data we need for our application in common data types like JSON or XML.

REST (Representational state transfer) is a form of data structure transformation, an architectural style for writing APIs. It uses simple HTTP methods to facilitate machine-to-machine communication. So, instead of using a URL for handling some user information, REST sends an HTTP request like GET, POST, DELETE, etc. to a URL to process the data.

RESTful API is a standard used in the design of APIs for web applications to manage resources. RESTful is one of the most commonly used API design styles today to let different applications (web, mobile, desktop...) communicate with each other.

The most important function of REST is to specify how to use HTTP methods (such as GET, POST, PUT, DELETE...) and how to format URLs for web applications to manage resources. RESTful does not prescribe application code logic and is not limited by application programming languages, any programming language or framework can be used to design a RESTful API.

How RESTful API Works

REST works mainly on the HTTP protocol. The above basic operations will use their own HTTP methods (CRUD method).

HTTP GET (SELECT): Returns a Resource or a list of Resources. As GET requests do not change the resource's state, these are said to be safe methods. if the resource is found on the server, then it must return HTTP response code 200 (OK) or 404 if the resource is NOT found on the server. And if GET API is not correctly formed then the server will return the HTTP response code 400 (BAD REQUEST).

Example URIs of HTTP GET.

HTTP GET http://www.yourdomain.com/products
HTTP GET http://www.yourdomain.com/products?minprice=10&maxpri
ce=20
HTTP GET http://www.yourdomain.com/products/1

HTTP POST (CREATE): Create a new Resource. When talking strictly about REST, POST methods are used to create a new resource into the collection of resources. Responses to this method are not cacheable unless the response includes appropriate Cache-Control or Expires header fields.

If a resource has been created on the origin server, the HTTP response code is 201 (Created) and contain an entity that describes the status of the request and refers to the new resource, and a Location header. If the action performed by the POST method might not result in a resource that can be identified by a URI. The HTTP response code 200 (OK) or 204 (No Content) is response status.

Example URIs of HTTP POST.

HTTP POST http://www.yourdomain.com/products
HTTP POST http://www.yourdomain.com/products/1

HTTP PUT (UPDATE): Update information for Resource (if the resource does not exist, then API may decide to create a new resource or not). If a new resource has been created by the PUT API, the HTTP response code should be returned 201 (Created). If an existing resource is modified, either the 200 (OK) or 204 (No Content) response codes should be returned.

What is the difference between the HTTP POST and HTTP PUT APIs? HTTP POST requests are made on resource collections, whereas HTTP PUT requests are made on a single resource.

Example URIs of HTTP PUT.

HTTP PUT http://www.yourdomain.com/products
HTTP PUT http://www.yourdomain.com/products/1

HTTP DELETE (DELETE): Delete a Resource. A successful response of DELETE requests SHOULD be an HTTP response code 200 (OK). The status should be 202 (Accepted) if the action has been queued. The status should be 204 (No Content) if the action has been performed but the response does not include an entity. And respone code 404 (NOT FOUND).

Example URIs of HTTP DELETE.

HTTP DELETE http://www.yourdomain.com/products/1

These methods or operations are often called CRUD corresponding to Create (C – HTTP POST), Read (R – HTTP GET), Update (U – HTTP PUT), Delete (D -HTTP DELETE).

Currently, most programmers who write RESTful APIs now choose JSON as the official format, but there are also many people who choose XML as the format, in general, it is easy and fast to use anyway.

Figure 3. RESTful API work mechanism

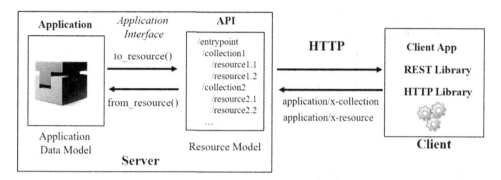

Figure 3 shows how Restful API works. From the client, the Rest/HTTP libraries will be referenced and invoked APIs, the Server will receive these requests and process the data and then return the result to the client through the APIs. The JSon data structure below illustrates a return result of the GET function.

```
{
    "status_code": 200,
    "data": [
    {
        "id": 1,
        "name": "john",
        "age": 20
    },
    {
        "id": 2,
        "name": "peter",
        "age": 25
    }
    ]
}
```

OVERVIEW VERT.X

Vert.X is a Toolkit, supporting many languages such as Java, RxJava, Kotlin, Javascript, Groovy, Ruby, Ceylon, Scala. There are many types of components on Vert.X that we can use and customize easily. All learning resources, source code, libraries, user manuals are located on https://vertx.io.

Vert.X – We can easily build and use any component or library we want.

Vert.X runs on top of the JVM – the Java Virtual Machine – allowing we to test our code and scale it instantly. So, we need to install JDK first.

Vert.X supports many different types of programming, including Back End programming support writing extremely good APIs. There is also extended support for building MicroService applications.

Vert.X – used by many major technology companies in the world: Vmware, Bosch, Cyannogen, Faunhofer, Redhat, Ticketmaster, Tesco, Swiss Post...

Figure 4. Vert.X architecture and operation
Source: Vert.X

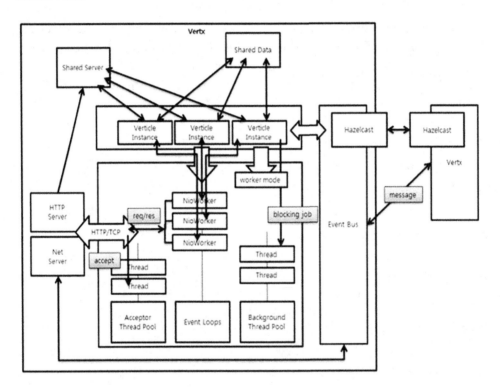

The core of Vert.X is based on the Hazelcast protocol. Hazelcast is an in-memory data grid. Hazelcast provides implementation of interfaces in Java such as Map, Queue, ExcecutorService, Lock... It is designed to be very lightweight and easy to use. Hazelcast ensures high availability and scalability. Distributed applications can use Hazelcast for distributed caching, synchronization, etc. Hazelcast is installed in Java language and client for

Java, C/C++ languages, C#... Hazelcast can also be thought of as a cache protocol (memcache protocol).

Inside there are 2 important components HTTP Server and Net Server. HTTP Server and Net Server Used to control network events and handle events. Net Server is used for events and handles its own protocol, and HTTP Server allows to register handlers for HTTP events like GET, POST, PUT, DELETE.

Vert.x has 3 types of thread pools:

Acceptor: Is a process to handle 1 socket. And 1 process is created on 1 port.

Event Loops: When an event occurs, it executes a corresponding handler. When the Event is done, it iterately reads another Event. When each event is attached to a process, by default Vert.x attaches 2 events to each CPU core thread.

Background: Used when the Event Loop executes the handler and requires an additional thread. You can specify the number of Threads in the backgroundPoolSize.

Verticle

When we implement a service, we inherit from AbstractVerticle which is called verticle. These verticles when invoked will be pushed into the Event loop.

Figure 5. Vert.X event loop
Source: Vert.X

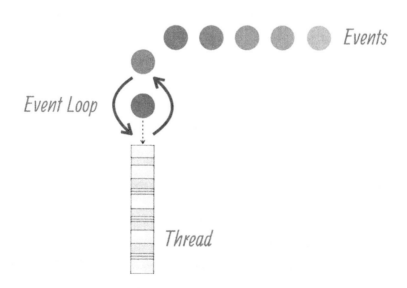

We can also set up multiple configurations for the verticle as well as deploy it multiple times:

Figure 6. Vert.X multiple deploying
Source: Vert.X

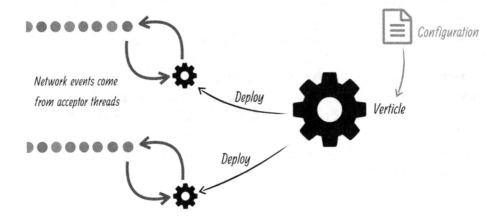

Event Bus

Event bus is the main tool by which different verticles can communicate asynchronously.

Figure 7. Vert.X event bus
Source: Vert.X

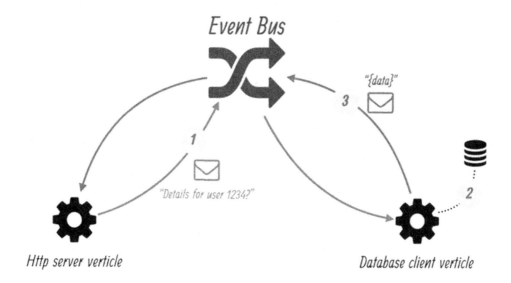

Http server verticle   Database client verticle

There is a single event bus instance for every Vert.x instance and it is obtained using the method eventBus.

The event bus allows different parts of your application to communicate with each other, irrespective of what language they are written in, and whether they're in the same Vert.x instance, or in a different Vert.x instance.

CREATE AND EMBED VERT.X IN KOTLIN PROJECT

In these sections below, we will demonstrate how to embed the Vert.X library in the application, create a website that listens on port 8080, How to build and deploy a Verticle in Vert.X, interactive HTTP GET, HTTP POST, HTTP PUT and HTTP DELETE, as well as how to use Postman to test these APIs.

To use Vert.X, from IntelliJ IDEA software, create a new Gradle project, select Kotlin/JVM as shown in Figure 8.

Figure 8. New Gradle project with Kotlin/JVM

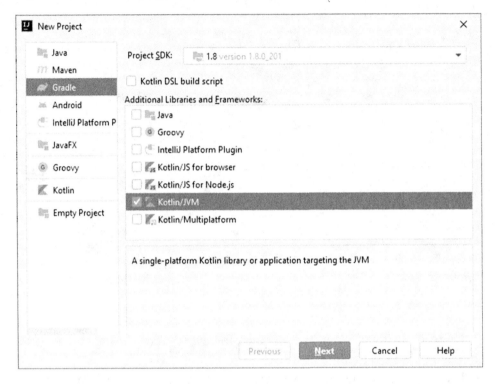

Press Next button and create project name is "HelloVertX", The project will be created as shown in Figure 9.

Figure 9. New HelloVertX project with Kotlin/JVM

To embed Vert.X in your project, go to the "build.gradle" file, and then we add the implementation for vertx as below (4.2.6 is current version on Mar 18/2022):

```
dependencies {
    implementation "org.jetbrains.kotlin:kotlin-stdlib"
    implementation 'io.vertx:vertx-web:4.2.6'
}
```

Above there is an Elephant icon, we click on this icon to compile and embed the Vert.X library into the project.

Figure 10. Embed the Vert.X toolkit

Then, in the kotlin directory, we create a Kotlin file with the name TestVerx. kt and write the code as shown in Figure 11 to create a website running on port 8080 using Vert.X.

Figure 11. Kotlin using Vert.X for Web

```
HelloVertX  src  main  kotlin  TestVertX.kt

Project ▼                    ⊕ Ξ ÷ ✿ —    TestVertX.kt
HelloVertX D:\kotlin\HelloVertX        1    import io.vertx.core.Vertx
  > .gradle                            2    import io.vertx.ext.web.Router
  > .idea                              3    import io.vertx.ext.web.RoutingContext
  > gradle                             4
  ∨ src                                5  ▶  fun main(args: Array<String>) {
    ∨ main                             6        var vertx = Vertx.vertx()
        java                           7
      ∨ kotlin                         8        var server = vertx.createHttpServer()
          TestVertX.kt                 9        var router = Router.router(vertx)
        resources                      10       router.route().handler { rc: RoutingContext ->
  > test                              11           var response = rc.response()
    build.gradle                      12           response.putHeader( name: "content-type", value: "text/html")
    gradle.properties                 13           response.end( chunk "Hello VertX Kotlin")
    gradlew                           14       }
    gradlew.bat                       15       server.requestHandler(router).listen( port: 8080)
    settings.gradle                   16    }
  ∨ External Libraries
```

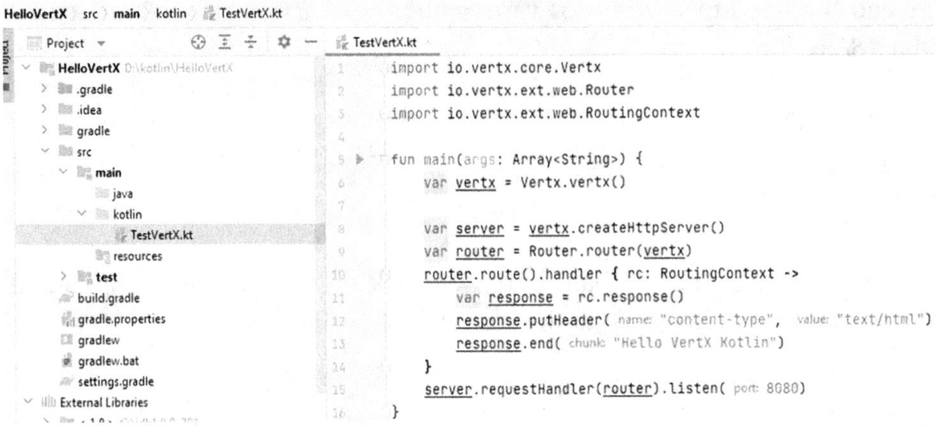

Table 1 shows the Kotlin code using Vert.X for web.

Table 1.

Listing 13.1: Kotlin Using Vert.X for Web
1
2 import io.vertx.core.Vertx
3 import io.vertx.ext.web.Router
4 import io.vertx.ext.web.RoutingContext
5 fun main(args: Array<String>) {
6 var vertx = Vertx.vertx()
7 var server = vertx.createHttpServer()
8 var router = Router.router(vertx)
9 router.route().handler { rc: RoutingContext ->
10 var response = rc.response()
11 response.putHeader("content-type", "text/html")
12 response.end("Hello VertX Kotlin")
13 }
14 server.requestHandler(router).listen(8080)
15 }
16

A Vertx object is created on command line 6, this object will create HttpServer on line 8 through the createHttpServer() function. Line 9 will create a Router object with a Vertx object as the argument. The Router object will call the handler command with the return parameter as a RoutingContext, this object will create HttpServerResponse through the response() function, the data will be output to the web screen thanks to HttpServerResponse. At command line 14, the program starts to initialize a web service on port 8080 through the listen() function..

The above program will create a website running on port 8080 and the content displayed is "Hello VertX Kotlin".

Figure 12. Run Kotlin Vert.X

To run the program, click on the blue triangle icon in front of main/ then select Run 'TestVertXKt'. Wait for the program to compile, then open the browser to see the results.

Figure 13. Website for Kotlin Vert.X

Figure 13 shows that opening http://localhost:8080/ will get the desired result. We can choose other ports, not necessarily 8080.

The source code of HelloVertx Project can be downloaded at the link https://github.com/thanhtd32/kotlin/tree/main/HelloVertX.

CREATE AND DEPLOY A KOTLIN VERTICLE IN VERT.X

In the previous section, we already know how to create a Website in Kotlin with Vert.X. In this section, we go into the technique of building classes that inherit from AbstractVerticle and how to deploy them. We should create an Event Loop for a group of transactions. For example, a group of transactions about Departments, Employees, Products, Customers, Invoices... and we can also collect 1 Verticle.

Each such Model class is a REST, but the RESTs can be grouped into an Event Loop (Create a common Verticle). This is also the architecture for later development of MicroServices systems.

To make it easy to understand, this lesson We will create a Verticle whose API is to get a list of Course names.

We create a new project with name "CourseVerticle", and add implementation for vertx, gson in the build.gradle file.

```
dependencies {
    implementation "org.jetbrains.kotlin:kotlin-stdlib"
    implementation 'io.vertx:vertx-web:4.2.6'
    implementation group: 'com.google.code.gson', name: 'gson',
version: '2.9.0'
}
```

The Gson library is used for convert object to JSon string.

After that, we create a new CourseVerticle Kotlin class extends from AbstractVerticle as shown in the Figure 14.

Figure 14. CourseVerticle Kotlin class

Next we override the start(Promise startPromise) method for the CourseVerticle class, it is shown in Table 2.

Table 2.

Listing 13.2: CourseVerticle Kotlin Class

1
2   import io.vertx.core.AbstractVerticle
3   import io.vertx.core.Promise
4   class CourseVerticle: AbstractVerticle() {
5   override fun start(startPromise: Promise<Void>?) {
6   super.start(startPromise)
7   }
8   }
9

When activating Verticle, the start function will be executed, the details of the code will be presented in the next pages. In this example we will return a list of courses, so add a listOfCourses method as shown in Table 3.

Table 3.

Listing 13.3: CourseVerticle Kotlin Class/ListOfCourses

import com.google.gson.Gson
1   import io.vertx.core.AbstractVerticle
2   import io.vertx.core.Promise
3   import io.vertx.ext.web.RoutingContext
4   class CourseVerticle: AbstractVerticle() {
5   override fun start(startPromise: Promise<Void>?) {
6   super.start(startPromise)
7   }
8   fun listOfCourses(routingContext: RoutingContext) {
9   var courses = *arrayOf*(
10   "Basic C#",
11   "Basic Kotlin",
12   "Advanced Java",
13   "Kotlin Android"
14   )
15   var gson = Gson()
16   routingContext.response()
17   .putHeader("content-type", "application/json;charset=utf-8")
18   .end(gson.toJson(courses))
19   }
  }

In the listOfCourses function, we declare an array of courses of type string, which will be passed by the GSon object to JSon using the gson.

toJson(courses) function. And this Json string will be returned to the client when calling the API. In the putHeader method of the Respone object, the content-type is application/json, so the data will be in Json format. In addition, we can replace it with XML.

Suppose we want to create API at URI /api/courses to see the entire list of courses, in the start function, we declare like Table 4, /api/courses will be passed to the Router object, then the listOfCourses function will invoked in the handler.

Table 4.

Listing 13.4: CourseVerticle Kotlin Class/Start
1   var router = Router.router(vertx) 2   router["/api/courses"].handler { 3   routingContext: RoutingContext? -> 4   listOfCourses(routingContext!!) 5   }

Router object will receive requests from HttpServer and is responsible for routing and creating API Methods. There are many methods provided by Router. (Get–>HttpGet), (Post–>HttpPost), (Put–>HttpPut), (Delete–>HttpDelete).

RoutingContext is used to handle requests in Vert.x-Web, each RoutingContext object will be created corresponding to a request Handler (can be get, post, put, delete ...). RoutingContext is used to access HttpServerRequest and HttpServerResponse to get data from the Client and output data back to the Client. In addition, it also helps us to access: Session, cookies, body.

Then the router object will be passed to initialize on port 8080. If the execution is successful, the complete() function will be executed, otherwise the fail function will be executed.

Table 5.

	Listing 13.5: CourseVerticle Kotlin Class/Start

1
2
3
4
5
6
7
8
9
10
11
	vertx.createHttpServer()
	.requestHandler(router)
	.listen(config().getInteger("http.port", 8080))
	{ result: AsyncResult<HttpServer?> ->
	 if (result.succeeded()) {
	startPromise!!.complete()
	} else {
	startPromise!!.fail(result.cause())
	}
	}

When the user invokes the API it will look like http://localhost:8080/api/courses

We have the full code of CourseVerticle as in Table 6.

Table 6.

Listing 13.6: CourseVerticle Kotlin Class/All Coding

```
1
2    import com.google.gson.Gson
3    import io.vertx.core.AbstractVerticle
4    import io.vertx.core.AsyncResult
5    import io.vertx.core.Promise
6    import io.vertx.core.http.HttpServer
7    import io.vertx.ext.web.Router
8    import io.vertx.ext.web.RoutingContext
9    class CourseVerticle: AbstractVerticle() {
10   override fun start(startPromise: Promise<Void>?) {
11   var router = Router.router(vertx)
12   router["/api/courses"].handler {
13    routingContext: RoutingContext? ->
14    listOfCourses(routingContext!!)
15    }
16    vertx.createHttpServer()
17   .requestHandler(router)
18   .listen(config().getInteger("http.port", 8080))
19   { result: AsyncResult<HttpServer?> ->
20    if (result.succeeded()) {
21   startPromise!!.complete()
22   } else {
23   startPromise!!.fail(result.cause())
24    }
25    }
26    }
27   fun listOfCourses(routingContext: RoutingContext) {
28   var courses = arrayOf(
29   "Basic C#",
30   "Basic Kotlin",
31   "Advanced Java",
32   "Kotlin Android"
33   )
34   var gson = Gson()
35   routingContext.response()
36   .putHeader("content-type",
37   "application/json;charset=utf-8")
38   .end(gson.toJson(courses))
39    }
40    }
41
```

HttpServerResponse allows us to control responses between the client and the server. It is created from RoutingContext, it can stream files and many more features. Next, we create a Kotlin class file RunVerticle.kt to call the CourseVerticle implementation like Table 7.

Table 7.

Listing 13.7: Run CourseVerticle
1 2 import io.vertx.core.Vertx 3 fun main() { 4 var vertx = Vertx.vertx() 5 vertx.deployVerticle(CourseVerticle()) 6 } 7

So we have completed the code, to execute we select the blue triangle icon in the main function in the RunVerticle.kt file as shown in Figure 15.

Figure 15. Run CourseVerticle

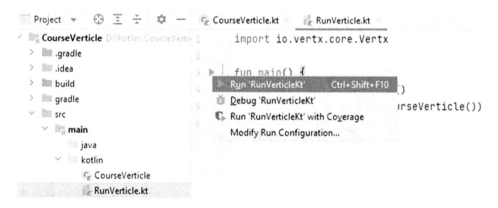

After the program compiles and executes Verticle, we open the browser and call the API http://localhost:8080/api/courses, we have the result as shown in Figure 16.

Figure 16. Result of api/courses

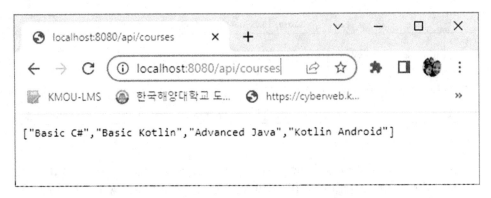

Observing the above output, we see a Json array of strings that are the course names returned when calling the API. This JSon string is handled by GSon, we can return more complex structures, it will be covered in the next sections.

The source code of CourseVerticle Project can be downloaded at the link https://github.com/thanhtd32/kotlin/tree/main/CourseVerticle

KOTLIN HTTP GET IN VERT.X FOR LIST OBJECT

In lessons on HTTP GET, POST, PUT, DELETE, we will illustrate on a product data set that includes information: Product code (int), product name (string), quantity (int) and unit price (float). So, we need to create a Product class that includes the requested information.

HTTP GET is one of the methods to create an API to retrieve data: Single data, list data, support for creating search and sorting functions, etc.

In this section, we will do 3 examples of HTTP GET, including: API get all products, API sort products ascending or descending, and API get a product by ID. These APIs will be tested on Postman. We create a project with name "ProductRestful", add the library Vert.X and GSon to project as in previous tutorials, class structures are shown in the **Figure 17.**

Figure 17. Result of api/courses

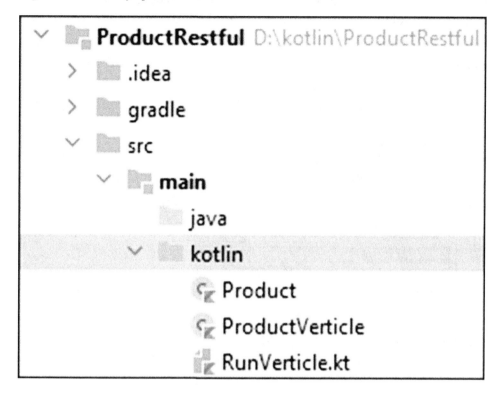

The Product class is used to create a structure for the product, including attributes id, name, quantity, and unit price. This class is demonstrated in Table 8.

Table 8.

Listing 13.8: Product

1
2
3
4
5
6
7
8
9
10
11
12
13
14
15
16
	`class Product {`
	`var id:Int = 0`
	`var name: String? = null`
	`var quantity:Int = 0`
	`var unitPrice:Float = 0f`
	`constructor() {}`
	`constructor(id: Int, name: String?,`
	`quantity: Int,`
	`unitPrice: Float) {`
	`this.id = id`
	`this.name = name`
	`this.quantity = quantity`
	`this.unitPrice = unitPrice`
	`}`
	`}`

Next, we create the ProductVerticle class, instantiate some objects in createExampleData() method like in the Table 9.

Table 9.

Listing 13.9: ProductVerticle
1 class ProductVerticle: AbstractVerticle() {
2 private var products = ArrayList<Product>()
3 fun createExampleData() {
4 var p1 = Product(1, "Coca", 2, 15f)
5 var p2 = Product(2, "Pepsi", 5, 20f)
6 var p3 = Product(3, "Aqua", 3, 25f)
7 var p4 = Product(4, "Sting", 7, 30f)
8 var p5 = Product(5, "Redbull", 3, 19f)
9 products.add(p1)
10 products.add(p2)
11 products.add(p3)
12 products.add(p4)
13 products.add(p5)
14 }
15 }

Continue to add the getAllProducts method behind the createExample() method to the ProductVerticle class to provide a list of Products for the API get all Products.

Table 10.

Listing 13.10: ProductVerticle
1 fun getAllProducts(routingContext: RoutingContext) {
2 var response = routingContext.response()
3 response.putHeader("content-type",
4 "application/json;charset=UTF-8")
5 var gson = Gson()
6 response.end(gson.toJson(products))
7 }

Finally, we add the start function to ProductVerticle as shown in Table 11.

Table 11.

Listing 13.11: ProductVerticle

```
1   override fun start(startPromise: Promise<Void>?) {
2   createExampleData()
3   var router = Router.router(vertx)
4   router["/api/products"].handler {
5   routingContext: RoutingContext ->
6   getAllProducts(routingContext) }
7   vertx.createHttpServer()
8   .requestHandler(router)
9   .listen(config().getInteger("http.port", 8080))
10  {
11  result: AsyncResult<HttpServer?> ->
12  if (result.succeeded()) {
13  startPromise!!.complete()
14  } else {
15  startPromise!!.fail(result.cause())
16  }
17  }
18  }
19
```

router["/api/products"] is declared, and port 8080 is used. When calling API we will use the following URI: http://localhost:8080/api/products
The full code of ProductVerticle is shown in the Table 12.

Table 12.

	Listing 13.12: ProductVerticle
1	
2	import io.vertx.core.AbstractVerticle
3	import io.vertx.ext.web.RoutingContext
4	import com.google.gson.Gson
5	import io.vertx.ext.web.Router
6	import io.vertx.core.AsyncResult
7	import io.vertx.core.Promise
8	import io.vertx.core.http.HttpServer
9	import java.util.ArrayList
10	class ProductVerticle: AbstractVerticle() {
11	private var products = ArrayList<Product>()
12	fun createExampleData() {
13	var p1 = Product(1, "Coca", 2, 15f)
14	var p2 = Product(2, "Pepsi", 5, 20f)
15	var p3 = Product(3, "Aqua", 3, 25f)
16	var p4 = Product(4, "Sting", 7, 30f)
17	var p5 = Product(5, "Redbull", 3, 19f)
18	products.add(p1)
19	products.add(p2)
20	products.add(p3)
21	products.add(p4)
22	products.add(p5)
23	}
24	fun getAllProducts(routingContext: RoutingContext) {
25	var response = routingContext.response()
26	response.putHeader("content-type",
27	"application/json;charset=UTF-8")
28	var gson = Gson()
29	response.end(gson.toJson(products))
30	}
31	override fun start(startPromise: Promise<Void>?) {
32	createExampleData()
33	var router = Router.router(vertx)
34	router["/api/products"].handler {
35	routingContext: RoutingContext ->
36	getAllProducts(routingContext) }
37	vertx.createHttpServer()
38	.requestHandler(router)
39	.listen(config().getInteger("http.port", 8080))
40	{
41	result: AsyncResult<HttpServer?> ->
42	if (result.succeeded()) {
43	startPromise!!.complete()
44	} else {
45	startPromise!!.fail(result.cause())
46	}
47	}
48	}
49	}
50	

To execute ProductVerticle, we proceed to create a file RunVerticle.kt kotlin and initialize the commands as shown in Table 13.

Table 13.

Listing 13.13: RunVerticle.kt
1
2   import io.vertx.core.Vertx
3   fun main() {
4   var vertx = Vertx.vertx()
5   vertx.deployVerticle(ProductVerticle())
6   }
7

Then we proceed to execute the main function, for the GET API we can test it on a web browser or on postman, uri http://localhost:8080/api/products

Figure 18. Test api/products on web browser

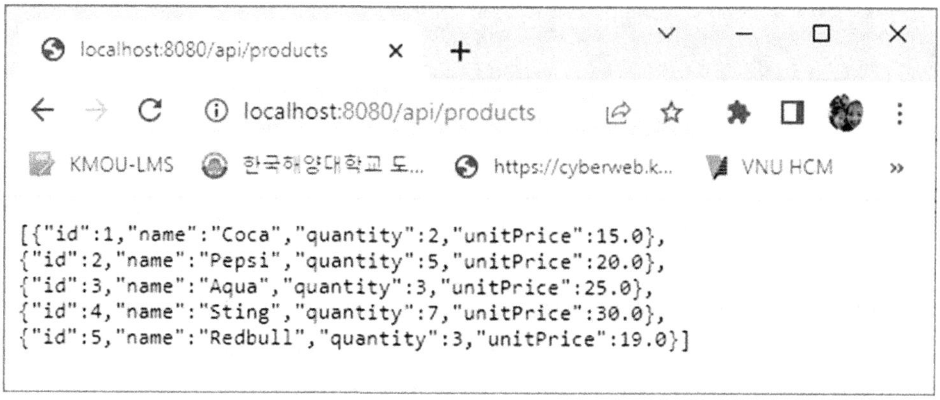

We can check the API products on the Postman, it is shown in the Figure 19.

Figure 19. Test api/products on Postman

Step 1, we choose GET method, step 2 we enter the API products, step 3 we click Send button, and in the step 4 we will see the result is returned from the server. The result is the JSonArray of Product.

The source code of ProductRestful Project can be downloaded at the link https://github.com/thanhtd32/kotlin/tree/main/ProductRestful.

KOTLIN HTTP GET IN VERT.X FOR SORTED LIST OBJECT

We continue to add an API to get a list of products but allow to sort by unit price ascending or descending, the parameter is passed to the program to automatically sort. We add a function getsortedProducts as in the Table 14.

Table 14.

Listing 13.14: ProductVerticle/getSortedProducts

```
1   fun getSortedProducts(routingContext: RoutingContext) {
2   var response = routingContext.response()
3   response.putHeader("content-type",
4   "application/json;charset=UTF-8")
5   //parameter taken from user
6   val sort = routingContext.request()
7   .getParam("sort")
8   if (sort == null) {
9   //it shows an error if there is no parameter
10  routingContext.response()
11  .setStatusCode(400).end()
12  }
13  else
14  {
15  if (sort.equals("desc", ignoreCase = true)) {
16  products.sortBy { x->x.unitPrice }
17  }
18  else
19  products.sortByDescending { x->x.unitPrice }
20  var gson = Gson()
21  response.end(gson.toJson(products))
22  }
23  }
24  }
```

Thus, the input parameter is [sort], if sort is desc, then sort products by descending unit price (sortByDescending), if sort is asc, then sort products by ascending unit price (sortBy).

Edit the start function of ProductVerticle class to create a sortedproducts API, it is shown in Tabl3 15.

Table 15.

	Listing 13.15: ProductVerticle/Start Edit
1	override fun start(startPromise: Promise<Void>?) {
2	createExampleData()
3	var router = Router.router(vertx)
4	router["/api/products"]
5	.handler(this::getAllProducts)
6	router["/api/sortedproducts"]
7	.handler(this::getSortedProducts)
8	vertx.createHttpServer()
9	.requestHandler(router)
10	.listen(config().getInteger("http.port", 8080))
11	{
12	result: AsyncResult<HttpServer?> ->
13	if (result.succeeded()) {
14	startPromise!!.complete()
15	} else {
16	startPromise!!.fail(result.cause())
17	}
18	}
19	}

Command line 4 and command line 6 above are modified to create the api/products and api/sortedproducts APIs. The Figure 20 shows how to call sorted products API.

Figure 20. *Test api/sortedproducts on Postman*

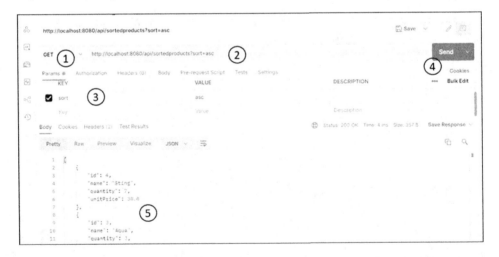

Step 1, we choose the Get method, step 2 we enter the API http://localhost:8080/api/sortedproducts, step 3, in the params tab, we enter sort in the KEY column, asc or desc in the VALUE column. Step 4 we click send button, and the sorted list of the Product will return in the step 5.

KOTLIN HTTP GET IN VERT.X FOR SINGLE OBJECT

We have known how to use HTTP GET to create APIs that get list of objects as well as sort objects by parameter. In this section we will use HTTP GET to create an API that queries an object when its id is known. We add code for getOneProduct function in ProductVerticle class as in Table 16.

Table 16.

Listing 13.16: ProductVerticle/getOneProduct

1   fun getOneProduct(routingContext: RoutingContext) {
2   var response = routingContext.response()
3   response.putHeader("content-type",
4   "application/json;charset=utf-8")
5   //get input id from URL
6   var sid = routingContext.request().getParam("id")
7   if (sid == null) { // if id not exist
8   routingContext.response()
9   .setStatusCode(400).end()
10 } else {
11 //convert id to int
12 var id = sid.*toInt*()
13 //find product by id
14 var p = products.*firstOrNull* { x->x.id==id }
15 var gson = Gson()
16 if(p!=null)
17 response.end(gson.toJson(p))
18 else
19 response.end("")
20 }
21 }

The function firstOrNull will return the Product if the id is existed and it will return null if id is not existed.

The getOneProduct function will receive an id to query whether any Product has the id as passed or not. The syntax http://localhost:8080/api/products/1, means get Products with id equal to 1.

The start function of ProductVerticle will be added to getOneProduct as shown in Table 17.

Table 17.

	Listing 13.17: ProductVerticle/Start Edit
1	override fun start(startPromise: Promise<Void>?) {
2	createExampleData()
3	var router = Router.router(vertx)
4	router["/api/products"]
5	.handler(this::getAllProducts)
6	router["/api/sortedproducts"]
7	.handler(this::getSortedProducts)
8	router["/api/products/:id"]
9	.handler(this::getOneProduct)
10	vertx.createHttpServer()
11	.requestHandler(router)
12	.listen(config().getInteger("http.port", 8080))
13	{
14	result: AsyncResult<HttpServer?> ->
15	if (result.succeeded()) {
16	startPromise!!.complete()
17	} else {
18	startPromise!!.fail(result.cause())
19	}
20	}
21	}

In Table 17, the command router ["/api/products/:id"] is added to create an API that queries products by id.

Then we run the main() function in the RunVerticle.kt file. The test results are illustrated in Postman in the Figure 21.

Figure 21. Test api/products/{id} on Postman

In the Figure 21, we test the API with api/products/{id} format. http://localhost:8080/api/products/3 it means, it will return the detail of the Product with id=3. We can try with many different ids, even those that do not exist to check the API's return is correct or not.

KOTLIN HTTP POST IN VERT.X

In the previous section, we learned to create Restful API HTTP GETs to get a list of data, sort the list, and view object details. In this article, we use the POST method to add new data to the Server. In this section, the document is using In-Memory Data. Store Product list in ArrayList. We can use many different types of databases for storage, such as MongoDB, MySQL, Microsoft SQL Server.

The Figure 22 illustrates how to convert between Kotlin Model Class and JSon Object Data. In the case of HTTP POST, we will pass to the Server a JsonObject with the structure of a Product as described. The program will convert this JSonObject to Kotlin Model Class to save the data.

Figure 22. Kotlin model class and JSonObject data

Kotlin Model Class

```
Product.kt
1    class Product {
2        var id:Int = 0
3        var name: String? = null
4        var quantity:Int = 0
5        var unitPrice:Float = 0f
6
7        constructor() {}
8        constructor(id: Int, name: String?,
9                    quantity: Int,
10                   unitPrice: Float) {
11           this.id = id
12           this.name = name
13           this.quantity = quantity
14           this.unitPrice = unitPrice
15       }
16   }
```

JSon Object Data

```
{
    "id": 8,
    "name": "TH True Milk",
    "quantity": 4,
    "unitPrice": 28.0
}
```

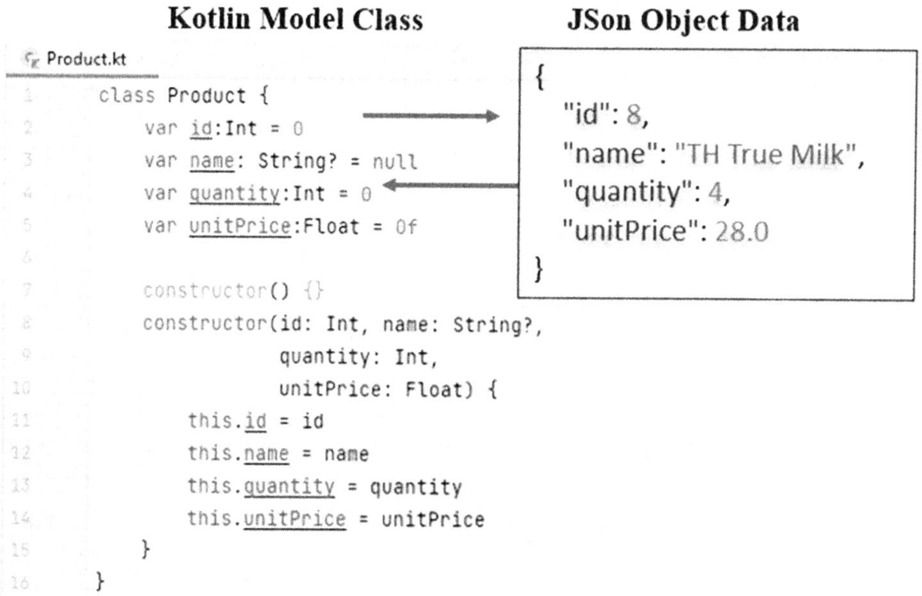

We add the insertNewProduct function in the ProductVerticle class, this function serves the HTTP POST API to add a new Product, the data passed to the API will have a JSon Object structure. The code for this function is illustrated in Table 18.

Table 18.

Listing 13.18: ProductVerticle/insertNewProduct

1   fun insertNewProduct(routingContext: RoutingContext) {
2   var response = routingContext.response()
3   response.putHeader("content-type",
4   "application/json;charset=UTF8")
5   try {
6   var gson = Gson()
7   var p =gson.fromJson(
8   routingContext.*body*.toString(),
9   Product::class,*java*)
10 products.add(p)
11 response.end("true")
12 } catch (ex: Exception) {
13 response.end(ex.message)
14 }
15 }

A Json Object data is transferred to Server, command line 7 → 9 will convert this Json Object into Kotlin Model class of Product. The object is then added to the products list. In the case of using a database, here we will save the object to the database. After successfully saving, the program will return "true" results to the client or if it fails, it will return error details to the client. Based on this result, the client side handles the next tasks.

Next in the start function of ProductVerticle, we add the following 2 commands to create the HTTP POST API.

```
router.route("/api/products*").handler(BodyHandler.create());
router.post("/api/products").handler(this::insertNewProduct);
```

The first command allows to receive data from the client sent via the Body tag, the second command helps to register the API /api/products with the POST method.

Table 19 shows the code details of the start function in the ProductVerticle class.

Table 19.

Listing 13.19: ProductVerticle/Start Edit
1 override fun start(startPromise: Promise<Void>?) {
2 createExampleData()
3 var router = Router.router(vertx)
4 router["/api/products"]
5 .handler(this::getAllProducts)
6 router["/api/sortedproducts"]
7 .handler(this::getSortedProducts)
8 router["/api/products/:id"]
9 .handler(this::getOneProduct)
10 router.route("/api/products*")
11 .handler(BodyHandler.create());
12 router.post("/api/products")
13 .handler(this::insertNewProduct);
14 vertx.createHttpServer()
15 .requestHandler(router)
16 .listen(config().getInteger("http.port", 8080))
17 {
18 result: AsyncResult<HttpServer?> ->
19 if (result.succeeded()) {
20 startPromise!!.complete()
21 } else {
22 startPromise!!.fail(result.cause())
23 }
24 }
25 }

Then we proceed to run the main function in the RunVerticle.kt file, then use Postman to test the HTTP POST API function, it shows in the Figure 23.

Figure 23. Test HTTP post in Postman

To test HTTP POST on Postman, we perform 7 steps as shown in Figure 23.

- Step 1: We choose method as POST
- Step 2: Select API http://localhost:8080/api/products
- Step 3: In the body tag, we select raw
- Step 4: In the body tag, we select JSON
- Step 5: Enter the JSON structure for the Product data that we want to upload to the Server. For example:

```
{
    "id": 8,
    "name": "TH True Milk",
    "quantity": 4,
    "unitPrice": 28.0
}
```

- Step 6: Click Send button
- Step 7: Results of success or failure when calling the API will be displayed, if successful, true, if failed, show details of the error sent by the Server. Figure 24 reviewing the product that has been successfully saved using the GET method, we see that the new object has been added to the list.

Figure 24. Result of HTTP post in Postman

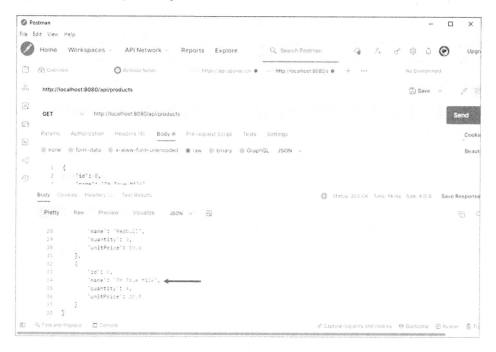

The result of converting Json to Kotlin Model class is illustrated in the Figure 25.

Figure 25. JSonObject to Kotlin model class

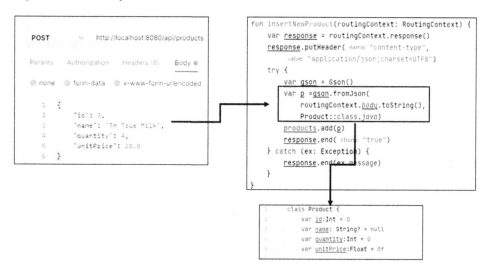

The data of the product that we want to send to the Server to add a new one will have the JSonObject format which is a string. When on the Server, the program will use Gson to convert this Json string into a Kotlin Model class. Once we have a model class, everything is considered complete, because we can arbitrarily process data on the object.

KOTLIN HTTP PUT IN VERT.X

We have used HTTP GET to query data, HTTP POST to add new data, HTTP PUT will be used to update data when calling APIs.

To update data, we also pass a JSonObject object to the Server. The program will convert JSonObject to Kotlin Model class, then proceed to check whether the object exists or not, if it exists, the program will update and return true, if not, return false. The code shown in Table 20.

Table 20.

	Listing 13.20: ProductVerticle/updateProduct
1	fun updateProduct(routingContext: RoutingContext) {
2	val response = routingContext.response()
3	response.putHeader("content-type",
4	"application/json;charset=UTF8")
5	var gson = Gson()
6	var p =gson.fromJson(
7	routingContext.*body*.toString(),
8	Product::class.*java*)
9	var pos=products.*indexOfFirst* { x->x.id==p.id }
10	if(pos!=-1) {
11	products.set(pos, p)
12	response.end("true")
13	}
14	else
15	response.end("false")
16	}

The command line 6→8 will convert JSonObject to Kotlin Model class Product. Command line 9 (indexOfFirst method) will check if this Product exists or not, if it exists, it will return the found position and update the data on line 11, then return true to the client. Otherwise, if not found, it will return false to the client.

Similar to HTTP POST, for HTTP PUT we also go to the start function of ProductVerticle class and we add the command:

```
router.put("/api/products").handler(this::updateProduct)
```

Run the program, and check on Postman for HTTP PUT to change the product information.

Figure 26. Test HTTP PUT in PostMan

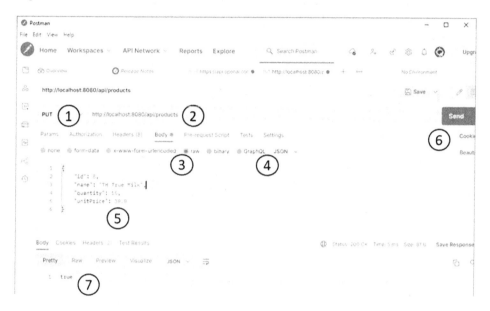

To test HTTP PUT in Postman, we perform 7 steps as shown in the Figure 26.

- Step 1: We choose method as PUT
- Step 2: Select API http://localhost:8080/api/products
- Step 3: In the body tag, we select raw
- Step 4: In the body tag, we select JSON
- Step 5: Enter the JSON structure for the Product data that we want to upload to the Server. For example:

```
{
    "id": 8,
    "name": "TH True Milk",
    "quantity": 16,
```

```
"unitPrice": 30.0
}
```

- Step 6: Click Send button
- Step 7: If the update is successful, the client will receive the value true otherwise it will receive the value false. Similar to HTTP POST, we can use the HTTP GET function to verify that this Product is up to date.

KOTLIN HTTP DELETE IN VERT.X

HTTP DELETE Method is used to invoke data deletion APIs. For example, in this case we will write API to delete Product when its Id is known.

We will build an API to delete products with the following URI syntax http://localhost:8080/api/products/{id}. So, in the start function of ProductVerticle, we need to add the command:

```
router.delete("/api/products/:id").handler(this::deleteProduct)
```

With the deleteProduct function shown in Table 21.

Table 21.

Listing 13.21: ProductVerticle/deleteProduct
1   fun deleteProduct(routingContext: RoutingContext) {
2   var response = routingContext.response()
3   response.putHeader("content-type",
4   "application/json;charset=UTF-8")
5   var sid = routingContext.request().getParam("id")
6   var id = sid.*toInt*()
7   var p = products.*firstOrNull* { x->x.id==id }
8   if (p!=null) {
9   products.remove(p)
10   response.end("true")
11   } else response.end("false")
12   }

Command line 5 will receive the id from the client, and command line 6 will return the id to a number, command line 7 will check if this product code exists or not, if it exists, it will remove it with the remove method at command line 9 and at the same time it returns true on line 10 to notify successful deletion, otherwise it will return false when deletion fails at line 11.

Below is the detailed code of the start function in the ProductVerticle class shown in Table 22.

Table 22.

Listing 13.22: ProductVerticle/Start Edit

```
1    override fun start(startPromise: Promise<Void>?) {
2    createExampleData()
3    var router = Router.router(vertx)
4    router["/api/products"]
5    .handler(this::getAllProducts)
6    router["/api/sortedproducts"]
7    .handler(this::getSortedProducts)
8    router["/api/products/:id"]
9    .handler(this::getOneProduct)
10   router.route("/api/products*")
11   .handler(BodyHandler.create())
12   router.post("/api/products")
13   .handler(this::insertNewProduct)
14   router.put("/api/products")
15   .handler(this::updateProduct)
16   router.delete("/api/products/:id")
17   .handler(this::deleteProduct)
18   vertx.createHttpServer()
19   .requestHandler(router)
20   .listen(config().getInteger("http.port", 8080))
21   {
22   result: AsyncResult<HttpServer?> ->
23   if (result.succeeded()) {
24   startPromise!!.complete()
25   } else {
26   startPromise!!.fail(result.cause())
27   }
28   }
29   }
30
```

We proceed to run the main function of RunVerticle and test on postman for the HTTP Delete case as shown in the Figure 27.

Figure 27. Test HTTP DELETE in PostMan

- Step 1: Choose the DELETE. Method
- Step 2: Enter URI http://localhost:8080/api/products/2 with 2 being the product id we want to delete.
- Step 3: Press the send button.
- Step 4: Returns true if the deletion is successful, false if the deletion fails

The source code of ProductRestful Project can be downloaded at the link https://github.com/thanhtd32/kotlin/tree/main/ProductRestful

KOTLIN AUTHENTICATION IN VERT.X

To secure Restful APIs, Vert.X also supports JWT Auth provider libraries, with many different security handling techniques, in this document we show how to use keystore with security code as SHA256. This process includes five main steps as follows.

- Step 1: Call the library "vertx-auth".
- Step 2: Create keystore files and copy to the project
- Step 3: Set Authentication requirements for APIs
- Step 4: Login to get Token
- Step 5: Use Tokens to access APIs

We create a Project "AuthenticationRestful", and then we create a MyVerticle Kotlin class and a Runverticle.kt as shown in the Figure 28.

Figure 28. AuthenticationRestful project

In the MyVerticle class, we have an api/users API to return a list of users, the code is like in Table 23.

Table 23.

	Listing 13.23: MyVerticle
| 1<br>2<br>3<br>4<br>5<br>6<br>7<br>8<br>9<br>10<br>11<br>12<br>13<br>14<br>15<br>16<br>17<br>18<br>19<br>20<br>21<br>22<br>23<br>24<br>25<br>26<br>27<br>28<br>29<br>30<br>31<br>32<br>33<br>34<br>35<br>36<br>37<br>38<br>39<br>40 | ```kotlin
import com.google.gson.Gson
import io.vertx.core.AbstractVerticle
import io.vertx.core.AsyncResult
import io.vertx.core.Promise
import io.vertx.core.http.HttpServer
import io.vertx.ext.web.Router
import io.vertx.ext.web.RoutingContext
class MyVerticle: AbstractVerticle() {
override fun start(startPromise: Promise<Void>?) {
var router = Router.router(vertx)
router.get("/api/users")
.handler(this::listOfUsers)
vertx.createHttpServer()
.requestHandler(router)
.listen(config().getInteger("http.port", 8080))
{ result: AsyncResult<HttpServer?> ->
 if (result.succeeded()) {
startPromise!!.complete()
} else {
startPromise!!.fail(result.cause())
}
 }
}
fun listOfUsers(routingContext: RoutingContext) {
var users = arrayOf(
"admin",
"user1",
"user2",
"user3"
)
var gson = Gson()
routingContext.response()
.putHeader("content-type",
"application/json;charset=utf-8")
.end(gson.toJson(users))
}
}
``` |

Illustrated in Table 23, API api/users will simulate returning a list of 4 users (admin, user1, user2, user3). Tabl 24 shows a command for RunVerticle. kt to run MyVerticle.
```

Table 24.

Listing 13.24: RunVerticle.kt

1 2 3 4 5 6	`import io.vertx.core.Vertx`
	`fun main() {`
	`var vertx = Vertx.vertx()`
	`vertx.deployVerticle(MyVerticle())`
	`}`

We execute RunVerticle.kt and call the API http://localhost:8080/api/users, the result will be 4 users as below returned to the client.

```
[
    "admin",
    "user1",
    "user2",
    "user3"
]
```

However, now we require that users who want to access the API api/users must log in first, otherwise, they will report an Unauthorized error.

So, we will create an API /api/login (HTTP POST), the user must call this API to login before accessing the api/users.

Then in the Step 1, we open the build.gradle file and add the Vert.X libraries for web and Vert.X for JWT authentication, along with Google Gson.

```
dependencies {
    implementation "org.jetbrains.kotlin:kotlin-stdlib"
    implementation 'io.vertx:vertx-web:3.9.4'
    implementation 'io.vertx:vertx-auth-jwt:3.9.4'
    implementation 'com.google.code.gson:gson:2.9.0'
}
```

JWT is a simple token used in web programming that makes it easier to authenticate users in the system (especially in Single Page Applications). Some of JWT's strengths: Easy token authentication, it contains data in JSON form and easy to communicate in multiple systems, compact, completely stateless.

In the Step 2, We create keystore files and copy to the project.

JWT in vertx has 3 ways to load keys: Using secrets (sysmetric keys), OpenSSL (pem format), and keystore files. In this document We use keystore with HS256 encryption algorithm. Here is the syntax to create a Keystore file:

```
keytool -genseckey -keystore keystore.jceks -storetype jceks
-storepass secret -keyalg HMacSHA256 -keysize 2048 -alias HS256
-keypass secret
```

In the above syntax, [secret] is the password, [jceks] is the JWT type, keystore.jceks is the file that will be generated, with the HS256 algorithm. We open the command and copy the keytool command above into the command line as shown in the Figure 29, a file keystore.jceks will be created in the computer.

Figure 29. Create keystore by keytool

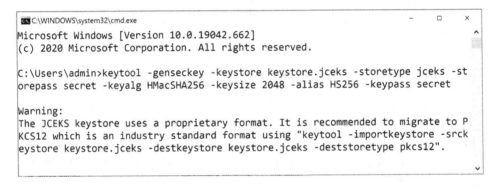

By default, the keystore.jceks file will be created in the current user, which file will we put in the project (in the project create a keys folder and copy this file in) as shown in the Figure 30.

Figure 30. Copy keystore file to keys folder in Project

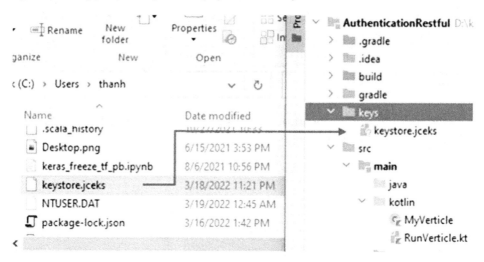

In the Step 3, we set the Authentication requirements for APIs. Specifically, when accessing the api/users API, the program will report an Unauthorized error when not logged in. We write the Authentication JWT with the command below.

```
var authConfig = JWTAuthOptions()
    .setKeyStore(
        KeyStoreOptions()
            .setType("jceks")
            .setPath("keys\\keystore.jceks")
            .setPassword("secret")
    )
var jwt = JWTAuth.create(
    vertx,
    authConfig)
```

The above command will create a JWTAuthOptions (authConfig) object, set the type to jceks, the path is where we store the keystore file and the file's password. Then the JWTAuth object will be initialized via the create (vertx, authConfig) function.

Then we set up Route APIs that require authentication, for example the following command when someone accesses API api/users will be told to require authentication:

```
router.route("/api/*").handler(authHandler(jwt))
router.get("/api/users").handler(this::listOfUsers)
```

The api/* syntax means that every API declared behind it must authenticate. The authHandler function is defined as follows.

```
fun authHandler(jwtAuth: JWTAuth): JWTAuthHandler {
    return JWTAuthHandler.create(jwtAuth, "/api/login")
}
```

The code that requires authentication when calling the full MyVerticle API is updated in Table 25.

Table 25.

Listing 13.25: MyVerticle

```
1
2    import com.google.gson.Gson
3    import io.vertx.core.AbstractVerticle
4    import io.vertx.core.AsyncResult
5    import io.vertx.core.Promise
6    import io.vertx.core.http.HttpServer
7    import io.vertx.ext.auth.KeyStoreOptions
8    import io.vertx.ext.auth.jwt.JWTAuth
9    import io.vertx.ext.auth.jwt.JWTAuthOptions
10   import io.vertx.ext.web.Router
11   import io.vertx.ext.web.RoutingContext
12   import io.vertx.ext.web.handler.JWTAuthHandler
13   class MyVerticle: AbstractVerticle() {
14   override fun start(startPromise: Promise<Void>?) {
15   var router = Router.router(vertx)
16   var authConfig = JWTAuthOptions()
17   .setKeyStore(
18   KeyStoreOptions()
19   .setType("jceks")
20   .setPath("keys\\keystore.jceks")
21   .setPassword("secret")
22   )
23   var jwt = JWTAuth.create(
24   vertx,
25   authConfig)
26   router.route("/api/*")
27   .handler(authHandler(jwt))
28   router.get("/api/users")
29   .handler(this::listOfUsers)
30   vertx.createHttpServer()
31   .requestHandler(router)
32   .listen(config().getInteger("http.port", 8080))
33   { result: AsyncResult<HttpServer?> ->
34   if (result.succeeded()) {
35   startPromise!!.complete()
36   } else {
37   startPromise!!.fail(result.cause())
38   }
39   }
40   }
41   fun authHandler(jwtAuth: JWTAuth): JWTAuthHandler {
42   return JWTAuthHandler.create(jwtAuth, "/api/login")
43   }
44   fun listOfUsers(routingContext: RoutingContext) {
45   var users = arrayOf(
46   "admin",
47   "user1",
48   "user2",
49   "user3"
50   )
51   var gson = Gson()
52   routingContext.response()
53   .putHeader("content-type",
54   "application/json;charset=utf-8")
55   .end(gson.toJson(users))
56   }
57   }
58
59
```

Executing the main function in RunVerticle.kt, checking Api/users will give an error as shown in the Figure 31.

Figure 31. Unauthorized after call api/users

In the Step 4, we will create a Login API to get Token. In the start function add the following two commands:

```
router.route("/api*").handler(BodyHandler.create());
router.post("/api/login").handler { ctx->login(ctx,jwt) }
```

The above code is to create the login API, which requires login (in this case, we will use JsonObject to pass the user+password to the server). The login function is shown in Table 26.

Table 26.

Listing 13.26: Login

```
1
2    fun login(context: RoutingContext, jwtAuth: JWTAuth) {
3    try {
4    var data = context.bodyAsJson
5     var user=data.getString("user")
6    var pwd=data.getString("pass")
7    if (!(user.equals("admin") &&
8    pwd.equals("123"))) {
9    return
10   }
11   val token = jwtAuth.generateToken(
12   JsonObject(),
13   JWTOptions().setExpiresInSeconds(60))
14   var cookie = Cookie.cookie("auth", token)
15   cookie.setHttpOnly(true).setPath("/").encode()
16   context.addCookie(cookie).response()
17   .putHeader("content-type", "text/plain")
18   .putHeader("Authorization", token)
19   .end(token)
20   } catch (ex: Exception) {
21   context.response().setStatusCode(401)
22   .putHeader("content-type",
23   "application/json")
24   .end(ex.message)
25   }
26   }
27
```

In Table 26, a User object in JSon format will be sent from the Client, it is stored in the bodyAsJson property of the RoutingContext object. In this case, we assume that the login account is admin/123 (of course, when deploying a database such as MongoDB, we replace this with a query that checks login data). If the login is successful, the program will return the token in the generateToken function with a time of 60 seconds (we can adjust this time). This token will be saved in a cookie and sent down to the Client for processing, based on this token, when using other APIs, the user needs to send the token to the Server to access the authorized APIs. Tabel 27 is the detailed code of MyVerticle when adding the login API.

Table 27(a).

Listing 13.27: MyVerticle
1   class MyVerticle: AbstractVerticle() {
2   override fun start(startPromise: Promise<Void>?) {
3   var router = Router.router(vertx)
4   var authConfig = JWTAuthOptions()
5   .setKeyStore(
6   KeyStoreOptions()
7   .setType("jceks")
8   .setPath("keys\\keystore.jceks")
9   .setPassword("secret"))
10   var jwt = JWTAuth.create(
11   vertx,
12   authConfig)
13   router.route("/api/*")
14   .handler(authHandler(jwt))
15   router.get("/api/users")
16   .handler(this::listOfUsers)
17   router.route("/api*")
18   .handler(BodyHandler.create());
19   router.post("/api/login")
20   .handler { ctx->login(ctx,jwt)}
21   vertx.createHttpServer()
22   .requestHandler(router)
23   .listen(config().getInteger("http.port", 8080))
24   { result: AsyncResult<HttpServer?> ->
25   if (result.succeeded()) {
26   startPromise!!.complete()
27   } else {
28   startPromise!!.fail(result.cause())
29   }
30   **}**
31   }
32   fun authHandler(jwtAuth: JWTAuth): JWTAuthHandler {
33   return JWTAuthHandler.create(jwtAuth, "/api/login")

Table 27(b).

34	}
35	fun login(context: RoutingContext, jwtAuth: JWTAuth) {
36	try {
37	var data = context.*bodyAsJson*
38	var user=data.getString("user")
39	var pwd=data.getString("pass")
40	if (!(user.equals("admin") &&
41	pwd.equals("123"))) {
42	return
43	}
44	val token = jwtAuth.generateToken(
45	JsonObject(),
46	JWTOptions().setExpiresInSeconds(60))
47	var cookie = Cookie.cookie("auth", token)
48	cookie.setHttpOnly(true)
49	.setPath("/").encode()
50	context.addCookie(cookie).response()
51	.putHeader("content-type", "text/plain")
52	.putHeader("Authorization", token)
53	.end(token)
54	} catch (ex: Exception) {
55	context.response().setStatusCode(401)
56	.putHeader("content-type", "application/json")
57	.end(ex.message)
58	}
59	}
60	fun listOfUsers(routingContext: RoutingContext) {
61	var users = *arrayOf*("admin","user1","user2","user3")
62	var gson = Gson()
63	routingContext.response()
64	.putHeader("content-type",
65	"application/json;charset=utf-8")
66	.end(gson.toJson(users))
67	}
68	}
69	

We proceed to run the main function in the file RunVerticle. Call the API api/login to get token as shown in the Figure 32.

Figure 32. Get token from api/login

To get the token, we call the API http://localhost:8080/api/login with the POST method, in the body entry JSonObject is the user object, in this case we illustrate it as admin/123. After you click Send, the API will return the Token string shown in item 5. We will use this token to pass it on to the Server when calling other APIs in the Step 5. When calling API/users, in the authorization (3) section, we select Bearer Token and paste the token in item 4, then click send to call API/users, the list of users will be returned as shown in the Figure 33.

Figure 33. Call API/users with Bearer Token

We have completed the chapter dealing with Restful API for Kotlin using Vert.X, API Methods like HTTP GET, HTTP POST, HTTP PUT and HTTP DELETE have been implemented, for each different type of method that we use. be suitable. In addition to handling security for the API, the JWT Authencation provider table is also implemented.

The source code of ProductRestful Project can be downloaded at the link https://github.com/thanhtd32/kotlin/tree/main/Authentication Restful

Readers can read more explanations of the conditional structure in the authors' books (Dmitry Jemerov, et al. 2017), and Programming book is referenced (Schild, 2019), and book (Ebel, 2019), and book (Späth, 2019), and book Vert.X (Ponge, 2020), and the book (Bailey et al., 2021).

EXERCISE

1. What is Restful API?
2. How does Restful API work?
3. Explain the function of HTTP GET, HTTP POST, HTTP PUT and HTTP DELETE.
4. What libraries in build.gradle are used to use Vert.X in Restful builds?
5. Present how to create and execute Verticle in Vert.X.
6. Present how to create GET, POST, PUT, DELETE methods in Vert.X.
7. Present how to use the Postman software (for calling GET, POST, PUT, DELETE methods).
8. Present how to create Authentication for APIs.
9. Given the JSon Object structure below, let's build the Kotlin Model classes to be able to use GSon to create the corresponding JSon.

```
{"items": [
  {"type":"CAD","value":18},
  {"type":"AUD","value":20},
  {"type":"EUR","value":19}
]}
```

10. From the class model learned in question 9, please use Vert.X to build APIs for data (GET, POST, PUT, and DELETE).
11. Use Vert.X's JWT Authentication Provider to build a security mechanism for the APIs in question 10.
12. Building a Complex application with Desktop and Mobile application using Vert.X.

Given a database of 3 tables:

*   Employee table includes columns: EmployeeID, EmployeeName, UserName, Password
*   Customer table includes information: CustomerID, CustomerName, Age
*   EmployeeCustomer table includes information: EmployeeID, CustomerID.
    Let's design a database using Mysql or Microsoft SQL Server, or MongoDB to store data for the 2 tables described above.

- Building Restful API using Vert.X to write all functions such as adding, editing, viewing data, deleting data.
- Building Desktop Application:
  + Login screen: When Employee logs in successfully, it will display the Customer operation screen corresponding to this logged-in Employee.

Figure 34.

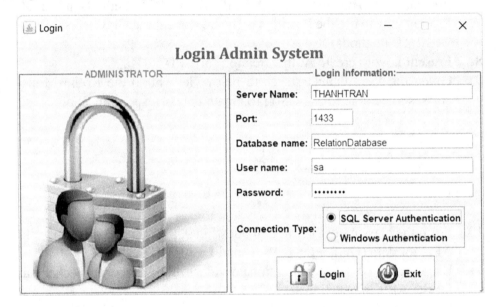

+ Customer operation screen: The operations of adding new, editing, deleting Customer will be stored for Employee login.

Figure 35.

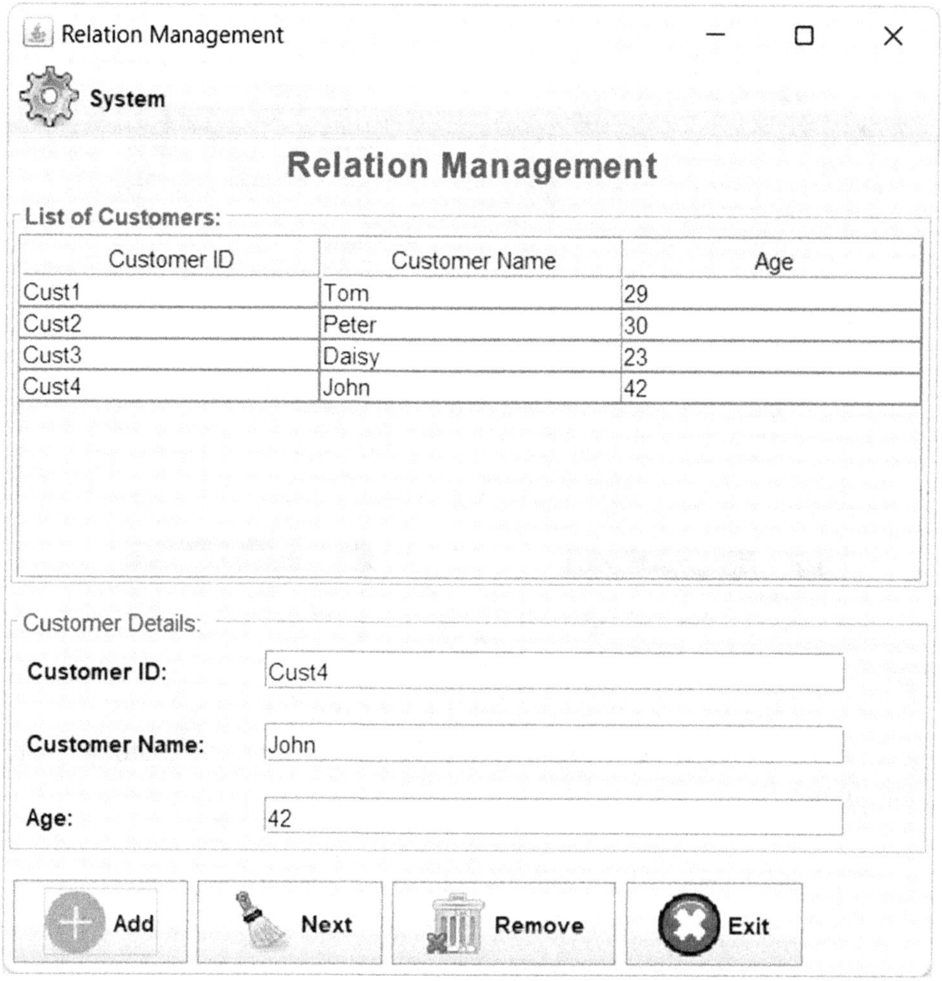

Restful APIs will be invoked to handle any changes to customer data.
- Building Mobile Application:
    + Login screen: When Employee logs in successfully, it will display a list of Customer of Employee manipulated in Desktop Application.

Figure 36.

Restful APIs will be invoked to handle any changes to customer data (edit, remove).

REFERENCES

Bailey, Greenhalgh, & Skeen. (2021). *Kotlin Programming: The Big Nerd Ranch Guide* (2nd ed.). Big Nerd Ranch, LLC.

Ebel, N. (2019). *Mastering Kotlin: Learn advanced Kotlin programming techniques to build apps for Android, iOS, and the web.* Packt Publishing.

Jemerov & Isakova. (2017). Kotlin in Action. *Manning*, 320–322.

Ponge. (2020). *Vert.x in Action Asynchronous and Reactive Java.* Manning Publisher.

Schild, H. (2019). *Java the complete Reference* (11th ed.). McGraw-Hill Education.

Späth, P. (2019). *Learn Kotlin for Android Development: The Next Generation Language for Modern Android Apps Programming.* Apress Publisher.

Tran, D. T., & Huh, J.-H. (n.d.). *Full source code of the book.* https://github.com/thanhtd32/kotlin

Compilation of References

Bailey, A., Greenhalgh, D., & Skeen, J. (2021). Kotlin Programming: The Big Nerd Ranch Guide (2nd ed.). Big Nerd Ranch, LLC.

Bailey, Greenhalgh, & Skeen. (2021), Kotlin Programming: The Big Nerd Ranch Guide (2nd ed.). Big Nerd Ranch, LLC.

Bailey, Greenhalgh, & Skeen. (2021). Kotlin Programming: The Big Nerd Ranch Guide (2nd ed.). Big Nerd Ranch, LLC.

Bailey, A., Greenhalgh, D., & Skeen, J. (2021). Kotlin Programming: The Big Nerd Ranch Guide (2nd ed.). Big Nerd Ranch, LLC.

Dmitry & Svetlana. (2017). Kotlin in Action. Manning.

Ebel, N. (2019). Mastering Kotlin: Learn advanced Kotlin programming techniques to build apps for Android, iOS, and the web. Packt Publishing.

Eckel & Isakova. (2020). Atomic Kotlin. Mindview LLC.

Eckel &Isakova. (2020). Atomic Kotlin. Mindview LLC.

Eckel, B., & Isakova, S. (2020). Atomic Kotlin. Mindview, LLC.

Eckel, B., & Isakova, S. (2020). Atomic Kotlin. Mindview, LLC.

Griffiths, D., & Griffiths, D. (2019). Head First Kotlin. O'Reilly Media.

Griffiths, D., & Griffiths, D. (2019). Head First Kotlin. O'Reilly Media.

Jemerov & Isakova. (2017). Kotlin in Action. Manning, 320–322.

Jemerov & Isakova. (2017). Kotlin in Action. Manning.

Jemerov, D. & Isakova, S. (2017). Kotlin in Action. Manning.

Jemerov, D., & Isakova, S. (2017). Kotlin in Action. Manning.

Ponge. (2020). Vert.x in Action Asynchronous and Reactive Java. Manning Publisher.

Schild, H. (2019). Java the complete Reference (11th ed.). McGraw-Hill Education.

Compilation of References

Schild, H. (2019). *Java the complete Reference* (11th ed.). McGraw-Hill Education.

Späth, P. (2019). *Learn Kotlin for Android Development: The Next Generation Language for Modern Android Apps Programming.* Apress Publisher.

Tran, D. T., & Huh, J.-H. (n.d.). *Full source code of the book.* https://github.com/thanhtd32/kotlin

About the Authors

Duy Thanh Tran recieved the President's Award (1st prize research Ph.D. Degree Award) at National Korea Maritime and Ocean University, Republic of Korea in Feb., 2023. Since July 2016, he has been a Full Lecturer in the Faculty of Information Systems, University of Economics and Law, Vietnam National University Ho Chi Minh City (VNU)-HCM, Vietnam. Also, he is Associate Editor (AE) at Human-centric Computing and Information Sciences, (HCIS), (SCIE IF=6.558). He received Best Paper Award at the 15th International Conference on Multimedia Information Technology and Applications (MITA 2019). He is co-author of books: *Basic mobile application development* (ISBN: 978-604-73-5672-0), *Advanced mobile application development* (ISBN: 978-604-73-5673-7), *Basic programming techniques* (ISBN: 978-604-73-7187-7), *Advanced programming techniques* (ISBN: 978-604-73-7493-9).

Jun-Ho Huh is an Assistant Professor in the Department of Software, Catholic University of Pusan, South Korea. He is Associate Editor at Human-Centric Computing and Information Sciences (HCIS), Springer, Berlin Heidelberg with FTRA (SCOPUS/ESCI indexed), Associate Editor at *Journal of Information Processing Systems* (JIPS), Korea Information Processing Society (SCOPUS/ESCI indexed), and Submission Editor at *Journal of Multimedia Information System*, Korea Multimedia Society.

Index

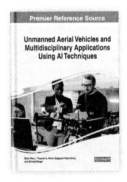

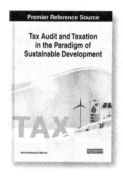
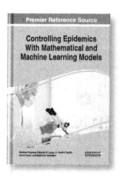

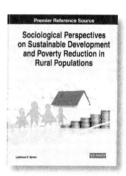

Printed in the United States
by Baker & Taylor Publisher Services